The opening of Antoine's Théâtre Libre (Free Theatre) in Paris in 1887 was one of the founding gestures of the modern theatre. This book investigates Antoine's exploration of the possibilities and limitations of stage realism, his concept of a workshop theatre for new writing and acting, his experiments and achievements in the *mise en scène* at the Théâtre Libre and the Théâtre Antoine, on the classics at the Odéon and in the early silent film. Chothia's study will be of interest to students and teachers of drama, theatre history, film studies and literature.

DIRECTORS IN PERSPECTIVE

General editor: Christopher Innes

André Antoine

What characterizes modern theatre above all is continual stylistic innovation, in which theory and presentation have combined to create a wealth of new forms – naturalism, expressionism, epic theatre, and so forth – in a way that has made directors the leading figures rather than dramatists. To a greater extent than is perhaps generally realized, it has been directors who have provided dramatic models for playwrights, though of course there are many different variations in this relationship. In some cases a dramatist's themes challenge a director to create new performance conditions (Stanislavski and Chekhov), or a dramatist turns director to formulate an appropriate style for his work (Brecht); alternatively a director writes plays to correspond with his theory (Artaud), or creates communal scripts out of exploratory work with actors (Chaikin, Grotowski). Some directors are identified with a single theory (Craig), others gave definitive shape to a range of styles (Reinhardt); the work of some has an ideological basis (Stein), while others work more pragmatically (Bergman).

Generally speaking, those directors who have contributed to what is distinctly 'modern' in today's theater stand in much the same relationship to the dramatic texts they work with, as composers do to librettists in opera. However, since theatrical performance is the most ephemeral of the arts and the only easily reproducible element is the text, critical attention has tended to focus on the playwright. This series is designed to redress the balance by providing an overview of selected directors' stage work: those who helped to formulate modern theories of drama. Their key productions have been reconstructed from promptbooks, revues, scene-designs, photographs, diaries, correspondence and – where these productions are contemporary – documented by first-hand description, interviews with the director, and so forth. Apart from its intrinsic interest, this record allows a critical perspective, testing ideas against practical problems and achievements. In each case, too, the director's work is set in context by indicating the source of his ideas and their influence, the organization of his acting company, and his relationship to the theatrical or political establishment, so to bring out wider issues: the way theater both reflects and influences assumptions about the nature of man and his social role.

Christopher Innes

Contemporary cartoon by Desiré Luc commenting on Antoine's eclecticism. He is shown as the promoter of Romanticism and Idealism as well as the Naturalism and Realism for which he is now remembered. The latter figure is represented wearing the cap of liberty and without the conventional fig leaf. (*Les Hommes d'aujourd'hui*, no. 341)

André Antoine

JEAN CHOTHIA

University Lecturer, Faculty of English,
and Fellow of Selwyn College, Cambridge

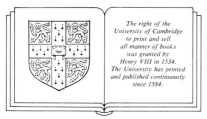

The right of the
University of Cambridge
to print and sell
all manner of books
was granted by
Henry VIII in 1534.
The University has printed
and published continuously
since 1584.

CAMBRIDGE UNIVERSITY PRESS

CAMBRIDGE

NEW YORK   PORT CHESTER

MELBOURNE   SYDNEY

Published by the Press Syndicate of the University of Cambridge
The Pitt Building, Trumpington Street, Cambridge CB2 1RP
40 West 20th Street, New York, NY 10011, USA
10 Stamford Road, Oakleigh, Melbourne 3166, Australia

First published 1991

Printed in Great Britain at the University Press, Cambridge

British Library cataloguing in publication data

Chothia, Jean
Andre Antoine, – (Directors in perspective).
1. France. Theatre. Directing. Antoine, André
I. Title   II. Series

Library of Congress cataloguing in publication data

Chothia, Jean.
André Antoine / Jean Chothia.
    p.   cm. – (Directors in perspective)
Includes bibliographical references.
ISBN 0 521 25219 9
1. Antoine, André, 1858–1943 – Criticism and interpretation.
I. Title.   II. Series.
PN2638.A64C48   1991
792'.0233'092–dc20   90-1672   CIP

ISBN 0 521 25219 9 hardback

SE

for Mary and Gordon

Contents

Illustrations

Preface

The opening of André Antoine's Théâtre Libre in Paris in 1887 marked the beginning of the independent theatre movement. It introduced the idea that change and innovation in drama and theatre would come from avant-garde theatre groups which had consciously set themselves apart from mainstream theatre, represented by the Boulevard, Broadway or London's West End.

Antoine's importance for subsequent theatre derives from his theatre work: his practical exploration of the possibilities and limitations of stage realism and the innovation and sometimes the excesses in acting and *mise en scène* that resulted. But, perhaps even more, it derives from his underlying idea that there ought to be a *théâtre d'essai*, a workshop theatre, where new plays and performance methods might be tried out regardless of their commercial prospects. This idea caught the imagination of theatre people abroad as well as in Paris and led with remarkable speed to the founding of the Théâtre Libre in Brussels, the Freie Bühne in Germany and the Independent Theatre in London, whilst, at home, the numerous rival ventures that were spawned began the process of continual revolution and counter-revolution which has characterized subsequent alternative and avant-garde theatre movements. The very term 'avant-garde' was introduced into dramatic criticism, in the early 1890s to describe the work of the Théâtre Libre and its symbolist rivals.[1]

The Théâtre Libre made its stand in the name of artistic integrity and against the profit motive. It became the home of ensemble acting and of plays which were true to experience and took risks. The closest analogy, and one to which Antoine himself repeatedly returned, is with the work of Courbet and Manet who, some two decades earlier, found an audience despite the hostility of the art establishment by exhibiting their paintings independently in *salons des refusés*. But whereas the new painting needed a single exhibition space and the new fiction a single sympathetic publisher, the new drama needed the whole paraphernalia of a theatre which could provide appropriate acting and *mise en scène* before it could hope to find its audience. It needed a new and different kind of theatre establishment. Believing that the 'wider public' had been sold short by commercial theatre and would value challenging new drama if given the chance, Antoine opened the Théâtre Libre in Montmartre, a location that provided an audience of artists, writers and Bohemians who were both interested in experiment and prepared to demonstrate their interest by subscribing for a season's tickets in advance.

The idea of the season subscription, indeed, besides securing Antoine's theatre, was an important enabling factor of the modern theatre. Through it, Antoine demonstrated that theatre, whether called free, alternative or fringe – the labels change but the idea remains – could survive, albeit precariously, even without rich and powerful patrons such as sustained the Saxe-Meiningen Company and Wagner's theatre at Bayreuth. It was immediately imitated and developed by Otto Brahm at the Freie Bühne, would be crucial in the work of the Old Vic Company and is a mainstay of the Royal Court now. Susan Glaspell, writing of the Provincetown Players' subscription list some thirty years later, would note:

> The people who had seen the plays and the people who gave them were adventurers together. The spectators were part of the Players, for how could it have been done without the feeling that it came from them, without the sense of them there, waiting, ready to share, giving – finding the deep level where audience and writer and player are one.[2]

The significance of the independent theatre movement for twentieth-century drama can hardly be overestimated. Every major dramatist since the 1880s has found a stage through the work of just such a company as Antoine's. Not only did the organization and achievement of the Théâtre Libre inspire the earliest of these – the Freie Bühne (Hauptmann), the Irish Players (Yeats, Synge, O'Casey), the Stockholm Intimate Theatre (Strindberg), the Moscow Art Theatre (Chekhov), the English Stage Society (Shaw, Galsworthy and Granville Barker) – through them, it provided the essential idea for subsequent companies such as the Provincetown Players (O'Neill) or Devine's English Stage Company at the Royal Court in the 1950s. Playwrights' theatres all, devoted to new writing and complementary new performance methods, they have worked outside and independently of the commercial mainstream and private patronage.

Whilst Antoine's importance as an initiator is widely recognized, the extent of his informing ideas and the theatre practice itself are not well known outside his own country.[3] This is partly the penalty of having initiated so many practices which have subsequently become commonplace in our theatre but it is also because, in contrast to directors such as Stanislavski, Craig or Brecht, Antoine left no sustained analysis of his practice, no equivalent of *My Life in Art, On the Art of the Theatre* or *The Messingkauf Dialogues*. Antoine's published writings, *Mes souvenirs sur le Théâtre Libre, . . . sur le Théâtre Antoine, Le Théâtre de 1870 à nos jours*, are anecdotal, informative about people and events but tantalisingly short on particular aspects of *mise en scène*. The ironic fact is that precisely because theatre is a performance art, whatever the quality of those performances, it is ephemeral except where the printed word survives to speak to subsequent generations so that the estimate of the achievement depends, in the long run, rather more on what survives in writing than on what was once done. Like Burbage and Macready, Antoine has become little more than an honoured name, his enterprise shrunk back to a few moments which thrilled and drew the largest headlines. These have survived, available to meet the needs of quick passing reference, so that the work is characterized by the real fountain on the stage, the actual beef carcasses hanging in the stage butcher's shop or the spectacle of Antoine's back, habitually turned to the audience.

The nature and effect of Antoine's innovation on a number of fronts crucial to subsequent European drama and theatre practice cries out for exploration and I have drawn on Antoine's letters, press statements and the five manifestos he published between 1887 and 1894, on his notes and sketches in the prompt books of certain plays and on photographs, contemporary accounts and his journalism of the 1920s and 1930s to piece together my account of some of his most significant productions and to delineate, if not a coherent theory, at least some of the most significant ideas underlying the working method. I would hope to identify some of the aspects of the practice which made the work compelling to contemporary commentators and to draw attention to the power and some of the inherent contradictions of realism, the style particularly associated with Antoine and, many would claim, still dominant, if in dilute form, in the theatre today.

It was originally my purpose to try to supply something of this need for information in relation to the Théâtre Libre alone, but it became increasingly apparent as I explored the material that, far from stopping with his bankruptcy and withdrawal from the Théâtre Libre in 1894, Antoine went on to three further phases of theatrical activity. First, at the Théâtre Antoine, he demonstrated that a repertory theatre could survive, could flourish indeed, on the Boulevard *and* become famous for its ensemble acting, its attention to *mise en scène* and as a training ground for writers, actors and régisseurs. Then, as director of the Odéon, he created a national theatre for France, where he demonstrated that with imaginative staging and programming the serious subsidized theatre could reveal the vigour and immediacy of the great works of the past and successfully revive the less well known as well as introducing new and foreign plays into the repertory. Finally, as the director of eight silent films, his encounters with the new medium helped to shape the development of cinema in France. I discuss some of the innovations and hazards of these later years in the second half of this book.

The importance of theatres such as Antoine's has lain not in their longevity but in the intensity of their brief activity and the opportunities each made available to a new generation of writers, actors and audiences. The intensity and opportunity apparent in the four successive areas of Antoine's work as a director is the subject of this book.

Acknowledgements

I wish to thank James B. Sanders for his generosity in making available material from his Antoine collection and Philippe Esnault for his contribution to my understanding of Antoine's film, *Le Coupable*. Michèle Thomas and the staff of the Bibliothèque de l'Arsenal; M. Rieupeyrout and the projectionist of the Cinémathèque française; the staff of the Musée Henri Langlois, Paris and, particularly, Mme Gigou of the ART collection at the Bibliothèque Historique de la Ville de Paris assisted in locating and making available to me material relating to Antoine's work. Annette Lenton's drawings made from my rough sketches and tracings and Claudio Villa's photographic work enabled me to reproduce material from the Bibliothèque Historique and I am especially grateful to them. Travel grants from the British Academy and the University of Cambridge facilitated research in Paris. Christopher Innes gave judicious advice on a late version of my manuscript; Victoria Cooper and Sarah Stanton of CUP have been unfailingly helpful and supportive and Chris Lyall Grant has been a meticulous and patient copy-editor.

Thanks for permission to reproduce pictures are due to James B. Sanders for the frontispiece, 15, 17, 46; to Roger Viollet for 1, 16, 27, 54; to the Bibliothèque Historique de la Ville de Paris for 2, 12, 22, 23, 24, 28, 40, 41; to the Trustees of the British Museum for 13; to the British Library for 31, 32, 35, 36, 37, 39, 42, 44; to the Bibliothèque Nationale, Paris, for 8, 9, 11, 14, 20, 21, 26, 29, 33, 34, and to the Photothèque of the Musée Henri Langlois, Paris, for 47 to 53. Other illustrations are from my own collection and were photographed by Claudio Villa.

I am grateful to Gilbert Orsini, Joel Janin, Rosemary Lloyd and Jean-Renaud Garel for assistance and hospitality in Paris and to John Rudlin, Judith Braid, Tristan Fonlladosa and Michael Tilby for help with certain matters of translation. Freda Hewish, Betty Chothia and my parents Mary and Gordon Sandham provided support on the home front where the encouragement and good will of Cyrus, Lucy and Thomas Chothia contributed more than they guess to the writing and completion of this book.

JKC

1 Who would give the signal?

The first performance of the Théâtre Libre, in March 1887, coincided with the first night of a La Scala tour and the première of an operetta at the Bouffes Parisiens. It is less surprising that most critics chose the Boulevard productions than that four from leading papers made the journey out to the suburbs. These greeted the occasion and particularly the performance of one of the four one-act realist plays performed, *Jacques Damour*, adapted by Léon Hennique from Zola's short story, in Messianic language. *Figaro* ran Fouquier's report on its front page whilst Jules Lemaître, the respected critic of *Journal des débats*, wrote:

So, last Tuesday, at about half past eight in the evening, you might have seen ghostly figures slipping along between the street-booths of Montmartre, carefully picking their way among the puddles of water in the road, around the Place Pigalle, scrutinizing through their eye-glasses the signs at the street corners. No passage; no theatre. Finally, we have recourse to a lighted wine shop and then we enter a steep, tortuous ill-lighted alleyway. A row of cabs is going up slowly in the same direction. We follow them. On each side, dim hovels and dirty walls; quite at the end a dim stairway. We seemed so many 'great-coated magi', seeking a hidden and glorious manger. Is this the manger where the drama, that decrepit old man, that dotard, will be reborn?[1]

The acting, the set, the play itself, evidently had power to surprise the critics, but the presence of the searching magi in that dim alleyway and the attention subsequently given in the press was an effect of the cultural moment and of assiduous advance publicity.

The work of French dramatists from Pixérécourt at the beginning of the nineteenth century to Sardou and Dumas fils in the present had been widely translated and had a stranglehold on theatre managements throughout Europe. Similarly, the declamatory acting style, taught at the Conservatoire, the prestigious school of the Théâtre Français, was universally imitated even though, powerfully formal in its great actors, Rachel, Got or Constant Coquelin, it tended in the second rank to bombast, stiffness and what Shaw labelled 'the French actor's peculiar mechanical cadence'.[2]

Although lip-service was still paid in France to Renaissance drama and the Comédie-Française proudly used the soubriquet *la maison de Molière*, there was in fact very little difference between the subsidized and the more sophisticated commercial theatres in what was actually performed. The repertoire of both had been dominated for thirty years by the work of a small group of dramatists: Scribe's dexterous social comedies; Sardou's highly formulaic plots of marital infidelity and reconciliation, and the social-problem melodramas of high finance and upper-middle-class adultery of Augier and Dumas fils who used a *raisonneur*, a sympathetic character, to voice the presumed values of the audience and point the moral. All were versions of the *pièce bien faite*, the well-made play whose plethora of incidents, fourth-act climax and optimistic denouement conformed to a pattern, skilfully reworked through scores of ingeniously varied events. Always glamorous, often titillating, these plays flattered the audience, offering amusement but not imaginative participation. As Henry James wrote, the 'good French play':

> serves its purpose to perfection, and French dramatists, as far as I can see, have no more secrets to learn. The first half dozen a foreign spectator listens to seem to him among the choicest productions of the human mind, and it is only little by little that he becomes conscious of the extraordinary meagreness of their material . . . Prime material was evidently long ago exhausted and the best that can be done now is to rearrange the old situations with a kind of desperate ingenuity. The field looks terribly narrow, but it is still cleverly worked.[3]

Theatre, the major nineteenth-century entertainment industry had by the 1880s become a profitable area of business speculation, the *pièce bien faite* its standard product.

Stirrings towards change in the theatre, to match those in the novel and the visual arts, were recurrently evident in Paris in the 1870s and 1880s, but they were spasmodic and without continuity. Montigny had worked, earlier in the century, for greater coherence in staging but the attempts were directed, as with Irving in England, towards the staple repertory. Reports of Wagner's innovations in the *mise en scène* did filter into France but although the *Revue Wagnérienne* was founded in 1885, Wagner's operas found public performance only in concert versions. The Saxe-Meiningen Company was never invited to perform in Paris and Ibsen's work was not known.

Attempts at innovation in the drama had foundered on weak texts or hostile audiences. After seeing the 1884 version of Zola's *Pot-Bouille*, Antoine, then a clerk in the Gas Company, had written of his shock at the 'contrast between the book so vigorous and so true and the platitude in five acts served up at the Ambigu by Busnach'.[4] When there was a powerful text, as with Becque's drama of rapacious bourgeois life, *Les Corbeaux* (1882), the staging had been unsympathetic and the reception even more so. The leading actor at the Comédie-Française, Constant Coquelin, had demanded extensive cuts, including suppression of the whole sequence in which the son parodies his father, and, the play having been withdrawn following a hostile press campaign, the Comédie actors voted not to take *La Parisienne*, Becque's next piece. Performed at the Renaissance (7 Nov. 1885), this play met with indifference from the public and hostility from the theatre's backers and the entrepreneur there retreated from further attempts at innovation.

The written word proved more successful, for the moment. Whereas melodramatic versions of his novels might not do much to alter fixed ideas in the theatre, Zola's weekly dramatic criticism and his famous essay 'Le Naturalism au théâtre', which addressed a young and radical constituency that included Antoine, Strindberg and many who would become Théâtre Libre writers and actors, did stimulate enthusiasm for reform. With Zola's assault on the French comedy in the early 1880s, 'the trend of the times', as Strindberg would later point out, had begun 'to exert its demands for reform even in the theatre'. A claim to moral regeneration and to a more clear-sighted patriotism than that which characterized the vested interests of the established theatre was implicit in Zola's identification of realist drama with demands for a theatre of scale and simplicity, truth and conflict, comparable with that of Molière and Racine. His journalism, in Antoine's words, 'prepared, educated and emancipated the public'. When, for example, the leading dramatists Augier and Sardou supported the ban on the dramatized version of *Germinal* on the grounds that what was acceptable in the privacy of the novel was not on the public stage, Zola had replied with a battle cry:

those who should be asked are those who press forward, those who bring forward a new art and who need the great air of liberty. Let them come and they will tell you that the theatre is dead if you close it to truth, to satire of the powerful and tears for the humble, to political and social evolution of which the future will be made.

(*Figaro*, 27 Nov. 1885)

It was hardly a coincidence that Ibsen's famous letter to Lucie Wolf, announcing his decision to abandon poetic drama, was written within a year of the publication of 'Le Naturalism au théâtre'. To its first-night audience, the Théâtre Libre seemed to offer the anticipated breakthrough.[5]

It was probably inevitable that the breakthrough should have come, as is so often the case with the innovative imagination, with a figure like Antoine, who was an outsider. He subsequently made much of the chance nature of his enterprise, writing:

The battle already won in the novel by the naturalists, in painting by the impressionists and in music by the Wagnerians was going to be carried into the theatre . . . Here then the field of battle, the occupiers of the place to be won, the troups ready for a possible assault; but who would coordinate so many scattered elements? Who would give the signal? Quite simply, chance. Without being the least aware of it, I was to become the animator of forces which I did not even suspect.[6]

However timely Antoine's appearance, the Théâtre Libre, far from being a chance affair, was the product of his long-standing excitement about the new achievements in the literary and visual arts and his dissatisfaction with the current state of the drama. Whilst he must have been surprised and delighted by, even perhaps afraid of, the massive interest and enthusiasm roused by his work, Antoine was able to recognize the importance of his undertaking and to use the response it generated. From the outset, he described his as a *vrai théâtre* – a professional theatre which for the moment had no money to pay its actors and, bypassing the commercial theatres of the Boulevard, insisted on comparing its achievements with those of the two state-subsidized houses, the Théâtre Français and the Odéon.

One of the huge new class of the *petite bourgeoisie*, Antoine was working between twelve and fourteen hours a day as a clerk in the Gas Company when he opened the Théâtre Libre. He had no direct access to the established literary and theatrical worlds but, as amateur and autodidact, was steeped in the products of both, sensitive to new literary ideas but alert to the need to adapt them to the practicalities of the stage if theatre was to be regained as a lively art. This combination of responsiveness to new ideas and understanding of theatre practice was what set Antoine apart.

Apprenticed at age thirteen to the bookseller Firmin Didot in rue Jacob, Antoine, afflicted by a 'fierce hunger for reading', patched up an education out of the exhibitions at the nearby Ecole des Beaux Arts, the small magazines of the new literary movements of Bohemian Paris and free evening classes. The exhibitions included the work of Manet, to whose 1872 exhibition he returned repeatedly to learn what was at stake; the little magazines included Zola's journalistic battles for Manet's *Olympia*, for the naturalistic novel and against the moribund theatre, and Catulle Mendès' *République des lettres* with its discussion of the novels of Flaubert, the Goncourts, and Zola, whilst the evening classes included Hippolyte Taine's History of Art course where Antoine learned about the importance of the cultural moment in the creation of new art. Antoine was, in other words, educating himself on the theory and practice, the battles for and eventual triumph of the new artistic and intellectual movements: impressionism, Naturalism and determinism. The lesson of his reading, his own experience and the classes he attended was that the new and the truthful in the arts would necessarily achieve prominence but only after a struggle against the status quo. In a *Figaro* interview of 1891, he said that Zola's 'Letter to French Youth' had been his catechism for ten years.

At the same time, having had, like countless other children, a seat with cherries and *eau de vie* for 50c at his local theatre, the Bataclan in the Marais, having thrilled to Taillade in melodrama and, more unusually, having watched, through the good offices of a neighbour, *La Chatte blanche* from the prompter's box at the Gaîté, he discovered a passion for the theatre. This he fed, once he had started work, by regular attendance at the Théâtre Français, eventually graduating to membership of the claque, leading the applause for 30 sous a night, and to occasional employment as an extra in crowd scenes.

Despite the legend, although disqualified by class, style and financial situation from entering the Conservatoire, Antoine was by no means untrained when he first performed for the Théâtre Libre. He had attended the theatre itself so continuously and so attentively that he patched up a Conservatoire-style training by knowing every major speech in the repertoire and the details of the organization and delivery of every scene by heart. His recitation of these scenes so impressed Marius Laisné, an acting teacher whose public evening course on diction he had attended, that Laisné took him on free as a private pupil. Laisné's other star pupil, Wisteaux, who became Antoine's close friend and the sounding-board for his ideas, would later, as Mévisto, be a founder-member and leading actor of the Théâtre Libre.

There is a long-standing tradition of serious discussion of ideas about theatre in France that has no parallel in England. As part of his own campaign for reform, Zola had cited Diderot's arguments for a more sensuous theatre language and a more realistic acting style. Antoine, by contrast, deeply moved by what seemed to him the totally absorbed acting of Mounet-Sully and the young Bernhardt, was stimulated to define his own ideas at the point where his observation clashed with Diderot's *Paradoxe sur le comédien*. When still only sixteen, he wrote to the leading actors of the Théâtre Français asking whether they thought the actor should deliver himself entirely into the emotions of the role or should remain self-possessed on stage, as Diderot had argued. Got's reply, quoted without further comment some twenty years later in the published version of the actor's journal, bears repeating for the clarity with which he reproduces both the matter and the urgency of Antoine's original enquiry:

Was Diderot really right in *The Paradox of the Actor* or, rather, does the actor excite emotion only when he experiences it himself? That is your question is it not?

Well, I would say, neither of these propositions is the truth or, rather, each is true on condition that they are brought together. Let me explain. The actor, like the singer, the instrumentalist, the orator, like all those who intend to work directly on a crowd, the actor must be double under pain of not being, that is to say that at the same time the artist performs and experiences, a kind of reasonable being must remain in him, standing aside, watching the active being and also the audience, and always capable of arrangements, of resourcefulness, and of nuances — a regulator, in short, as they say in mechanics.

So, sir, that is my opinion, and I can only thank you for having chosen me to arbitrate or at least advise in this delicate discussion.

Although too shy to follow up an invitation from Coquelin to come and discuss the question, Antoine did keep Got's letter and throughout his life would return to consideration of what would be for him, as actor and director of actors, the central paradox of the acting profession: that the role must be thoroughly controlled and rehearsed but that the persuasive actor will lose his or her self-consciousness and appear to become the character.[7]

His correspondence during four years' enforced absence on military service in Algeria reveals his obsessive interest in French theatre. 'What's new in Paris?', he wrote to Wisteaux in February 1880:

I relished your account of *Charles IX* and I am quite of your mind. The play is as fine as it is remarkable; if I remember rightly, there is a scene, that of the King's Council, which is quite masterly . . . I'm also waiting, when you're ready, for details of Sardou's *Daniel Rochat* which, I gather, is on on the 16th. Alas, I guess I shan't see that . . .

I would never have believed that I would feel so deprived at not being able to go to the theatre (I don't know what I wouldn't do to spend a single evening at the Théâtre Français). The other day a third-rate company here gave a performance of *La Tour de Nesles* in which I figured as an extra.   (*Correspondance*, p. 34)

But distance also seems to have matured his ideas and, after his return to Paris in 1882, his commentary on the acting and *mise en scène* of the Théâtre Français became notably more critical.

What free time he didn't spend at the Théâtre Français he devoted to acting and directing for the amateur Cercle Gaulois whose members contributed 8 francs a month and performed on Sundays. It is evident from his letters that he had quickly become one of the moving spirits of the Cercle and thought continually about the theatre and his own possible place in it. Years, not just of dreaming and thinking on Antoine's part but of critical watching and rigorous amateur experiment, were behind the production Fouquier and Lemaître came to see in March 1887, at the tiny Théâtre de l'Elysée des Beaux Arts of a prologue and four one-act plays. 'Un préfet', by Arthur Byl, 'La Cocarde', by Jules Vidal, 'Mademoiselle Pomme' by Alexis and Duranty and *Jacques Damour*, adapted from a Zola short story, by Léon Hennique, made up the first programme of Europe's first independent theatre.

The first soirée: *Jacques Damour* (30 Mar. 1887)

It was Poor Theatre with a vengeance. The Cercle Gaulois had split over Antoine's scheme of presenting new plays, especially plays associated with Zola and Alexis, and its establishment had refused support for the project. Whilst this forced Antoine to find 100 francs rent, a full month's wages, to hire the Cercle's theatre, it also enabled him to draw in actors he respected from the rival Cercle Pigalle and to adopt a new, more resonant, name. The perception that practical and rhetorical advantages could be seized even from financial exigency, evident in this initial break with the Cercle Gaulois, is characteristic of Antoine's subsequent approach to theatre management.

The name chosen, the 'Théâtre Libre' or 'Free Theatre', announced intent and, with its echo of Victor Hugo's call for a 'théâtre en liberté', also claimed comparison with the heroic struggles of French theatre in the past. Although, as Lemaître's comment makes apparent, the poverty was not without glamour for the audience, it was real enough for Antoine and his company. Rehearsals took place in a billiard-room whose rent was the price of drinks from the bar below; the stage furniture, from Antoine's mother's living-room, was wheeled across Paris in a hand-barrow, and Antoine himself, despite the demands of his job, wrote and delivered some 1,300 letters in an effort to fill his 349 seats.

Hennique's play only uses the climax of Zola's story about the communard, Jacques Damour, in which Jacques, having fled France following the failure of the commune, returns after the amnesty to find his child is dead and that his wife, believing him drowned, has remarried. The strength of the central scene, in which the haggard Jacques and his bluff and comfortable rival, Sagnard, discuss who is Félice's rightful husband, depends not on physical action or heroic posturing, but on the tension generated when the audience is made to witness a situation in which, for all its emotional intensity, there is no evident right or wrong. The onus of feeling and moral judgement is not borne by a conventional *raisonneur* as in the *pièce bien faite* but weighs directly on the audience.

The impression of authenticity the production gave depended, in part, on the accurate observation and precise placing of appropriate stage properties which were listed carefully on Antoine's script as:

> 2 coffee cups on round table
> bottle cognac on round table
> death certificate in bureau drawer
> some small change on a plate on little cash table
> 1 bottle wine and 4 glasses on buffet
> 1 newspaper with Sagnard

The simplicity and accuracy of setting and costume were thrilling to an audience accustomed to lavish scenic decoration, and Antoine's mother's furniture, solid and worn, gave the set substance and helped convey that central tenet of Naturalism: that environment is character. But equally important was the way presentation of character within environment contributed to the dramatic structure of the play.

Using terms that would become familiar in subsequent discussion of Antoine's work, La Pommeraye noted of the opening scene, in which the lower-middle-class family is discovered at table, that 'this scene of calm, of

1 Stage of the theatre, Passage de l'Elysée des Beaux Arts, Antoine's first theatre. The footlight guard is visible across the front of the stage. Commentators claimed that illusion was impossible in such a tiny theatre. (Photo Harlingue-Viollet)

peace and of intimate joy is put before the audience with truth, without trickery and without emphasis' (*Paris*, 4 Apr. 1887). But the significance of the scene derives less from the fact that the on-stage world looks remarkably like the real world than from the way that impression of real, lived lives is used to shape the audience's response to what follows. The impression of everyday domesticity creates a sense of the habitual and secure that Jacques' entrance will destroy.

Although Lemaître claimed that illusion was impossible on such a tiny stage, where people in the audience felt they could reach out and touch the actors, there was widespread comment on the naturalness and on the care and accuracy of the acting. Henry James, who saw the play in London, wrote in the character of Dorriforth in his dialogue 'After the Play':

When the appointments are meagre and sketchy, the responsibility that rests upon the actors becomes a still more serious thing, and the spectators' observation of the way they rise to it a pleasure more intense. The face and voice are more to the purpose than acres of painted canvas, and a touching intonation, a vivid gesture or two, than an army of supernumeraries.[8]

Antoine, as Jacques, demonstrated a capacity (that would become famous) for holding a dramatic silence and for drawing audience response by sheer bodily control. La Pommeraye had seen no 'professional actor who [had] composed character, face, clothes, bearing, allure, gesture, expression, better' than Antoine, 'all were true and gripping'; Paul Alexis wrote in *Cri du peuple* that, 'as well as his perfect diction, he has SILENCES which transport the whole theatre' (10 Mar. 1887), whilst for the actor Charles Mosnier, who first saw this production when it toured to Nancy:

The vision of Antoine on the threshold nailed me to my seat. I will always remember the life-likeness of his slow arrival. I recall that his silences were held a long time and as to his expression . . . when he began to speak between his teeth, what truth, and what beauty.

('André Antoine', vol. I, p. 35)

This matter of the held silences is germane to discussion of Antoine's work as director. In a period of cavalier adaption of plays, one of Antoine's most firmly held beliefs was in the integrity of the dramatist's text. He held that the director's task was the interpretation of the dramatist's imagined world for the theatre. Accordingly, he made few alterations to Hennique's or to any other dramatist's script. The small changes he did make, however, which usually involved simplification of a climactic moment and the use of silence and gesture, contributed importantly to the intensity of feeling and to the stage-worthiness of the play.

At the end of *Jacques Damour*, the shallow Sagnard, full of bonhomie now the problem is resolved in his favour, presses Jacques first to a meal and then, when that is refused, to a drink. Antoine cut Jacques' lines here and emphasized the gulf of experience that separated him from the other characters by playing him as scarcely able to speak before the ruin of his dream of a domestic haven. The conviviality of the family, by contrast, is emphasized when they relax back into their habitual attitudes. The version Antoine played ends like this:

SAGNARD: To you! (*They drink in silence*)
BERRU: Good, this wine! Hey, Damour?
VOICE OF PAULINE (*outside, calling*):   Mummy! Mummy!
FELICE: Just coming.
DAMOUR: (*putting his empty glass on the table*):   So, goodbye everyone.
CURTAIN

By cutting Jacques' actual departure and the family's polite farewells at the door, with which Hennique had ended his script, and by finishing instead with a fast curtain on the line, 'Voilà, adieu tout le monde', which, in the French, is worryingly double-edged, Antoine confronts the audience with the raw emotion and empty future of the loser.

The great paradox of Antoine's career, that the first exponent of playwrights' theatre was the creator of director's theatre, is already apparent in this opening production. The argument is that if the play is to live on the stage and be completely coherent, someone must take control of all aspects of production: casting, setting, lighting, stage movement, must, that is to say, replace the co-ordinating function of the old stage-manager by the interpreting function of the modern director. In acting as interpreter, the director cannot help but interpose his own imagination between those of the audience and the playwright.

The second soirée: *La Nuit Bergamasque* and *En famille* (30 May 1887)

If his opening night awoke literary Paris to recognition of a new talent, Antoine's second experimental evening proved that the Théâtre Libre was no mere firecracker and Antoine, for all his protestations to the contrary, no wide-eyed innocent caught up in a current he could not resist. Clearly, he realized from the outset that choice of programme was crucial in creating and sustaining the curiosity and allegiance of an audience.

Despite press interest, the enterprise could have foundered after its first initiative. The wealthier Cercle Pigalle, indeed, put on their own rival evening of advanced plays with some success in May 1887 but, having no further programme planned, soon faded from the competition. Antoine, by contrast, set about finding new scripts. Rejecting proffered work from Byl and Vidal, authors of the unsuccessful plays of the first soirée, he approached the writer Bergerat, who was a journalist and a well-respected poet. Charmed that the adventurous new company whose work had created such a stir wanted the play the Comédie-Française had refused, Bergerat gave Antoine his verse comedy *La Nuit Bergamasque* for the second soirée and became a loyal supporter. It was an adroit move because not only did Bergerat's name, comparable with Zola's in its claim to seriousness, promise to stimulate the attention of the press but, being a verse comedy set in a fantastic oriental world, the play presented a dramatically effective contrast, for actors and audience alike, with *Jacques Damour* and with the raw one-act prose play, *En famille* by the unknown Oscar Méténier, with which it was to be paired.

The programme made the claim to eclecticism that Antoine would continually reaffirm in the face of critics who labelled the theatre as naturalist, and established a practice to which he would largely hold of combining in a single programme the famous with the unknown, the relatively safe with the risqué, the lyric with the realist, the full length with the one act. The inclusion of Bergerat also enabled Antoine to develop the analogy between his own work and that of Manet for, as well as presenting new work, his theatre would demonstrably be a *salon des refusés*, performing plays rejected by a blinkered or timorous art establishment.

If this attention to variety even within a programme of avant-garde plays is telling, equally telling for Antoine's future development as a director is his evident capacity to identify the talented and single-minded amongst his prospective actors and ruthlessly to bypass the rest in casting his second soirée. Of the seventeen who had performed in March, Antoine made Baston his régisseur and kept as actors only Barny, Pinsard, Méré, Brevern and Burguet, bringing in Luce Colas from the Cercle Pigalle and his proven friend Wisteaux who, as Mévisto, was earning his living as a cabaret singer. He assembled in this way a group who, with Mlle Deneuilly (Pauline Verdavoine), his future wife, would be the core of the company in its first two years. As telling, too, is the impression of there being something remarkable about the *mise en scène*, the 'care and attention one could not overpraise', that audiences were beginning to perceive in Antoine's staging.[9]

There are three photographs of Méténier's play, the first extant photographs of any play in performance, and they serve to demonstrate the solidity and the meagreness of an Antoine realist set in the early days of the Théâtre Libre (see fig. 2). The setting is a secondhand shop: the characters are dealers, receivers, petty crooks and a prostitute. Plain cloth is hung between the fixed pillars at the back of the stage and at the front the characters are gathered around a table. Coat-stands of old clothes pressing in around the table serve both to signify the trade and to make the stage space seem more cramped than it actually is. The action presents a transitional state between Théâtre Français convention and Antoine's fully-fledged realist method. The actors are uninhibited about sitting in the presence of the audience, and the table is not only sited in a prominent position at centre front of the stage but is accurately equipped with the bottles and covers of a family mealtime. Each actor creates an impression of being absorbed in his or her part by responding with eyes and bearing to the speaker, but it is notable that Alexis and Mévisto, who stand to make their speeches, are still using the large arm gestures of the Théâtre Français, and that the actors are so grouped around the table that everyone faces forward towards the audience and Mévisto and Antoine, at opposite ends of the table, assume the kind of position they would subsequently repudiate as distractingly awkward in order to avoid turning their backs on the audience.

Perhaps most thrilling for the audience was the coupling of Méténier's play with Bergerat's. Antoine never allowed doubling within a play because of the need for the actors to be absorbed in their roles. But such absorption is for the duration of the play only, assumed with the dialogue and costume.

2 *En famille*, Théâtre Libre, 1887. The first known photographs of a play in
performance. In the second picture, Albert stands to sing; in the third,
Auguste, standing to explain why he cannot join the festivities, describes
the execution of a family friend. Stands of old clothes act as indicators of
the family trade. The placing of the table at centre front becomes a recurrent
element in Antoine's staging (cf.fig.10)
From stage right: Auguste (Mévisto), Albert (Alexis), Amélie (Luce Colas),
Mère Paradis (Barny), Père Paradis (Antoine, in his first old man role)

The action was fully prepared and rehearsed beforehand, each part composed
by the actor and director. And, just as Antoine avoided type-casting his
actors, so he could, and did, ask them to take parts in two or even three plays
performed in the same programme. It was, therefore, in keeping with their
acting skills that Mévisto, Barny and Antoine, having inhabited Méténier's
lower-middle-class living-room, should appear after the interval in Bergerat's
fantasy, the virtuosity and contrast displayed contributing to the delight for
the Théâtre Libre audience.

  Bergerat recalled that rehearsals took place in hallways, in the storeroom
of the couturier for whom Barny worked or in the basement of a brasserie,
but that Antoine, 'perhaps the most original figure in our dramatic world',
electrified his actors with his gift for organization and his authority.[10] The

prompt book for *La Nuit Bergamasque*, with Antoine's detailed stage directions written out on plain sheets interleaved with the text, demonstrates how fully Antoine attended to the *mise en scène* from the outset. Individual stage positions and sequences of moves are noted, as they will be in the prompt book for *Julius Caesar* at the Odéon some twenty years later, with quickly sketched stage plans, small crosses to define positions and arrows to register particular movements. And, as there, the demarcation between writer and director is evident: although Bergerat's stage directions which were not in accord with Antoine's notion of the play, most notably in the boudoir scene of Act III, are boldly crossed out, markedly few cuts or alterations are made to the *words* of the play.

I would argue that in order to define his own imaginative space as director, Antoine needed to be absolutely clear that the dramatist's prerogative was located in the dialogue, although, as will be evident in the discussion of his productions of Tolstoi, Ibsen, Strindberg and Hauptmann, where he was working with contemporary scripts of the first order that were themselves attentive to environment and staging, Antoine also followed the dramatist's stage directions scrupulously.

Briefly, Bergerat's play, derived from a Boccaccio story, is the tale of an old miser, Enobarbus, who values his hoard of gold more than his wife and is robbed of both: the one by his impoverished nephew, the other by a love-stricken gallant. Having been made to demonstrate his own capacity to speak verse at his first meeting with the dramatist, Antoine was attentive to the way the lines were spoken, registering frequent voice directions, 'très langoureuse', 'très lyrique', in his script and noting that all the scenes must be alert to the light, tripping quality of the verse, that the actors must register the metre and the echoic rhymes.

To suit the tone of this play, and against his own impulse to low-key internalized playing, which had been so striking in *Jacques Damour* and which he would use for *En famille*, Antoine wanted a *commedia dell'arte* style of performance and asked his actors to slightly exaggerate their gesture and to give attention to the mime sequences and the way in which facial expression could extend the comedy. He also seized on the possibilities for high farce.

In Act II, Enobarbus, equipped with dark lantern, digs up the hoard he has hidden from his heirs, echoing Volpone's corrupt eroticism as he apostrophizes it. The soliloquy is overheard by the two young men, Myrio and Bruno. Antoine used deliberate, literal upstaging as, separate but absolutely parallel in their actions, the two young men peep up from behind the wall at the rear of the stage then, climbing on to the wall, compel audience attention as they simultaneously register that the mistress Enobarbus addresses is merely his gold.

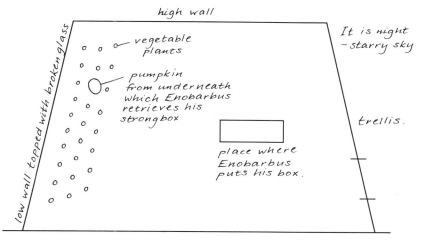

high wall

It is night
– starry sky

low wall topped with broken glass

vegetable
plants

pumpkin
from underneath
which Enobarbus
retrieves his
strongbox

trellis.

place where
Enobarbus
puts his box.

3 *La Nuit Bergamasque*, Théâtre Libre 1887. The sketch reproduces a stage plan from the prompt script showing the set for Act II, Enobarbus' garden with distribution of plants. Bruno and Myrio will appear over the back wall to catch Enobarbus addressing his gold. The annotations are translations of Antoine's notes

The comic pitch is heightened when they suddenly both leap from the wall and intercept Enobarbus who immediately sits to conceal his hoard. Bruno sits at one end of the bench while Myrio towers over the miser, then Myrio sits at the other end and each moves in, encroaching on the old man's space:

BRUNO: It's hot.
MYRIO: Very hot.
ENOB: A plague on you. You're suffocating me.
BRUNO: This is – my friend Myrio.
(*Enob. looks at him. Myrio greets him: all in Italian Comedy Style.*)

This exaggerated looking, pushing, greeting is echoed and extended in the next act when each of the male characters enters, in turn, through the window of Fatima's boudoir into an increasingly fast action of disguise and recognition which culminates in Fatima and the maid throwing Enobarbus' bag of money to and fro, whilst Enobarbus runs frantically between them.

But, even in farce, Antoine was conscious of the difference between mainstream acting and what he was aiming for, recording, when Bergerat brought Jean Coquelin to rehearsals of *La Nuit Bergamasque*:

in rehearsing me in my role, he seemed to attach an exaggerated importance to the preparation of what he calls effects. I think this method of interrupting the acting to glance at the public as if to say, 'Now you are going to see how funny this is', is exactly the opposite of what I would like to do. (26 May 1887)

No one glances at the audience from Antoine's stage.

In setting this play, Antoine explores the stage space using different heights and planes: figures are placed on the wall, over the wall, in and out the windows; they stand, they lounge, they sit in comic rows. Enobarbus scrabbles, digging on hands and knees. The boudoir scene is arranged at an angle to the audience which not only emphasizes the windows through which the various entrances and exits would be made, but has the practical consequence of better backstage space for the accurate timing of sudden appearances at the windows and incident-free, tumultuous exits.

Such an alignment facilitates mobility of action. But it also alters the relationship of the audience to the action, putting them not behind the fourth wall but as if they were in a corner of the room itself. At the time, Antoine seemed not to have registered this, nor its appropriateness to realist drama. *En famille* was set square to the audience as *Jacques Damour* had been, but this angling of the set at the second soirée is prophetic. After experimenting with the fourth wall, Antoine would look again at the angled set in his search for ways of representing the fluidity of life. Reprinting Strindberg's 'Preface to *Lady Julie*' for distribution to his audience at the première of the play in 1893, Antoine noted that, amongst the ideas for renovation in the theatre, 'decor arranged at an angle, the suppression of the ramp, lighting from above' were already common in his theatre (13 Jan. 1893). Once he had facilities to build each set from scratch at the Théâtre Antoine and, especially, the Odéon, this would be a favourite alignment for interior sets and, thirty years later, pursuing the same end, he would be the first in the French cinema to reject the fixed filming angle in favour of a camera which would move into the frame, taking the audience into the action.

This production made bigger demands than the everyday clothes and living-room furniture of earlier ones and, despite their limited resources, the company met them heroically. Each actor was responsible for making his or her own, historically accurate, fifteenth-century costume. The set, especially the kitchen-garden scene – for which he introduced a mass of potted plants, a leafy trellis, a wall topped with broken glass – was charming in its strangeness and reality, its key points being the bench and, with mock-heroic charge, a spreading pumpkin plant under which Enobarbus' gold was hidden.

The combination of the real and the strange raises interesting questions about Antoine's style. He would later protest the readiness of critics to fix the naturalist label on him, arguing that he was open to a great range of different kinds of drama. The claim is quite true: by the end of his second year he could claim to be the leading French patron of poetic as well as of naturalist drama, having produced nine verse plays, one pantomime and one tragi-parade amongst his new work. It is clear, moreover, that the magical quality of *La Nuit Bergamasque*, Banville's *Le Baiser*, Mendès' *La Reine Fiammette* derived from the decor as well as from the lyrical speaking of the language. But what is also evident is that, even where it is decorative or fantastical, it is both substantial and spatially functional.

This is wholly characteristic of Antoine. The world inhabited by the play might be remote from the everyday world but within its own terms it is represented as real. Its elements may be strange, distant, fanciful, but they are solidly present, not two-dimensional hardboard cut-outs nor sketches painted on a rippling back-cloth. Carpets and silken cushions signify the luxurious eastern boudoir; real vegetables and a pumpkin, the garden. Colour, and the line and plane of stage space are already important (see fig. 3) and light will become so, but they are used as suggestive components of the picture, never sufficient in themselves as light, boxes or screens would be to Appia or Craig and their twentieth-century followers, and it is a picture that is always figurative, never abstract.

The excitement generated by the first soirée, the announcement that *Jacques Damour* was taken for the Odéon and the curiosity stimulated when Antoine turned not to Médan, as might have been anticipated, but to Bergerat for his next programme, ensured a full and glittering house. *L'Action* had called the first soirée 'brilliant' but accounts of the second gave almost as much attention to listing the audience as to reviewing the plays. Got recorded in his journal:

And what an audience. Besides the more or less leading lights of the press, Sarcey, Vitu, Blavet, La Pommeraye etc., Lockroy, for his last day at the ministry, with G. Ollendorff, G. Hugo, and Daudet; Rodin, the sculptor of the admirable gate of hell of the Arts Decoratifs; Puvis de Chavannes, the compère Carjat, Coquelin cadet, and so many others, art students, photographers, journalists, monologuists, decadent poets, shady characters, parvenus or parvenants, with or without their wives, all those indeed who make a pretence to being in the swing of things, as they say.   (p. 249)

And, with interesting insight, he compared this debut with that of Molière and Béjard's *L'Illustre Théâtre*.

Despite the publicity and the support from prospective authors, it was a huge undertaking for Antoine. Coming from a family of small clerks and earning only 1,800 francs a year, he could hardly have been in a worse financial position to launch a theatre company. He was conscious of the temerity of his idea, registering his apprehension in his letters to Pauline Verdavoine and noting in his diary shortly after the first soirée:

These performances . . . seem to have passed all our expectations at the first stroke.
    Byl and Vidal waited for me at the Gas Company and, very moved themselves, told me it was absolutely necessary to continue. It is the advice of Paul Alexis, and I sense strongly that everyone around me awaits a new initiative, but with whom and to what end? These productions are expensive and I won't recover for a long time the 300 or 400 francs they have cost me.   (4 Apr. 1887)

Charles Mosnier, a member in 1887 of the leading amateur company of Bordeaux, later noted pointedly that nothing could have prevented its president who was capable, talented and, unlike Antoine, rich, from similarly creating something except, 'ideas and the will to impose them on the whole world' (vol. I, p. 27).

If Antoine's claim to having been taken wholly off-guard was not quite the *comédie d'ingénuité* his sceptical biographer, Francis Pruner, has claimed, it is clear that his long preparation and late beginning meant that when the opportunity did present itself and the glittering audience proved ready to flock to the hard benches of Krauss's little theatre, Antoine was ready to meet it, gratified but not overwhelmed by the sudden attentions of the writers and actors he had admired from a distance.

His professionalism is evident in the way that, immediately after the second soirée, he entered on a period of intense preparatory activity for the coming season. By June, he was looking for ways to establish 'a solid and permanent organization for the Théâtre Libre' and planning a full season's programme, liberally spiced with famous names to attract an audience. A letter to Hennique, announcing that he planned to begin with adaptations of Zola's story *Captain Burle* and, from the rival naturalist faction, of Goncourt's *Sœur Philomène*, demonstrated the magnitude of his aspirations:

I believe that Paul Alexis will complete the evening. Next, we will have a special translation of *The Power of Darkness* by Tolstoi. Then something by J. Richepin, a one-acter by M. Mallarmé, one from Descaves . . . I have been appealing everywhere and await decisions from Catulle Mendès, Becque, Maupassant, Mirbeau, Bonnetain, Coppée etc.

You see the season could be interesting, but won't you, who brought me good luck with *Jacques Damour*, give me anything further?   (22 June 1887)

He had promises of plays from the poets Banville and Mendès; had nipped Byl and Vidal's scheme for a rival theatre in the bud by inviting them to adapt the Goncourt work; had written to Bonnetain at *Figaro* and Sarcey at *Le Temps* and received publicity for his search for unpublished plays, and had had 2,000 brochures printed on credit, when, early in July, Porel offered him his 'oldest youthful dream, magically realized': the chance to make his debut at the Odéon in an Augier revival at 500 francs a month. The offer demonstrated how far he had come from that dream and how seriously he was taken even if, as Céard and Zola believed, it was made to silence an upstart rather than to promote a new talent.[11] He began delivering his brochures by hand the next day, having refused the offer.

Within three weeks, Antoine had resigned his job to devote his time properly to the Théâtre Libre. What financial security he had came from a scheme mapped out with M. Paz, who became the theatre's first administrator, to offer a season's guaranteed seats in return for an advance subscription of 100 francs. The Théâtre Libre would never have a theatre of its own, but once the first twenty-four subscriptions were received he gave his company a base by renting premises in rue Blanche, which would become its permanent offices and rehearsal rooms.

2 The fourth wall: Antoine and the new acting

Sœur Philomène (11 Oct. 1887)

The realistic texture of Antoine's productions had excited the naturalists amongst his supporters from the outset. With *Sœur Philomène*, in October 1887, the attention of observers generally shifted from the composition of the audience and the daring choice of writers to what was happening on the stage. The success of the two experimental evenings had increased Antoine's willingness to challenge stage conventions and the results were considerable.

With this first production of the first full season, the indulgent and patronizing note largely vanished from press accounts and no paper subsequently missed a Théâtre Libre opening. Drama critics, like Vitu of *Le Figaro*, were compelled to acknowledge that 'all these young people play with a very studied care, not like amateurs, society people or hams but as true artists' (12 Sept. 1887). Edmond de Goncourt, from whose novel *Sœur Philomène* was adapted, recorded finding in the production an effectiveness which he had not observed in the script. This effectiveness lay in, 'the combination of subtlety of feeling, style and action with theatrical realism'.[1]

Goncourt's lukewarm comment about the script is telling. The Byl and Vidal adaptation was, in fact, innovatory in its avoidance of the melodramatic climaxes and multiplicity of events that had characterized earlier stage versions of naturalist novels, but it needed an innovatory theatrical imagination to perceive this. As with Hennique's version of Zola's *Jacques Damour*, there was no attempt to dramatize the whole novel. The script, which became the model for subsequent Théâtre Libre adaptations, concentrated instead on a single sequence of intense psychological conflict. The nun, Philomène, struggles to assert her faith in the face of her feeling for her atheistical colleague, the doctor Barnier, whilst he must face himself and his past when he recognizes a dangerously ill patient in Philomène's hospital to be Romaine, his former lover, forced on to the streets by poverty after following him to Paris from her village. Such a script, thin on plot, dense in social and psychological implication, demanded the kind of concentrated energy from its actors which Antoine was developing at the Théâtre Libre.

Although appalled by the subject-matter, which questioned religious faith and acknowledged on stage the realities of contemporary poverty, desertion and prostitution, the conservative Sarcey, nevertheless, found great qualities

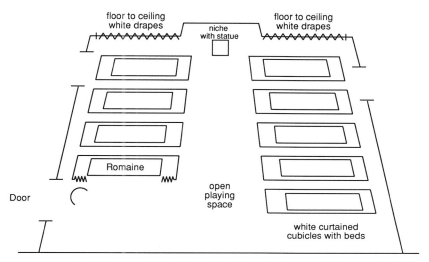

floor to ceiling
white drapes

niche
with statue

floor to ceiling
white drapes

Romaine

Door

open
playing
space

white curtained
cubicles with beds

4 *Sœur Philomène*, Théâtre Libre 1887. Stage plan for Act II showing the arrangement of the stage and the acting space, based on descriptions and a photograph of the scene

of 'observation, imagination and style' in the production. The *Gaulois* critic stressed the 'simplicity of means' through which Antoine achieved immense effects, whilst Ganderax of the influential *Revue des deux mondes* acknowledged that his scepticism evaporated before the naturalness of the first act in which the characters came and went, eating and chatting between operations, washing their hands at the small fountain at the back, until the scene rose to a climax in a heated defence by Barnier (Antoine) of the integrity of the nuns which was 'punctuated by an oath which is the guarantee of his sincerity'. It was less the shock of the oath which made this moment for Goncourt, too, 'hugely effective' than the fact that, instead of standing piously, Antoine uttered it 'stretched out, lying back against the table', so that his very coarseness of word and gesture 'underlin[ed] his defence of these holy women'. The stage action seems to have absorbed the attention of the commentators despite their preconceptions.[2]

Another example of what proved at once so stylish and so real in the production came in the second act, where it was not a single gesture that impressed but a carefully constructed sequence of action. The scene, which represented the hospital ward, was, apart from a crucifix over the door at the front and a statue of the Virgin Mary at centre back, entirely set in white: white hangings, white covers to the iron beds, white habits for the nuns. The dying woman lay in a bed at right front of the stage. Two rows of beds, nine altogether, placed to give the illusion of parallel lines seen in perspective, ran from left and right front towards the centre back of the stage, where the statue was placed. In the final sequence of the play, Philomène (Deneuilly) walked in silence the length of the two rows away from the audience to lead the *oremus* at the statue. The orchestration of Deneuilly's soft voice, praying at the back of the stage, the communal responses of the sick at mid-stage and the random sounds of the dying woman at the front, rambling during the 'Our Father' then singing during the 'Hail Mary', divided attention between two rival kinds of desolation, and forced the audience into consciousness of that desolation and of the private feeling behind the public role Philomène must assume.

The play ends with an exchange whose organization is reminiscent of the ending of *Jacques Damour* in the way it shifts the weight of feeling and interpretation on to the audience. Barnier enters on the physically static scene of the *oremus*, his movement across the stage to the bed of the now silent Romaine breaks the physical stillness and the ritual pattern of voices:

PHIL:	Holy Mother	*Response*:	Pray for us
	Mother of Christ		Pray for us
	Mother so pure		Pray for us

A quick exit having been orchestrated for the other characters, Barnier and Philomène face each other across the bed of the dead Romaine as he attacks the vanity of her prayers and she of his science. In a brief exchange, spoken quietly, she then states that she is not a woman, only Sœur Philomène; he asks her to forgive him; she replies that only God can forgive. Saying she'll finish by making him believe, he exits abruptly and she kneels to pray by Romaine's bed. Each word, tone, gesture, stage position, contributes to the audience's gripped attention. In a final small but significant gesture, Antoine had the actress drop her prayerbook and sob as the curtain fell.

For all the sequence seemed 'real', 'sincere' or 'natural', the draining of colour from the stage, the prominence of the religious icons, the arrangement of the stage furniture and people, the counterpoint of voices, the skilled use of silence and of expressive gesture were all carefully contrived to contribute to the total scenic image. The effect was due less to either the issues or the stage set, as such, than to Antoine's use of the stage space and his organization of the relationships of objects and people within that space and to the belief each of the actors created in the living presence of his or her character on the stage and the emotional interaction between them.

Just what was new about Antoine's staging is worth fuller discussion. Various nineteenth-century actors had created a flutter of critical excitement by introducing bits of everyday activity, sitting to deliver a speech or turning away from the audience to speak up stage or to exit. Earlier in the century,

Bocage had quarrelled with the Gymnase for his defiance of acting convention, including the obligation to face the audience continually; Montigny, at the same theatre in the 1840s, first, according to Dumas fils, 'had chairs changed in position by characters while they were speaking, . . . began ladies knitting during the dialogue when previously they never had anything in their hands but a fan or a handkerchief' and 'added many little pieces of business to give the dialogue life, to make it appear more rapid', and Marie Dorval and Frédéric Lemaître appalled the Comédie and charmed their Boulevard audiences by an absorption in their parts that led Gautier to write that Dorval, 'had cries of poignant reality, sobs to break the heart, intonations so natural, tears so sincere, that the theatre was forgotten and one could not believe that the grief was assumed'. Antoine himself recalled having seen Mounet-Sully, in *Zaire* in the 1870s, so abandon the rules of politeness under pressure of the part that he committed the solecism of turning inwards to the centre stage.[3]

Throughout the century, then, there had been moves towards realistic behaviour on stage, but the reported impression of what was happening at the Théâtre Libre is on a quite different scale. The previous examples of realistic performance had not notably altered audience expectations because they were piecemeal, attributed to the individual genius or rashness of particular actors and not linked with evident changes in dramatic texts or with a generally available acting style. Whilst individual actors might seem to become absorbed into the world of the play, the neo-classic conventions of presentational acting, endorsed by Napoleon at the beginning and energized by the genius of Rachel at mid-century, remained the model for teaching at the Conservatoire, and for performance on the French stage.

The habitual playing place of nineteenth-century theatre was the front third of the stage, so that faces were clearly lit and figures were not obscured by the shadows thrown by the footlights into the stage area. Leading actors habitually assumed the centre front of the stage, beside the prompter's box (as Henry Irving, for example, continued to do even after his organization of the *mise en scène* had become famous). And actors stood still to speak and receive lines. All was motivated by the rule that dialogue should be directed forward to the audience. As late as 1923, Antoine could still write:

French actors are unable to speak a word without asking you to be a witness. They speak not facing but turning their backs or sides to each other. If the tenor or young premier has a declaration to make to the young première he will stand behind her in order to remain completely visible, not to her to whom he addresses himself, but to you.

(*Conferencia*, 1 Mar. 1923)

Powerful acting certainly existed within the presentational style, as Antoine was the first to admit in his memories of Mounet-Sully and the young

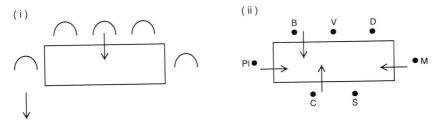

5 Seating around a table. (↓ playing direction)
(i) May 1887, *En famille*, based on photographs in fig. 2.
(ii) October 1887, reproducing Antoine's own sketch for Act I of *Sœur
     Philomène*. The leading speakers, B (Barnier) and M (Malvoire) are placed
     in dominant positions. The two with their backs to the audience are
     very small roles

Bernhardt, but something rather different was being developed at the
Théâtre Libre.

Conscious of the need to make the most of the depth of his tiny stage and
of the dramatic effectiveness of dividing audience attention between
different spheres of action happening simultaneously, Antoine had already,
in his two experimental evenings, used the back wall and windows for
entrances and exits and as a place from which silent characters could watch
the action at the front of the stage. In *Sœur Philomène*, his attempts to create a
more life-like stage action resulted in a significant shift of the centre of that
action.

An incident in the first act of *Sœur Philomène*, in which a group of medics
meet at lunchtime, epitomizes the development. Whereas the actors in *En
famille* had imitated reality by sitting at table and even eating and drinking on
stage, but had followed current stage convention in standing to deliver their
major speeches and arranging themselves so that everyone around the table
faced the audience, not only did characters now give their important
speeches seated, as if talking to each other, but their seats, placed on all sides
of the table and turned in to it, appeared to ignore the audience altogether.
The actors were playing towards each other, as if in a room, and not out to
the audience, as if in a picture frame (see fig. 5). This seemingly small change
was one of many in the production which demonstrated that the crucial shift
to illusionist theatre had taken place. The audience–stage relationship had
been altered. In moving the centre of the acting area from the middle of the
front plane to the middle of the stage area, and requiring his actors to play in
to the stage space rather than out to the audience and never to glance
knowingly at it, Antoine had moved the focus of the action from the
auditorium to the stage (see fig. 6). The actors, no longer playing directly to

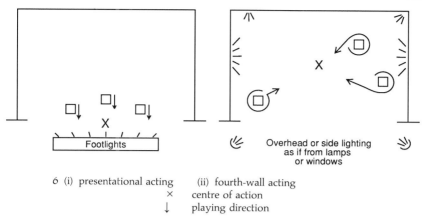

6 (i) presentational acting   (ii) fourth-wall acting
                 ×   centre of action
                 ↓   playing direction

the audience, are, by implication, no longer playing for it. No longer the acknowledged core of the action, the audience experiences the illusion of looking in on another real, self-centred world, of being the unseen witness of a moment of actual existence. Each audience member becomes a voyeur, a chance eavesdropper in whose unacknowledged presence the most intimate concerns of the characters are revealed. Jean Jullien supplied the felicitous phrase when he described the barrier between stage and audience as 'a fourth wall, transparent for the public, opaque for the actor'.[4]

If the illusion of the reality of the on-stage world were to hold, it followed that evident audience-focused conventions must be avoided and elements which might draw attention to the fact of performance, or to the pre-existent and conned script, suppressed. Aside and direct address become impossible, soliloquy absurd, unless motivated by loneliness, drunkenness or imminent breakdown. A hundred years later, the illusion-breaking tactics of Beckett's *Waiting for Godot* still make an impact because, despite the proclaimed revolt from realism, the expectations of the audience remain those created by Antoine and his dramatists.

But there is a paradox in all this. The audience of the *Sœur Philomène* scene only seems to be ignored. Illusionist theatre is not less artificial than other theatre, it is differently artificial. It is the shaped imitation of reality that makes the action more credible and more gripping. What happens on stage is not life but ever more thorough make-believe. However close to conversation what is spoken might appear, it remains dialogue, written to be spoken as if spontaneous but not, in fact, spontaneous, and much fuller awareness of the whole stage is demanded from the silent actors if they are not to distract attention from the less obviously positioned principals. Such a disposition, indeed, necessitates ensemble rather than star acting. The more natural-seeming grouping requires much greater attention to blocking if the main speakers are not to be masked. In overturning the old conventions, Antoine found that he must invent new ones in order to persuade his audience to believe in the reality of the fictional life presented on stage.

Although the rhetoric might occasionally make it appear that illusion and reality were confused in Antoine's theatre, the practice did not. There is no evidence whatever in Antoine's set-sketches, in photographs of the plays in performance or in eyewitness accounts that he ever set pieces of furniture, backs to the audience, along the front line of the stage, as has sometimes been claimed.[5] To someone with Antoine's theatrical sense transparency was the most crucial of the fourth wall effects. If the actor, being mobile, could and, on occasion, did turn away from the audience, the furniture, being inanimate, could not. It was arranged to look as natural as possible but without obscuring the view of the stage.

Sarcey, with his customary acuity, perceived the skill that had gone into making *Sœur Philomène* appear so natural and declared:

no more convention is their cry, and their plays are full of convention . . . go and watch students eating. When the conversation is animated all speak at once. That is the true truth. In the theatre that can't happen. Because it is necessary that the public hear, and that they hear the characters who are principals in the drama. These men have therefore condemned the others to absolute silence.   (*Le Temps*, 18 Dec. 1887)

He was right in fact if not in tone. Precisely because he aimed at illusion of the most complete kind, Antoine had to use artifice. If his actors were to eliminate reference to their private selves in projecting their characters, they needed acting skills as well as a sympathetic imagination. Theatrical skills were more not less crucial in the illusionist theatre. Antoine may well have become the first great *metteur en scène* because he engaged seriously with the claims of illusion and realised that, if it were to be sustained, the interacting elements of staging must be subject to a single organizing consciousness. Many of the innovations in theatrical practice that have been most unquestioningly adopted throughout Western theatre follow directly from this: attention to technique, belief in ensemble, intensive rehearsals, the carefully devised *regiebüch*. Like Wagner before and Stanislavski after him, Antoine, from the second soirée onwards, dimmed the house lights so that the audience might concentrate attention on the lit stage world and ignore each other.

Antoine's practice was ahead of his rhetoric at this time, for the stage world is not coterminous with the real world, however fully it might have the capacity to arouse real emotion. No doctor rushes from the auditorium to offer his services when Ibsen's Hedwig shoots herself. The audience might be thrilled into silence at a crowd scene but no one flees the theatre in fear or tries to join the mob. The seemingly real, the impression of spontaneity was what Antoine was continually working to achieve, which is why those critics, like Sarcey, who repudiated what they felt was his theoretical naïveté, repeatedly found themselves seduced by the on-stage action.

For the majority of the audience, the illusion Antoine created in *Sœur Philomène* clearly did compel belief. Far from being cool observers from beyond the fourth wall, they found themselves drawn experientially into the on-stage action. The production was thrilling in its truth-to-life, its observation. Ganderax felt 'the communication of ideas and emotions between this humble stage and this little auditorium' that derived from the belief created that 'these characters are not theatrical heroes but creatures sharing our humanity'. Antoine had achieved one of those mysterious moments of great theatre in which audience attention is made alert, feeling is quickened. What is astonishing is that, despite frequent failures, evenings that ended with the house in stony silence or hostile uproar, he would go on to achieve this kind of success again and again in the course of the next seven years.

It is, I think, valuable to enquire further into what was involved in the Théâtre Libre's illusionist acting style and what factors contributed to Antoine's development of it. It was not just the naturalness of the acting in *Sœur Philomène*, the fact that there was, 'nothing forced, nothing melodramatic', as *Gaulois* put it, 'no effects, no cries, no big gestures', that so impressed the audience. It was the inwardness of the performances. The very voice and bearing of the actors seemed in character; they seemed to be living their parts. Deneuilly, for example, spoke with 'a choked voice, as if suffocated by the interior struggles from which Philomène will emerge victorious' (*Figaro*) and Sarcey, despite his hostility to realist drama, was forced to admit that Antoine 'created great effect with his sometimes incisive, sometimes husky voice'. Jean Jullien, indeed, wanted to call the Théâtre Libre company 'interpreters' rather than 'actors' to avoid the implication, suggested by the common word, of self-display and pretentious diction at the expense of the subtle character distinctions inherent in the dialogue of the new drama.[6]

It is evident that, at its best, Antoine's own acting was compelling, despite the fact that his voice, like Irving's, seems not to have been particularly powerful. It is evident, too, that the acting developed in his theatre was an extension of his own style. The actor Méré, who was with Antoine from the beginning, recalled that even at the Cercle Gaulois:

He spoke as no one had before — he did not recite, he did not declaim . . . he spoke, he seemed to converse with other actors just as in life . . . If he had to laugh, his laughter gushed out naturally — if he had to weep, you saw him shed real tears — if he had an angry scene, people hid.

Le Théâtre Libre — Le 9 Octobre 1887

Monsieur Le Comte de Villiers de l'Isle-Adam, Monsieur Jules Vidal, Monsieur Arthur Byl vous prient de leur faire l'honneur d'assister à la Représentation qui sera donnée au Théâtre Libre, le Mardi 11 courant, à 8 h ½

L' Évasion
Pièce en un acte en prose.

Sœur Philomène
Pièce en deux actes en prose.

7 Subscriber's ticket for *Sœur Philomène*, 1887, printed in the form of an invitation issued in the names of the playwrights (to Jean Jullien, journalist and subsequently Théâtre Libre author)

Intelligence was crucial and that word, often coupled with a note that the voice was not strong, recurs in accounts of his quality as an actor from the note on his failed Conservatoire audition, 'de l'intelligence, du naturel – organe médiocre', to Sarcey's admission that, 'Antoine has no voice but by force of understanding succeeds in subduing and stirring his audience.'[7]

Whilst he never questioned the skill of Got, Mounet-Sully or Bernhardt, Antoine was clear that those skills were inappropriate to his theatre. The fundamental battle was for characterization by the actor and against display of a stage personality. In Antoine's house there would be, as George Moore reported, 'no taking the stage, no playing to the gallery'. The traditional seductiveness of the actor, the titillation of the audience by self-display, what Antoine even described as, 'solicit[ing] at any price the approval of the public', was sternly rejected. It is a fundamental change from playing to, to playing for, an audience and one that, departing from the practice of centuries, helped establish the dominant twentieth-century mode. This does not mean, however, that the audience abandoned its customary role easily. Demonstrative audience response to a particular 'turn' still punctuated performances. 'Who does not remember Antoine in *La Sérénade*', wrote Jullien. 'He had three replies to make, no more, three replies both drab and grey, and it was enough to make the whole room applaud.'[8]

As I have already suggested, despite the legend, Antoine was by no means the first to turn his back on the audience. His achievement was to provide notable consistency in his own and his company's acting and to promote it with a rhetoric to counter that of the Conservatoire and the neo-classical tradition. The Conservatoire's hold on entry to the respectable end of the acting profession meant that attitudes in mainstream theatre were self-perpetuating. An Englishwoman who studied at the Conservatoire in 1896 later recalled that complete production was not attempted. Each trainee was, 'more or less fixed in a certain line of parts; the conventional types of the theatre of the day. Comedy, tragedy, leading juvenile, soubrette, heavy lead etc.' and was trained by an experienced actor: 'for every phrase there was only one determinable inflection . . . which when once found should never be allowed to vary'. Emphasis was placed on what the Conservatoire textbook called *la seule inflexion juste*, not on the interaction of characters within plot and environment.[9] Whilst Antoine's personal animosity against the Conservatoire which had refused him a place is undeniable, his recognition that influence and fixed attitudes governed audition procedures led him to attend to what was wrong with Conservatoire training methods, and this provided the basis for his own ideas of acting.

The way actors spoke their words was important. Antoine attacked both the habitual nasal sing-song, developed to enable projection in the vast theatres of the beginning of the century, and the cherished Théâtre Français' enunciation, what Charles Mosnier labelled, 'l'Ar–t–i–cu–la–tion' (p. 31) in which all elision was forbidden, all 'e's open and all particles given full weight so that the dialogue was slow and declamatory and all voices vibrated ('la Vibrrration'). Such mannered diction, appropriate, perhaps, to the alexandrines of Racinian tragedy and adaptable to the habitual rising inflections of melodrama and the polished repartee of mid-nineteenth-century *haut-bourgeois* comedy, did not equip the actor to bring out the expressive sub-text of the low-toned, often colloquial prose of the new drama. Being amateurs and therefore untrained in the conventional mannerisms, the Théâtre Libre actors had freedom to find their own voices whilst being alert to the 'varieties, the unforeseen, the nuances of life, the indirect intonations, the eloquent silences' (Odéon lecture, 1903).

How far the charges of inaudibility brought against the conversational style are to be believed is questionable. Coquelin wrote:

> The theatre is not a drawing room; it is absurd to address an audience of fifteen hundred in a theatre as if one were talking to a few friends in the chimney corner; without increase in tone inaudibility is certain; without clearer articulation we shall be unintelligible.
>
> (*The Art of the Actor*, p. 45)

Sarcey claimed that the verse of Mendès' *Le Reine Fiammette* was so badly spoken that he hardly heard a word although the press was in ecstasies and that the dialogue in Jullien's *Le Maître* couldn't be heard beyond the second row of the stalls, although 'the play, which [he] personally found mediocre, had a very great success and the word masterpiece was uttered'. In part, these are statements of resentment at the absence of an expected rhythm and declamatory resonance. The concentrated attention so frequently registered could not have been commanded if the audience really could not hear, and some physically static sequences evidently depended on expressive vocal capacity. Goncourt wrote of the extended court scene of *La Fille Elisa* that, 'there is not an advocate at the Palais capable of pleading a cause like Antoine pleaded yesterday' and Lugné-Poë, although his memoir of Antoine is marked by extraordinary personal malice, insisted that Antoine taught him to speak. His own consciousness of lacking voice had, however, been the one factor that had caused Antoine to hesitate after the success of his first soirée and on more than one occasion a sympathetic critic, such as Frank Fay, noticed that he had to strain to hear because of the 'speed and softness' of the enunciation, so it is probable that, in the effort to avoid histrionics, lines were occasionally thrown away.[10]

What is quite clear is that bodies had to be as expressive as voices in Antoine's theatre. At an obvious level, this meant that actors must demonstrate consciousness of each other when speaking and avoid the deliberate turn towards the audience to emphasise a point or to acknowledge applause. More subtly, it meant that a narrow range of formal hand and arm gestures must give way to a use of the whole body in which stance and movement would convey the age, social class and mood of the character and smaller, more life-like gestures would alert audiences to nuances of interaction between characters, so that fixed attention, a pencil moved, a suddenly overturned cup, a touched hand, would be expressive. His actors had to be aware that 'at certain moments their hands and feet could be more eloquent than a tirade' (Mosnier, p. 610). The reiterated jokes about seeing only Antoine's back were more than matched by comments about how much he conveyed even when neither speaking nor obviously gesticulating. Coquelin evidently had Antoine in mind when he wrote:

I know all that can be said in favour of these 'back effects'. Certain actors gifted with a fine plastic presence are very fond of them; and the back muscles have their own means of expression, they bend, they crouch, straighten themselves, arch back, they can even at a pinch seem to be listening.   (*The Art of the Actor*, p. 46)

Costume, bearing, voice, manner of speech, could all provide important signals to the character's physical, social and psychological being. Even when he gained the resources to employ designers and seamstresses, the actors in Antoine's theatres always had ultimate responsibility for their own costumes, their hair and make-up, the very mud on their boots.

If Antoine was an outstanding actor some of his colleagues, Mévisto, Mlle Barny, Mme France, Luce Colas, Arquillière, Janvier, Gémier, Grand, Joubé were amongst the best of their generation as even the most hostile and sceptical critics had, at times, to acknowledge. But, more than this, it is clear that the company as a whole, including those weaker members who lacked the skill or stamina to become professional actors, so acted together that the stage event was often spell-binding. Absorption in the action, mutual physical awareness, eye contact, the expression of the character's condition in the bearing of the actor is apparent even in the dingiest or the most evidently posed of the photographs of Antoine's productions that I have unearthed from the early *En famille* onwards.

The idea of ensemble acting had been revived for the modern period by the Saxe-Meiningen Company and was one of the elements of their work that Antoine most admired – and most envied – when he saw the company perform in July 1888. 'In whatever direction you look', he wrote, 'you fix your eyes on a detail in the situation or character. The power is incomparable.'[11] Allowing for patches of raw and ragged acting as new actors took the place of experienced ones, lured away by commercial theatres, Antoine's company had a qualitative consistency that continually astonished, a consistency derived from shared belief and dependent on intensive training and rehearsal.

Antoine's emphasis on versatility was both adversarial and fundamental to the way his troupe was trained. Whereas a leading Comédie actor had the right to all the parts in his or her particular line in any given season, type-casting seemed deadening to Antoine. Each new play must make new demands on the actors who must extend their skills by playing a wide range of roles. Although he himself excelled in elderly peasant parts — Akim in *Power of Darkness*, Père Rousset in *Blanchette*, Père Fouan in *La Terre* — one of his outstanding roles was the young Oswald in *Ghosts*, another, the lover in Banville's lyrical *Le Baiser*, whilst in *La Sérénade* Mévisto was cast as the weak old father for the express purpose of demonstrating his range to Got, and Antoine took a bit part with three replies. Antoine took eighty-three different roles in his time with the Théâtre Libre and Gémier, who, having failed to get a place at the Conservatoire, joined Antoine in 1892, played forty-two roles in three years. Such a system demanded extraordinary discipline and nervous energy from the actors, even more so at the Théâtre Antoine where the repertoire changed nightly and each actor had to carry numerous roles. There, as at the Théâtre Libre after its first year, however exhausting the demands might be, there was always a press of actors wanting to learn through working with the company.

The manner of work, the long hours of intensive rehearsal, Antoine's own single-mindedness created a fierce company spirit. Those not prepared to give everything to the Théâtre Libre, left. From July 1887, Antoine got himself into the Conservatoire auditions and in August 1888 he advertised for young people who wished to learn their métier to join him. He also, increasingly, attracted professional actors, like Marie Defresnes of the Comédie-Française, Louise France who had played soubrette roles with Coquelin, Henry Mayer from the Vaudeville, Mlle Meuris, a first-prize winner at the Conservatoire, from the Théâtre du Parc in Brussels. Impressed by the Théâtre Libre, they came to work and learn in its environment, as did Conservatoire students or candidates. The great coup came in May 1889 when Damoye, having won the Conservatoire tragedy prize and, therefore, the right to make his debut at the Comédie-Française, did so with Antoine instead. Many of the actors of the next generation, indeed, had their training not with the Conservatoire but with Antoine.

The difference between the two styles was demonstrated in the often disappointing results when Théâtre Libre plays were taken by mainstream houses. Professional actors took over the words, but not the inwardness in performing them, and the realistic set was not sufficient to establish belief. As Henry James had observed of an early attempt at realism, 'if the chairs and tables were very natural, the actors were rather stiff'. Hennique later contrasted the unconvincing effect the fine figure of Paul Mounet made playing Jacques Damour with the thrill Antoine created playing the part as 'a poor miserable creature', La Pommeraye found that the Odéon actors spoke too emphatically to convey an impression of conversation between humble people and another critic finding the Odéon actress 'too straight in bearing, too young, too distinguished' as Jacques's wife, said that the Théâtre Libre actors by contrast had 'truly entered the skins of their characters. They were inexperienced but one felt that they acted on the stage without awareness of the presence of the public.'[12]

Such impressions were commonly recorded even by critics who declared themselves hostile to naturalist acting and habitually insisted that they could not hear in Antoine's theatre: Sarcey wrote of a Théâtre Libre revival at the Bouffes du Nord, 'Antoine gave to this old man a *je ne sais quoi* of gravity and mystery to which the other did not attain'; Doumic wrote, of an Ancey failure at the Odéon, that the lines 'demanded to be spoken with simplicity and naturally' and that the actors were 'very inferior this time to those of the Théâtre Libre', and Hector Pessard wrote in response to the failure of a Becque revival at the Comédie-Française that, 'M. Antoine's back is less destructive of my scenic illusion than these faces narrating their private business to the gentlemen of the orchestra stalls.' Antoine wrote of the same production that:

When Mlle Reichenberg attacks the first scene of *La Parisienne* with her actressy voice and when M. Prud'hon replies to her in the tones of Dorante, they immediately falsify Becque's prose, and they did this for three hours the other evening without respite . . . Most of our actors, from the moment they appear on stage, seem driven to substitute their own personality for the character whom they should make live; instead of themselves being subsumed in their character, their personality takes the character over. Thus, the other evening, we had Mlle Reichenberg and not Clotilde; M. Prud'hon, Le Bargy and de Feraudy, but not Becque's people at all.

Certainly, although Becque had come to be valued as a major dramatist, despite the increasing imitation of illusionist acting his plays did not achieve notable success until they were performed by Antoine's company at the Théâtre Antoine in the later 1890s.[13]

At this distance in time, when illusionist acting is the norm, improvisation is not uncommon and the Stanislavski system has been developed into the Strasburg Method, it is all too easy to assume that we understand what was meant by realistic acting in Antoine's day. In deriding stylized gesture and declamation, Antoine was not advocating that actors play themselves or indulge their own emotions. Each must engage in an act of imaginative identification with the character for the duration of the stage performance, after which the actor would become him or herself again. So Mévisto could play first the mad murderer in Icres's realist *Les Bouchers*, uttering his furious tirades in a 'thunderous voice' and carry equal conviction when he returned after the interval to speak prophecies 'with perfect lyricism', in flowing beard and white robes, as Jesus Christ in Darzens's miracle play, *L'Amante du Christ*. His triumph in both parts outraged militant Catholics, unable to perform as disciplined a separation between the actor and his part as Mévisto's own. Other critics would delight in asking, 'Did you recognize in the little father Matthiew, played by M. Antoine, the young and elegant intern of immediately before? This variety, this art of diverse composition of different roles is what characterizes true artists.'[14]

The absorption in the part, so crucial to naturalistic acting, must be founded on extensive preparation. Plays usually went into intensive rehearsal some three weeks before performance, at the rue Blanche studio and on stage with lights and props when possible. Where there were problems, as with the casting of the lead in Curel's *L'Envers d'une sainte*, for which some twenty-four different actresses were tried, rehearsals might stretch over months alternating with new, less problematic, productions. Antoine's attitude to his actors combined the egalitarian and the despotic. Although he called them his 'companions' and always addressed them by their titles, he was demanding and often impatient. Lugné-Poë claimed that he worked on them by a combination of terror and naive charm but that when he claimed he would make a great performer of one of them, he did (*Le Sot du tremplin*, p. 93).

Scenes were worked over and over, lines, gestures, stance, were plotted with remarkable attention to detail and all movements were recorded in the prompt book so that any slip could be immediately rectified. The actors had to seem to live their parts, speak as if experiencing the exact emotion, but must not improvise in any way, nor alter lines nor miss a recorded move-ment. Mosnier's contract included the agreement, 'never under any circum-stances to modify the *mise en scène* or the interpretation of the entrusted role' (p. 273). Antoine insisted that his actors listen to the text and think, understand, imagine their character on the basis of what was said and done there and on their experience of people they had observed in the real world so that, through their mimetic skills, they could eliminate their private selves and reproduce the character the author had imagined. Writers who sat in on rehearsals were amazed at the very long hours Antoine and his casts worked, but also at their concentration on the play itself. For Antoine, the answer to Diderot's paradox, to the question of how a part could be both constructed and lived lay in thorough training and rehearsal. Much later, he would complain that Desjardins was under-rehearsed in a Comédie-Française *Cinna*. The bizarre *mise en scène* meant that 'the actor was not positioned to launch one of the finest cries of the French stage' (*L'Information*, 8 July 1919). There is no sentimental insistence on losing oneself in a part in such a statement.

Which is not to say that Antoine did not also perceive that on occasion a more than normal transforming power has seemed to energize a performance, leading the actor to experience briefly a total loss of self. Various actors since have attempted to articulate an experience of such absorbed playing in reminiscences and autobiographies and audiences and critics have realised when they have been present at a 'really great performance'. Antoine's own performance as Oswald in *Ghosts* seems to have been of this frighteningly complete kind. Whilst George Moore reported that 'the drama seemed to be passing . . . deep down in our hearts in a way we never felt before', Antoine described his experience as a kind of madness in which, 'from the beginning of the second act I remember nothing, either of the audience or the effect of the show and at the fall of the curtain, I found myself shaking, enervated and unable to get a hold on myself for some time'. If such mysterious loss of self happens, it does so involuntarily within a performance, but the performance must have been rehearsed in every detail.[15]

With the change from presentational to illusionist acting, emphasis is shifted to the script and away from the individual actor. Self-promotion has no place. Jules Lemaître went so far as to say:

I am entirely in favour of impersonal comedians; perhaps the Théâtre Libre goes to the other extreme and turns each actor and actress into a mere machine; still, that is preferable to your mummer who would fain rewrite each of Shakespeare's plays to suit his own individuality . . . actors and actresses are on the stage to present your creations to the public, not to invent your parts for you. The great wish of every sensible dramatist must be to work with a good all-round company, innocent of the star and original genius.

Antoine's description of the role of the actor in relation to the text often sounds remarkably similar to Gordon Craig's suggestion that the actor is essentially an instrument, a marionette. Replying in 1893 to a Comédie actor, Le Bargy, who had asked him to persuade Curel to modify his role in *L'Amour brode* to make it more sympathetic, Antoine wrote that the actors' métier:

is to interpret as best they can characters of whose genesis they know nothing. They are, in reality, mannequins, marionettes more or less perfect, depending on their talent, whom the author clothes and manipulates according to his whim . . . the actor's ideal must be to become a keyboard, a marvellously tuned instrument on which the author can play at will.

And he appealed to Le Bargy to work to change attitudes at the Comédie-Française. Intriguingly, when he left the Comédie ten years later Le Bargy, who had succeeded at the Conservatoire the year Antoine failed, joined Antoine's company and in 1919, as drama critic of *L'Information*, attacked the Comédie for seeming no more alive than its façade.[16]

References to discipline were as common in press accounts as exclamations of wonder at the truth and naturalness of the acting, but such impersonality was not cold. Critics struggled for language to describe the mutuality and intensity of Théâtre Libre acting and its power to absorb the attention of its audiences. An impression of what they meant can be recouped from Antoine's films, from the interaction of the mother and child in *Coupable*, for example.

The rhetoric of amateurism was important because it emphasized the claims Antoine made to fresh seeing. His actors could engage in a direct reading of each fresh text unspoiled by the preconceptions of blinkered training and dogmatic practice. In his May 1890 manifesto, Antoine took delight in quoting Stendhal's claim that he had seen a perfectly performed play only once, 'in Italy, by ordinary actors, in a barn', and in noting that there were amongst his actors an architect, a dressmaker, a wine merchant, a telegraphist and various clerks and shop assistants. But the demands Antoine made on his actors, rehearsing daily from 2.00 pm and usually well into the night, were such that, although there was a continual coming and going of genuine amateurs and Curel in 1891 noted that Théâtre Libre actors still worked without pay, 'sustained by a touching conviction of serving art and a blind trust in their chief', very few of the regular actors were able to continue in fully paid work outside the theatre, unless, like Pinsard the architect, they took tiny parts.[17]

By 1890, according to Lugné-Poë, who was paid from 60 to 70 francs a programme to act as régisseur, the company was composed of professional or semi-professional actors, or people like Janvier who juggled work and the Théâtre Libre until they had the confidence and reputation to give up work.[18] The fact that virtually all the company was able to go on a long summer tour that year demonstrates that few were tied by consistent outside work. The Théâtre Libre soon came to be seen as an alternative training school, 'a kind of practical and accessible Conservatoire', as Antoine called it, and many of the actors taken on by mainstream theatres came back when they could for his Sunday productions.

The success of an invited performance by Antoine and Marie Defresnes in Brussels with actors from the Théâtre du Parc, in January 1888, which 'raised in a single evening a month's salary at the Gas Company' (approx 120 francs), enabled Antoine to arrange for the whole company to play *Tout pour l'honneur* at the Molière there. After this, they regularly returned to Brussels, and also toured to London, St Petersburg, Berlin, Amsterdam and, from 1890, made annual summer tours of the French provinces. Of the 14,279 francs earned in touring and public performances at the Menus Plaisirs in the 1888–9 season, for example, something under a third went into the Théâtre Libre funds and the rest was shared amongst the actors. Whilst the theatre never made enough to pay its actors consistently for the monthly performances or for the long rehearsal hours that led up to them, such tours and occasional public performances encouraged actors to remain with Antoine for surprisingly long periods.

3   Extending the repertoire

The Power of Darkness (11 Feb. 1888)

Mid-way through his first full season, recording the success of his first production of a foreign play, Antoine wrote:

> The performance of *The Power of Darkness* was a triumph. Tolstoi's play appeared to everyone to be a masterpiece. We had there the best and most important press imaginable; M. de Vogüé, all enthusiasm, came to find me to say that he was going to do an article for *La Revue des deux mondes*. The pressure for seats was such that they are demanding a public performance. Apart from anything else, the receipts will be welcome because I haven't a sou and I scarcely know how we shall be able to give the next show.
>
> (12 Feb. 1888)

The huge success of this play marked the proper arrival of the Théâtre Libre into public consciousness, and initiated a pattern of open performances of the most successful productions which brought in desperately needed cash. Although Antoine had feared that heavy snow would deter audiences from venturing to the public performance at the theatre on the outskirts of Paris, the theatre was packed, attendance, 'stupefying' (18 Feb. 1888), and the 4,000-franc profit secured the rest of the season.

Having demonstrated the importance of a carefully observed environment in creating a believable stage world in his earlier productions, Antoine used set, properties and costume to thrilling effect in *Power of Darkness*. Most of the previous Théâtre Libre plays had demanded a lower-middle-class living-room with humble domestic furniture and everyday costume for interior settings, whilst exterior scenes, the *commedia* garden of *La Nuit Bergamasque*, the faerie forest of Banville's *Le Baiser*, had required a degree of fantasy but little specificity. The demands of *Power* were altogether more rigorous. The quest for authenticity led Antoine, via his translator, to the Russian *emigré* community and permission to use antique costumes and to borrow icons, rugs, samovars brought from Russia. These, furnishing the stage, brought colour and strangeness to it and, for all they emanated from a quite different social stratum from that of Tolstoi's characters, created an *impression* of authenticity.

That the success came with a foreign play and was followed up by Antoine in the next few years with the French premières of work by Ibsen, Strindberg and Hauptmann, among others, was to have far-reaching implications for

European theatre. It takes an act of imagination now, when works by Brecht, Pirandello, Sartre, Beckett, Bond figure in the repertoire of theatres throughout Europe, to realize what an innovation it was to introduce Tolstoi's play to a French and, thereby, to a European audience. Previous to this, the custom in France, on the rare occasions when foreign works were played, had been to adapt them to local taste, as was done in the Comédie-Française's *Hamlet*, cannibalized by Dumas and Meurice in 1886. The Saxe-Meiningen Company was never invited to France and even when Wagner's opera had become an international *cause célèbre* no place could be found for it on a French stage. The planned staging of *Lohengrin* at the Eden Theatre in May 1887 had, indeed, been prevented by a ban. And here was Antoine, in the capital of European theatre, claiming a huge success for a play which had been banned in its own country and which he offered in a scrupulously close translation that made no concessions to the customs of the French stage and with a staging concerned, above all, to avoid the sentimental exoticism of the Opéra Comique and evoke an authentically Russian peasant world.

In contrast to the Théâtre Libre's first experimental evening a year previously, the leading critics, faced with several premières had, without exception, opted for that at the Théâtre Libre and had seen their choice vindicated. Across the political spectrum, from *La Petite République's* judgement that 'never [had] tragic horror and thrilling reality been pushed further than in this fine drama' to *L'Événement's* claim that 'M. Antoine's troupe created a marvel in *The Power of Darkness*', the press agreed that this was an 'immense success by acclamation' and that the applause that greeted the end of the fifth act was unlike anything witnessed for a long time in the theatre. The scholar-critic, Vogüé, well known for his championing of Russian mysticism against French Naturalism, said in his review that he had been fearing disaster, Antoine's Waterloo, but, in the event, 'this was Austerlitz; when the curtain fell on the final scene in a storm of acclamation, the public was transported', whilst not a few commentators shared the opinion expressed most sharply in *La République française's* comment, 'If I were a Parisian theatre director, I would not be proud of myself, especially today. What? To suspect the existence of a drama the equal of *Power of Darkness* and let escape me the marvellous windfall of its production.'[1]

Drunkenness, self-seeking, jealousy, betrayal, characterize the world of the play whose plot includes both the murder of an elderly husband, Peter (Cernay), by his wife, Anisya (Dorsy) and her lover, Nikita (Mévisto), and the expedient killing of the child of the adulterous liaison by Nikita and his mother, Matriona (Barny), until, in the final moments of the play, Nikita experiences a transformation, brought about by his father, old Akim (Antoine), a Tolstoian saintly fool, and, confessing his guilt, seeks penance.

Whilst the Médan group saw the play as typical of French Naturalism, Antoine was aware, as with his subsequent work on Ibsen and Hauptmann, that he was dealing with a play of a different kind and calibre from anything so far attempted. In praising a Pitoëff production of 1921, he would write that, 'our French interpretation, perhaps longer and more lyrical, hardly had this savour. With Pitoëff's company, Tolstoï's masterpiece takes another character, it is no longer the great Aeschylean drama that we created at the Théâtre Libre, with our Latin mentality, but a village tragedy, evidently much closer to the conception of the master.'[2]

For all its generosity to Pitoëff, the comment has significance for our understanding of the power of Antoine's own production and also, perhaps, even at this early stage, for his ambitions that would eventually surface at the Odéon. His apprehension that something lyrical and Aeschylean underlay the habitual concern with the substance of the real world enabled him to mount a production that was at once convincingly Russian, rooted in credible peasant activities and attitudes, and convincingly pertinent to the imaginative life of each member of the audience. It made him peculiarly well able to hold the opposing tendencies of Tolstoï's play in fruitful relationship. The powers of light and darkness are, indeed, pitted against each other in the play in a struggle for a man's soul. But, for all his mysticism, Tolstoï inhabited a nineteenth-century world and was responsive to its intellectual life and determinist philosophy. Whilst environment is certainly not everything, it figures as large in his plays as it does in his novels. In addition to Antoine's tried ability to create belief in environment, the play demanded a new sense of imaginative scale. Antoine's ability to communicate this to the cast and through them to the audience helps to explain why, when in Vogüé's terms a supposedly doctrinaire realist group came into contact with a primitive miracle play, the result was Austerlitz not Waterloo.

The matter of the translation was significant. The play, written in 1886 and banned the following year, was especially appropriate to Antoine's theatre because it was the work of a 'grand refusé' and because of its subject-matter and form. Tolstoï, who had become famous throughout France since the early 1880s, had used peasant argot, 'a locution', according to the London *Daily Telegraph* (19 Feb. 1888) that, although 'doubtless accurate', was 'tiresome, loathsome and repulsive in the extreme', to depict a peasant life of Zolaesque drunkenness and degradation. But, having been announced, production was held up because not only was the dialogue of Halpérine's published translation judged stiff, even academic, by Antoine but Halpérine had rarely given French equivalents for Tolstoï's idiomatic phrases, preferring to explain the Russian idiom in scholarly footnotes. Antoine commissioned a literal translation from a Russian, Pavlowski, and Méténier, author of *En famille* and an expert in underworld argot, produced from this a much rougher and more colloquial text which Faguet, amongst others, claimed people bilingual in Russian and French found 'of marvellous and absolutely literal fidelity'.[3]

Antoine was making a claim for the integral text but also for the director's responsibility for the translation. Forty years later, still holding to this, he wrote that it was not enough 'that a translation should be intelligent and faithful, to give the true movement and character of the work; it is necessary, too, that the adaptor has a genuine sense of dramatic composition and the gift of dialogue'. What is more, he took care to have the author endorse the version he planned to play and to publish the endorsement.

Méténier was able to produce a letter from Tolstoi's daughter which read:

Gracious sirs,
  My father says he has received your proofs; he strongly approves your translation and sends you some small corrections he has found necessary. He is very pleased to see *The Power of Darkness* staged and, above all at the Théâtre Libre,

and suggested alternatives for about twenty words. In much the same circumstances, Prozor's claim to be the single authorized French translator of Ibsen would be overridden with the publication of a correspondence in which the dramatist expressed his pleasure that the Théâtre Libre planned to première his work in France and his enthusiasm for the Darzens translation of *Ghosts* whose 'truth to the original' brought his consent 'in spite of [his] agreements with M. Prozor'. Ibsen's care in the matter is demonstrated in his comment that:

The word *Haandsraekning* does not have a double meaning. It implies the idea of a benevolent help in danger. By this word Osvald wishes to say that should the need arise, he wants someone to consent to give him the poison should he not be in a condition to take it himself.

Prozor's publishers were, moreover, later told by Ibsen that he could not refuse a second play – *The Wild Duck* – to the theatre that had first performed his work in France.[4]

The adversarial position adopted by some outsiders before the production demonstrates vividly the fixed beliefs against which Antoine was pitted in playing a foreign work. For all the subsequent wisdom about the play, Antoine had certainly not seized it out of the eager grasp of other Parisian directors and, indeed, a supposedly supportive Céard had written to Zola before the production that he feared that the slow tempo and obscure characters would leave the audience bored.[5] Just before the opening Halpérine, with the supporting opinions of leading dramatists, argued in a six-column article in *Justice* (6 Feb. 1888) that the play was great literature but could not feasibly be staged. A gleeful Antoine recorded these opinions in his May 1890 manifesto and again in his memoirs. Augier, Sardou, Dumas fils each acknowledged it a marvellous play but not playable and especially not in France. 'From the point of view of the French stage', wrote Dumas fils:

> I do not believe that M. Tolstoi's play would be possible. It is too sombre, none of the characters is sympathetic and the language which Akim, for example, speaks, would, in fact, be incomprehensible to us. The Nikita, so strange and so true would only appear boring at the outset and hateful at the end.

Sardou demonstrated how unbridgeable the gulf seemed between what was artistic or literary and what was good theatre, judging it 'cruelly true and very fine' but 'made to be read and not seen', whilst Augier found it, 'less a play than a novel in dialogue whose boredom would be unsupportable on the French stage'.

What is surprising here is how confidently Antoine's opponents expose their own flanks in making their claim for the well-made play, the strong plot, the clear moral statement, acknowledging that in the established theatre the strange and the true were, as Zola and Antoine had claimed, less important than optimism, polished language and familiar stereotypes. Dumas fils did, indeed, attempt to cover himself by adding, with a dismissive thrust at the Théâtre Libre's coterie audience, that 'a performance given before a lettered and refined public in an auditorium which would contain no more than 300 or 400 people, where women were in the minority, could leave a profound literary impression, but that would be all'. It was precisely such sneers that Antoine, so recently a member of the general public himself, rejected. One can see why the clamour for a public performance and its ardent reception were so gratifying to him and, indeed, wherever the play wasn't banned, as it was in London, for example, it was included in the Théâtre Libre tour repertoire and it was regularly revived for the general public at the Théâtre Antoine.

After resolving the matter of the translation, Antoine had a further brief but significant struggle before he could properly begin rehearsals. Zola, Méténier and their naturalist associates, whilst approving Antoine's choice of play and version, had less confidence than Antoine in his company. They took Tolstoi's play to be determinist and insisted that the figures deformed by their environment must be as strongly and convincingly represented as the single, wholly good character who seemed untouched by it. Since Antoine had cast himself as Akim, they wanted a professional actress, Marie Laurent, who had played the lead in the melodramatic Busnach version of Zola's *Le Ventre de Paris*, to play his adversary, Matriona, but Antoine had already decided that this role should go to Barny, his leading actress and loyal colleague from Cercle Gaulois days.

At the end of October, it was announced in *Figaro* that Laurent would play the part. Antoine merely recorded his scepticism in his diary, but Laurent left voluntarily after a series of stormy rehearsals, and shortly afterwards Antoine, noting his doubts about some of the actors, had the satisfaction of recording, 'Mévisto will be strong in Nikita . . . I am sure of Barny, of Luce Colas and of Lucienne Dorsy, who have already proved themselves in our earlier shows' (4 Feb. 1888).

It must have been peculiarly satisfying when, amongst the general praise for the acting, one reviewer, recalling a famous Lucretia Borgia performance, commented with unconscious irony that 'Mlle Barny was physically a Marie Laurent. Impossible to speak more truly, justly and be more terrible and more true in the role of Matriona.'[6] Whilst this was not Antoine's last battle to assert his control over casting, it was an important step on the way. After he had subverted a star-studded production of Porto-Riche's *La Chance de Françoise*, in the following season, by casting himself in a walk-on part and giving all his attention to the play with which it was paired and had stubbornly refused to accept Goncourt's judgement as to which part Mévisto should play in *La Patrie en danger* until Goncourt capitulated, authors no longer attempted to challenge his judgement in this matter.

The struggle was no mere whim on Antoine's part, but an assertion of faith in his own judgement and in his company. He needed to work with his own people precisely because unself-centred, ensemble playing was crucial to his conception of theatre and of Tolstoi's play. The frequent comments on the remarkable impression of ensemble suggest that the audience, accustomed to the star system, did experience something lived and interactive in the performance which made a triumph out of a play judged unplayable. One after another, critics tried to find words to describe 'the art truly rare and surprising' of the Théâtre Libre actors, 'some unknown, others very new to the profession', in this production. Hector Pessard wrote:

Perhaps I still haven't the custom of praising the interpreters of the play as I should. I beg them to forgive me if I haven't said at sufficient length how much I admire the talent with which they imitate the Russian peasants painted by Count Léon Tolstoi. They are perfect, in their accurate costumes. They do not raise their voices, they do the most terrible things quite naturally. They are true peasants, never hurrying, advancing slowly towards their goal, not looking towards the effect but for all that striking the first blow.

(quoted, 1890 manifesto)

In rehearsal, each actor, and there were twenty-one in the cast, had had to work to understand the psychological development of his or her own character and the necessities and pressures of the world in which that character lived. The texture of peasant existence was to be demonstrated in the detail of non-speaking as well as speaking parts. The low-key sequences were to be as fully prepared as the climactic ones, so that the audience response to sequences of horror or intense feeling would be grounded in belief in the characters' existence at more commonplace moments of the action. The high notes would develop out of the lower ones.

Antoine's own role of Akim is a case in point. Akim's language is repetitive:

> Sin fastens on to sin — sin drags sin after it and you're stuck fast, Nikita, fast in sin. Stuck fast in sin, I mean . . .

his meandering around an idea; his optimistic catch-phrases and general benevolence in the face of the squalid and despicable activity around him, have such an air of foolishness that the sharp characters' abuse of him functions as a distorted reflection of the audience's own response. His bemusement at the ways of the world, his shock that Nikita, now wealthy, had stopped working, his puzzlement at the notion that money would accrue interest as it lay useless in a bank, give the moral position a comic edge. It would have been easy enough for the actor to present a caricature, but Antoine clearly did not. He avoided the creaking voice and bent back of the quaint stage gaffer and developed an uncluttered performance that eschewed both histrionic gestures and fussy mannerisms. Most importantly, he played with total conviction: the self-conscious actor was never allowed to upstage the character. The comedy was poignant because it remained implicit, left to the audience to perceive. As Faguet, generally hostile to the Théâtre Libre's work, was forced to admit:

He composes with a care for detail, an art of subordinating every inflexion and every gesture to the principal trait, which is the first condition of his art and which is the distinctive mark of his talent. This saint of Holy Russia, this poor being, narrow, pure, holy, this abbé Constantin of the Steppes, one feels in his fixed gaze, in his gesture, brief and direct, sober and obstinate, one feels in all his being that this divine soul married with the intelligence of a child, is held in a definite formula, inflexible as monastic rule and that life passes it without bending it, almost without touching its lustre the more like water on the stone of a temple.   (1888, p. 13)

And Lugné-Poë wrote later that 'Antoine was an astonishing actor and those who saw him as Akim in the *Power of Darkness* will certainly agree with me.'[7]

Faguet's statement that Antoine composed his part with great care for detail seems to catch the essence of the acting style. Activity for activity's sake was not part of the stage method. The culture of a peasant world was evoked not just in the costumes: Nikita's leg bindings, the coarse fabric of the overgarments, the many layers of clothing worn or the brilliance of the women's headscarves, but in music and stage action. There was rhythmic accompaniment to the spinning of Act I; keening lamentation at the Act II death, and a celebratory song and dance at the Act V wedding which filled the stage with sound and movement. A drunken Nikita lurched and staggered but, unlike a comic stage drunkard, beat his wife viciously.

The actors accompanied the bad-tempered cross-talk, the jibes, the love-making, with the unceasing activity of those who need to press on with their work if they are to make a living. In the course of Act I, Peter mends a horse collar, the women spin. In Act II, an exterior scene, Anisya beats hemp and Nikita ploughs whilst they await Peter's death. In Act III, Anisya weaves at the loom. A labourer is heard off-stage, as if working in the stockyard outside. The audience's ready acceptance of such activities as the believable context for the action is evident when it emerges that Nikita's digging later in the play, which at first seems to be the same kind of activity, is in reality a preparation for the infanticide and, therefore, directly functional in the plot. The initial acceptance makes the horror that accompanies recognition all the stronger.

Religious phrases are mouthed by Tolstoi's characters in the middle of the most nefarious deeds: 'It's God's will', says Matriona of Peter's death by poisoning; 'God has sent the right guest at the right time', says Anisya at one of Matriona's entrances, and the innocent Akim enters after the lust and murder of Act II with the words, 'Peace be to this house.' The irony is perceived by the audience but not the characters (an effect J.M. Synge would extend in his peasant drama). Occasionally, such a phrase signals knowing hypocrisy as when Nikita, in Act I, crossing himself, declares publicly, 'By God, and may I never leave this spot if I know anything about it', and then, alone on stage later, says, 'How strange it was when I crossed myself before the icon. It was just as if someone shoved me. The whole web fell to pieces at once', a sensation that offers crucial preparation for the redemptive confession at the end of the play. Not only did Antoine hang an icon on the wall, but he had both good and evil characters cross themselves before it, which intensified the ironic effect of Tolstoi's dialogue whilst also suggesting the fixed habits of the peasant community.

As for the setting, the script required an exterior scene that included a porch, a fence beyond which were fields, a yard where wedding celebrations for a large crowd could be held and an interior that represented a credible Russian living and working environment. Working from two models made by Jules Antoine, his architect brother, and materials from the stores of the Théâtre Montparnasse, Antoine and his designer, Bertin, built their set, with its practicable stoop, its yard fence and its back-cloth of fields and, for its interior, solid walls to box in the close, constricted communal life and a solid Russian fireplace with bed space above for the sick Peter. Whilst it was not strictly true that, as *Le National* claimed, 'in this moving play decorators and machinists have nothing to do', since it was one of the Théâtre Libre's most

8 Interior set for Théâtre Antoine revival of *The Power of Darkness*.
Decor by Menessier.
From stage right: Marina (Méry, originally Deneuilly); Nikita (Marquet,
originally Mévisto); Akoulina (Jeanne Lion, originally Luce Colas). (*Le
Théâtre*, 138, Sept. 1904. Phot.Bibl.Nat., Paris)

ambitious sets to date, it was the case that the total stage scene was geared to
interact expressively with the dialogue and to concentrate 'interest on the
subject itself and the manner in which it is interpreted', rather than on the
spectacle as such. The audience were never invited merely to enjoy the local
colour: the lamentations at Peter's deathbed were at once traditional,
haunting and false-faced; Akim had to assert himself against the gaiety of the
authentically imitated wedding festival — 'laughter' and 'accordion music' is
repeatedly written in on Antoine's script of the final scene — to compel the
attention and confession of Nikita.

Pictures of Antoine's 1904 revival at the Théâtre Antoine (figs. 8 and 9)
demonstrate both the achievement and some of the problems of the realist
set. They show, as do most pictures of subsequent productions, that whereas
with attention to detail convincing interiors could be created, exterior scenes
were much more problematic. The dresser, equipped with crockery, the
animal-skin covers strewn on the sleeping-place above the brick stove, the
solidity of the peasant furniture, ring true, as do the steps, porch and
outbuildings of the exterior scene. But, however well painted, the bushes and

9 Exterior set for the revival of *The Power of Darkness*. Although the actors seem rather stiff, because they are holding their poses for the photograph, the importance of eye contact and interactive positioning of the characters is evident.

From stage right: Nikita; Matriona (Grumbach, originally Barny); Anisya (van Doren, originally Dorsy). (*Le Théâtre*, vol. 138, Sept. 1904. Phot.Bibl.Nat., Paris)

trees are clearly man-made: they fail to live and the use of real hay bales or – as in *La Terre* (see fig. 34) – of real grass and plants only serves to emphasize the artificiality.

After his play had been banned by the Russian censor, Tolstoi had substituted a more oblique version of the scene in which Nikita and Matriona bury the illigitimate child alive, in which the burial, taking place off-stage, is revealed gradually through the on-stage conversation of an inquisitive small child and an old man who half guesses, half hears what is happening. Whilst the early, direct version might seem worryingly close to 'doll, spade and dark lantern' melodrama, Antoine's choice of it is not surprising. Not only did the oblique version seem conciliatory, but the original version made greater demands on the audience's feeling. A growing consciousness of the enormity of the deed, which is seen to succeed the horror of Nikita's action, helps prepare for his eventual transformation. Antoine evidently saw the scene as pivotal and, throughout the play, had his Nikita (Mévisto) develop hints of remorse latent in the text: reeling at the end of Act I after uttering an idle blasphemy and sobbing in Act III when, having been denounced by Akim, he refuses a drink. By the end of the burial scene, his frantic state contrasted sharply with the calm efficiency of Barny's Matriona.

The impression the actor gave of being physically possessed was evidently a crucial part of the power of Mévisto's performance, accounts of which reveal the anomaly of an audience responding to the intense feeling generated by illusionist acting with the traditional means of acknowledging not the character but the skilful actor. As *La Patrie* reported:

In the first act, he expressed with extraordinary power of concentration the quasi-bestial love that pushes him to Anicia; he touched perfection in the scene where he buries the corpse of the child murdered by him and, a little later, he brought anxiety and remorse to the rending cry, 'Oh my mother what have you done to me?' with a gradation so strong and so accomplished that the whole room broke into applause.   (13 Feb. 1888)

If this provides a reminder of the limits of illusion, particularly in an audience accustomed to reward virtuoso acting, it also demonstrates how fully our present-day theatre has, by comparison, absorbed the social behaviour introduced by illusionist acting. However impressed we might be today by, for example, the cry, 'Oh mother, mother, / What have you done?', uttered by an actor playing Coriolanus, we don't assert our right to acknowledge it until the end of the scene.

The impact of the production was quickly felt outside the Théâtre Libre. After the public performance at the Théâtre Montparnasse, the company performed Act III at a Franco-Russian fête organized by *Figaro* in March in honour of the Russian ambassador. (No one seems to have found this odd, despite the Russian state's ban on the play.) It was felt outside Paris, too. Otto Brahm, preparing to open the Freie Bühne on the model of the Théâtre Libre, registered his own excitement at the play, whilst Antoine's touring production in Brussels at the end of the month (Feb. 1888) caused a furore, stimulating the founding of the Belgian Théâtre Libre and making an impact on the as yet unknown Maeterlinck.[8] Banned by the English censor when Antoine toured to London later that year, the play came to signify dramatic innovation and courage and, in the course of the next forty years, was repeatedly performed by independent companies. Antoine's role, Akim, was one of the first played by Max Reinhardt.[9] Stanislavski staged it, as did Pitoëff, the leading realist of the Cartel de Quatre, whilst the production by New York's Theatre Guild helped shape the writing of *Desire Under the Elms*, Eugene O'Neill's play about lust, child murder and greed for possession in rural New England. And it is no coincidence that when a production was finally permitted in England, in 1928, it was directed by J.T. Grein, who had been the founder of the English Independent Theatre. Antoine revived it (along with *Ghosts*) as one of his last productions at the Théâtre Antoine before he moved to the Odéon, where he staged it successfully in 1907, 1912 and 1913.

Ghosts (30 May 1890): *The Wild Duck* (17 Apr. 1891); *Miss Julie* (16 Jan. 1893)

After this epoch-making production, Antoine explored other sources of new foreign plays and by the summer of 1888 was already interested in Ibsen's most notorious and most frequently banned play, *Ghosts*, described subsequently in *Figaro* as, 'perhaps the most daring and most terrifying work in the contemporary repertoire' (9 Oct. 1889). Although Ibsen's play had, unlike *Power*, been produced elsewhere in Norwegian, in both Chicago in 1882 and Scandinavia in 1883, and in German translation in 1886, the Saxe-Meininger German production had been *in camera* and Ibsen's work, still unproduced in France, had only begun to be known there after two articles about it appeared in the *Revue d'art dramatique* in 1887. The French theatre bibliographer, Mme Horn-Monval, has described as 'a record without precedent in the foreign theatre in Paris', the appearance within ten years of '45 of the most outstanding works of the greatest Scandinavian dramatists' at the Théâtre Libre and the Théâtre d'Œuvre, adding that it had been achieved 'as if by the turn of a magic ring'. In February 1898, Antoine successfully challenged the censor's ban on public performance of *Ghosts* and in 1906 *The Wild Duck* revival prepared for the Théâtre Antoine, transferred to the Odéon as the first Ibsen production on a subsidized stage.[10]

Whilst there is no denying Antoine's achievement in introducing important contemporary foreign writing to the French stage, in recognizing that it was, indeed, important and in making the scrutiny of foreign writing an essential part of the future agenda of Lugné-Poë and of independent theatre generally, the story was evidently not as simple as Antoine's own account in his published diary suggests. Before staging *Miss Julie*, Antoine had refused Strindberg's *The Father*; after *The Wild Duck*, he let the initiative for further productions of Ibsen go to Poë at the Théâtre d'Œuvre where *The Father*, too, was staged in 1894, whilst *Ghosts* was not performed until 1890, two years after it had first been proposed and nearly a year after the Freie Bühne, Berlin's answer to the Théâtre Libre, had stolen a march and performed the German version for its opening production.

Quite why *Ghosts* met with such delay is unclear. Certainly, this time it proved even more difficult to find an appropriate translation and Antoine refused to rush to performance without one. He rudely rejected Hessem's French translation of the German version, after a reading at the Théâtre Libre in September 1888, on the grounds that it was tedious and very probably inaccurate. Céard wrote to Zola that Hessem had translated it into Belgian patois and the scenes were so slow and colourless that the theatre would have been emptied before the middle of Act II. The next French version available, made by Prozor in spring 1889, was mooted for production in December, but proved stilted and, whilst evidently reasonably accurate, was more than twice as long as the Norwegian original. As Paul Ginisty had concluded in an article on the Prozor translation, 'the time has still not come to attempt a production on the French stage'. Céard then attempted to produce a more theatrical version of the text but abandoned it on the grounds that the Prozor and possibly the Ibsen original were too misty. Eventually Darzens, the chronicler of the Théâtre Libre, came up with a literal translation and proceeded to make a workable text, endorsed by Ibsen, specifically for Antoine.[11]

Perhaps as he became more familiar with the play Antoine himself had become nervous that his public, conditioned by the *pièce bien faite*, would not understand Ibsen's play or share his sense of its power and importance. The published version of his diary gives no inkling of this, but the text he finally used was considerably more of an adaptation than anything else he ever performed. The major cut in *Power*, of Akim's moralizing in the final sequence of the play, had, characteristically, eliminated wordiness to increase the force of the ending and, as with the ending of *Jacques Damour* and *Sœur Philomène*, had compelled the audience to attend to the minutiae of gesture and interaction between the characters. His version of *Ghosts*, however, cut some of the longer or more complicated speeches, notably those about fire insurance and, perhaps fearful of audience derision, Oswald's account of his joy in the Bohemian life of Paris in the warm south. Less honorably, given Antoine's declared belief in textual integrity, nervous that the audience would identify Pastor Manders as the author's *raisonneur* after the manner of the well-made play, he cut the part considerably and eliminated Mrs Alving's account of her attempted flight to him. Even so, some commentators expressed their puzzlement at Manders' failure to emerge as a trustworthy *raisonneur*, whilst others announced their sympathy for his position. Faguet judged the idea, 'very original, very profound even though the play is very badly made' (*Le Soleil*, 3 June 1890). The experience seems to have reinforced Antoine's belief in the integrity of the writer's text. He never again tampered with a script in this way, and not only was the translation he had made for *The Wild Duck* 'an absolutely scrupulous translation, strictly conforming to the Norwegian text', but, when *Ghosts* was revived at the Théâtre Antoine and the Odéon, most of the cuts had been made good.[12]

Whatever the reasons for the delay, once engaged in rehearsal Antoine's commitment to the piece was evident. Two of the company's most experienced actresses, Barny and Luce Colas, were cast as Mrs Alving and Regina and, although the parts of Engstrand and Pastor Manders were taken by two 20-year-old newcomers, Janvier and Arquillière, these were destined to become, with Gémier, the core of the professional company at the Théâtre Antoine. Antoine himself took Oswald, 'the finest role an actor could play'.

It is notoriously difficult to articulate the effect of powerful drama without recourse to the nebulous language of mysticism. George Moore began his account by describing the discomfort of the poky, crowded theatre, the irritating noise of latecomers, the doubts Céard had expressed about the play beforehand so that he could demonstrate that such cares had evaporated before the compelling presence of the production. He seemed to have 'lived through a year's emotion' in the half hour of Act III when Oswald tells his mother how much he likes Regina and she, in a scene that is 'simple in its dire and doleful humanity', is forced to reveal that the maid is his half-sister. The word 'simple' comes up repeatedly in Moore's recollection as he attempts to convey his belief in the actors' projection of the truth of Ibsen's terrifying dramatic ironies. Of Antoine's compelling performance as Oswald, discussed briefly in chapter 2, Moore wrote:

> Antoine, identifying himself with the simple truth sought by Ibsen, by voice and gesture, casts upon the scene so terrible a light, so strange an air of truth, that the drama seemed to be passing not before our eyes but deep down in our hearts in a way we had never felt before.[13]

Here, and again when he writes 'the brain reels, even as poor Oswald's brain is reeling', Moore catches the essence of illusionist acting, what we mean when, in popular speech, we say 'the actor *was* the part'. Antoine's voice was 'querulous with incipient disease', he showed the 'nervous irritation of the sick man', his voice at the end had become toneless, while Barny conveyed Mrs Alving's pent-up fears with feeling that stopped the heart as she cried, 'ghosts, ghosts', revealing a situation 'so supremely awful, so shockingly true'.

Comments on the performance of *The Wild Duck* similarly imply that Antoine caught something of the resonance and mystery of Ibsen's text even whilst creating a convincing impression of 'real people living in scrupulously accurate surroundings'. 'You will recall', wrote the critic of *Courrier français* of Mlle Meuris' Hedwig, 'in what a strange, poignant way she repeated after Gregers the words, "dans les profondeurs de la mer"' (5 July 1891). The figures, sitting, leaning, addressing each other, adopted notably natural postures in these productions and were clearly not projecting their own personalities. Mlle Meuris acted with a girlishness that revealed the 'sparkling and charming caprice of the spoiled child, greedy for treats and forgetful of more serious things'. Antoine, as Hjalmar, re-created with 'inimitable exactness of observation all the states of being of this feeble, vainglorious creature, this phraseur, incapable of any effort of will'. The operative word is 'observation'.[14]

The actors, especially those playing characters different in age, attitude or social condition from themselves, not only observed other people but extended their range by adapting expressive gesture, bearing and manner to their own use. So, Antoine puffed contentedly at a pipe in the opening scenes of *Ghosts*; Luce Colas, when Regina's true relationship to the family was revealed, shot a notably resentful look at the champagne and tossed her head before pushing violently out through the door which, being solid, swung behind her, and Barny twisted her hands through her hair while, as Mrs Alving, she listened in speechless horror to Oswald's reiterated, 'the sun, the sun'. Studied, adopted, perfected in rehearsal and reproduced at each performance, such gestures are the stuff of illusionist acting and part of its paradox. They help the actor to imagine the character, to 'build' it, and are eventually picked out for comment by the critic for their 'truth', 'naturalness' or 'simplicity'.

It is interesting to note that Antoine used the first person in his pencil notes on his own script of *The Wild Duck*: 'I walk and fasten the door of the room', 'I sit down', and names actors rather than characters in his marginal notes as if, in learning the part, the actor's personality predominates over the character, but it is the characters' initials which figure in his organization of the *mise en scène*, the numerous marginal sketches in which relative and changing positions on the stage are worked out. The surviving text of *Ghosts* is a cue script for Antoine's role of Oswald, suggesting that the company worked from cue scripts while the régisseur used the full text. Alterations to the pencilled movements and directions for Act II show Antoine rethinking positions in rehearsal to achieve the exact movements he wanted and the necessary intimacy for the truth-telling duologue between Oswald and Mrs Alving.

The setting and *mise en scène* of *Power of Darkness* had been particularly impressive. In his subsequent productions of foreign plays, Antoine developed the idea that environment, crucial in determining character, must be authentic to the play's origins. Norway or rural Sweden must be as strongly present now as Russia had been earlier. The peasants of Hauptmann's *Weavers* must seem not Breton or Burgundian but Silesian, and those of Verga's *Chevalerie rustique* must seem Sicilian. The process of exploration and making strange in the production of these plays demonstrated both their availability and their difference from the French repertoire.

In working on *Ghosts*, Antoine noted that Ibsen's five years' experience as

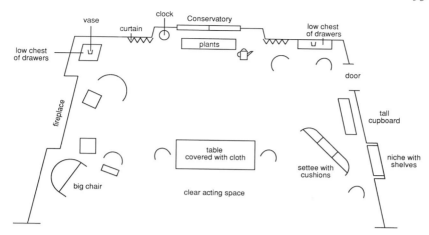

10 *Ghosts*, Théâtre Libre 1890. The stage plan, drawn from a photograph of Antoine's production, shows his attention to the author's stage directions. Much of the action took place around the front table.

metteur en scène in the Norwegian theatre was reflected in the stage directions and the theatrical suggestiveness of the dialogue. Since this was a playwright who, unlike many of the French naturalist writers, knew how to use the stage, he reproduced minutely whatever Ibsen specifically asked for and listened for further indications in the dialogue.

The opening words of *Ghosts*, Engstrand's 'Oh, comme il pleut', reinforced by Pastor Manders' comments on the foul weather and Oswald's depressive complaints about the gloomy north were rightly taken by Antoine as key indicators of mood and interpreted literally by him. The actors were equipped with appropriate greatcoats and umbrellas, Engstrand entered with wet clothes and the umbrella Manders handed to Regina at his entrance was dripping. The greyness and mist of Norway was continually present, painted on the back-cloth, seen through the practicable conservatory windows at the centre back of the stage and emphasized by the dim stage lighting, whilst a recurrent rain effect provided, in Sarcey's words, a 'bass note, continuous and melancholy, which accompanie[d] the drama and accentuate[d] its gloom' (2 June 1890). The power of the ending of the play was emphasized by the disruption of the pattern of synaesthesia when, Mrs Alving having drawn the curtain to let in the new day, the back-cloth was for the first time brilliantly lit as if with a morning sunshine that the audience had to reconcile with the horror of a now collapsed Oswald, reiterating his toneless cry for the sun from his chair at the front of the stage. As George Moore noted, just

11 *The Wild Duck*. Set for the Ekdals' living-room. The doors at the back
are open to show Old Ekdal's attic on an inner stage area. The stage is
roofed with a heavy beamed ceiling and lighting is from skylights and table
lamps.
Although this photograph is usually dated 1891, it is more probably a
photograph of the Théâtre Antoine revival, 1906. (Phot.Bibl.Nat., Paris)

before the end of the play, 'the boy answers not in tragic phrases, but in
words so simple and so true that, listening, the heart turns to ice'.

On his *Wild Duck* régisseur's script Antoine noted all the properties
mentioned in the stage directions or the dialogue and carefully detailed
instructions for the set. For Act II:

Large room in the form of an attic. At the right, part of a sloping roof, with large windows
half hidden by a blue curtain. Towards the back in a corner at the right, the entrance door,
in front, on the same side, a door leading to a bedroom. At the left, two doors; between
them a cast-iron stove. In the wall at the back a double door through which one must pass
to get outside. The arrangement and the furniture of the room are poor. Between the two
doors at the right, not quite against the wall, a sofa with a table and some chairs. On the
table a lighted lamp covered with a lampshade. In the corner a cooking-stove, an old
armchair. Here are the equipment and apparatus of photography. On the wall at the back,
left of the double door, shelves on which are placed some books, some boxes and bottles
with chemical products, some utensils and other objects. Some photographs, some
brushes, phials and colours ready on the table.

The steeply sloping ceiling of this Ekdal family room increased the effect of
claustrophobia (fig. 11). The doors at the back were set so as to enable

glimpses of the inner attic – almost an inner stage – in a way that helped the audience to identify that area with the key phrase, *les profondeurs de la mer*, and with the eventual disaster for Hedwig. Two extant sketches of the first and fourth act of the play show Antoine using lighting to create atmosphere. Lamps help to give the illusion of wealth at the Werle house-party in the opening act, shadows and patches of light, what Sarcey called, the 'crazy taste for night effects', in the other, intensifying the impression of indigence. The drawback to this expressive and detailed set was that an interval of an hour was needed to enable the scene-change to be made.

Antoine's emphasis on significance in his selection of stage properties was particularly appropriate to the work of Ibsen and Strindberg, where unnecessary items could give false messages to an audience learning to respond to a new dramatic method and find meaning in the multiple elements of the stage picture. In *The Wild Duck*, the properties represent Hjalmar's trade and the small domestic circumstances of the family. The photographic equipment has often been ignored in subsequent productions, but it was an important signifier in a period when photography was frequently regarded, on the one hand, as second-class image-making – the art form for the aspirant without genius – and, on the other, as the form which, unlike painting, could not distort but showed things exactly as they were. Even more than the spreading pumpkin plant of Bergerat's *Nuit Bergamasque*, this photographic paraphernalia had both solid presence and metaphoric force. In *Miss Julie*, similarly, the stage properties, the caged bird that is subsequently decapitated, the boots waiting to be polished, the dense green foliage and scented flowers of the midsummer night decorations, are significantly interactive with the dialogue.

For all George Moore's declaration that there had not been so deep or pronounced a success since *Power of Darkness*, the strangeness of Ibsen's and, even more, Strindberg's work tested the Théâtre Libre *habitués*. Antoine acknowledged that the response to *Ghosts* in the theatre was mixed: whilst 'the effect on some was profound, for the majority astonishment gave way to boredom', but claimed that 'a true anxiety gripped the audience during the last scenes'. The response to *The Wild Duck* was largely favourable, despite bursts of quacking from a disruptive element, and to *Miss Julie*, largely hostile, although several commentators, among them the critics of *Le Soir*, *Le Courrier français* and *Mercure de France*, found the play strange but admirable and praised Antoine's daring in having staged it.

Where Tolstoi's play was assimilable by the wider audience, perhaps because of the ultimate remorse of Nikita, because its picture of the peasantry was recognizable to readers of Zola's fiction, or because of its colour, its dances and its energy, Ibsen's writing, with its middle-class settings, its

12 Sketch by Ferdinand Bac of the final scene of *The Wild Duck* showing
the characters gathered around the dead Hedwig. The roofed stage, inner
room and lighting from a (transposed) skylight are all featured in the sketch.
(*Le Théâtre Libre Illustré*, 27 Apr. 1891)

parodic echoes of the well-made play (Sarcey was particularly disturbed by the use of the cynical Relling as *raisonneur*) and its use of images and key-words, proved more disconcerting. Many of the reviewers, particularly in the right-wing press, appealed to their readers' xenophobia. Some claimed not to have understood *Ghosts* whilst others felt that, even if Ibsen was a genius, his northern gloom was inimical to French taste. 'I feel in it a power that overcomes me', wrote Adolphe Brisson, 'an imagination that I wonder at; but I find some singular lacunae and impenetrable obscurities' (*Parti national*). Although declaring the conception, 'distinguished, original and profound', Faguet found the play 'badly made'. Commenting on *The Wild Duck* in *Gaulois*, Pessard invoked 'limpid French gaiety' and warned against the 'menacing invasion' of the foreign that threatened 'to submerge our national genius', and Sarcey, comparing the play's structure unfavourably with that of French drama, claimed to find the symbolism completely obscure and wrote:

Ibsen makes no effort to present his characters to you nor to expose the idea of the piece. The characters arrive on the stage and talk of their affairs without our knowing who they are and what these affairs might be. During the first two acts it is impossible, absolutely impossible, in spite of the most sustained attention, to divine what the question is and why the people who speak say these things and not others.   (4 May 1891)

Puzzled or hostile, as many of the reviewers were, they were demonstrably facing something unfamiliar with which they coped according to their own prejudices, and the length and liveliness of their accounts helped make Ibsen a household name in France and, even where hostile, served to stimulate interest and familiarity, so contributing to the notable advance in sympathy that took place between the production of *Ghosts* and that of *The Wild Duck* a year later.

If curious about Ibsen, all the French naturalist writers were as hostile towards the newcomer, Strindberg, as Goncourt had always been to foreign interlopers on his territory. Not only had Strindberg no international reputation, his philosophy was suspect and he was, unlike Ibsen, evidently a misogynist. *Miss Julie*, moreover, disrupted expectations even more seriously than Ibsen's plays had done. Although it had the logic of a two-act play, it was performed in one act whose centre was held by a midsummer dance. Henri Fouquier answered Strindberg's claim in the play's Preface that the wind of change was blowing from the south with his own that 'a wind of madness' was blowing from the north (*Figaro*). But although, to Strindberg's disappointment, Antoine had balked at *The Father* when offered Strindberg's own French translation in 1888/9, he did have the Preface translated for distribution to the audience of *Miss Julie*. He seems to have regarded the play as the expressive-realist answer to the Maeterlinck symbolism that Lugné-Poë was promoting at the Théâtre d'Œuvre. He showed his interest in the play by including it in his tour to Amsterdam in May and to the French provinces in June of 1893. He also revived his production for the play's first properly professional performance, at the Théâtre Antoine in 1899.

The Preface, written four years earlier and partly in response to news of Antoine's work at the Théâtre Libre, gratified Antoine and outraged many critics, who saw it as merely an extreme restatement of Antoine's own principles. In a way, this was just what it was. Antoine's practice found an echo in Strindberg's claims:

> when one has only one set, one is entitled to demand that it be realistic . . . Even if the walls have to be of canvas, it is surely time to stop painting them with shelves and kitchen utensils.
>
> . . . I have few illusions of being able to persuade the actor to play to the audience and not with them, though this would be desirable. I do not dream that I shall ever see the full back of an actor throughout the whole of an important scene, but I do fervently wish that vital scenes should not be played opposite the prompter's box as though they were duets milking applause. I would have them played at whatever spot the situation might demand.
>
> . . . if we could get rid of the side boxes (my particular *bête noire*) with their tittering diners and ladies nibbling at cold collations, and have complete darkness in the auditorium during the performance, and first and foremost, a *small* stage and a *small* auditorium — then perhaps a new drama might emerge, and the theatre might once again become a place for educated people.

Although Sarcey might mock at the absurdity, the set Strindberg requested and which Antoine produced does indeed represent stage realism taken to its logical extreme where it confronts the audience with theatre's artifice.[15]

The stage for *Miss Julie* was set on the bias, in the asymmetric way borrowed from late impressionist painting, with the kitchen furniture, the oven and table, partly on and partly off the stage, as if the audience were, indeed, catching a transitory glimpse of a fragment of another existence, a slice of life. Although he had not used such an effect before, Antoine's set for *Les Fossiles*, also in the 1892–3 season, showing the same room from a different angle in each of the three acts, represented a comparable attempt to reduce the fixity of the audience's relationship to the stage. Antoine would attack the seeming rigidity of the stage set again in his Shakespeare productions, but he only really solved the dilemma Strindberg's stage directions indicate in the new medium of film, where he discovered the fluidity of which he was always finally cheated in the theatre. Rather than set the camera square before a film set, Antoine would catch a corner of a room or ask his actors to walk not direct to the camera but at an angle across and past it.

The January 1893 performances of *Miss Julie* marked the beginning of a new series of foreign plays at the Théâtre Libre and of interaction with foreign independent theatres. Hauptmann's *Weavers*, a Freie Bühne play, followed in May then Björnson's *A Bankruptcy* in November, and Hauptmann's *The Assumption of Hannele Mattern*, in February 1894. This burst of activity which, in part, signalled Antoine's growing dissatisfaction with many of the French plays he was offered, a development which I will discuss more fully in chapter 4, proved a drain on Antoine's always scanty resources and was cut short by the bankruptcy and dissolution of the Théâtre Libre.

The production of each of these foreign works, so much more demanding on Antoine both as actor and director than the majority of the plays he otherwise performed, was an act of faith and theatrical daring. They demonstrated to audiences and writers that the drama could accommodate much fuller exploration of human character and condition than was apparent in Zola–Goncourt derived plays whilst still keeping faith with contemporary life and thought, and Ibsen's influence began to be felt in the scripts the theatre subsequently received. They seem also to have provided something of a transforming experience for Antoine himself, as if revealing the possibilities of major drama and his own part in presenting it.

Certainly, it was an extraordinary achievement to have broken through the nationalistic barriers of French theatre but, after the dissolution of the Théâtre Libre, Antoine seems to have lost interest in contemporary foreign writing. Although he retained his loyalty to the foreign plays he had already produced, regularly touring them and reviving them at both the Antoine and the Odéon, he attempted no new Ibsen, Strindberg or Tolstoi nor, more surprisingly, any of the new generation of foreign writers, Shaw, Chekhov, Synge, Gorki, whose work might have seemed to tune with his own. The initiative for new work passed to Lugné-Poë who, having finally broken with Antoine, had opened the Théâtre d'Œuvre in 1893, where he played mainly Maeterlinck and Ibsen in the Prozor translations, and somewhat slanted to emphasize symbolist elements.

It was probably less the case, as Antoine claimed, that there was now no longer the need for his initiative, than that, having worked with the most imaginatively powerful drama of his own time, the idea was growing of tackling the great foreign plays of the past and, most notably, Shakespeare, unadapted versions of whose work were still unfamiliar in France at the turn of this century.

4 Crowd scenes and lighting: Some experiments with the *mise en scène*

At the end of his first season, Antoine's idea of a playwrights' theatre which had drawn international as well as national attention had made his the most widely discussed of all Parisian theatres. He had staged twenty-four previously unperformed plays. His own qualities as an actor were acknowledged. His company had gained the right to be judged by professional standards and young actors, professionals in minor theatres and students enrolled at the Conservatoire were eager to be trained in the new acting. There was now no lack of potential subscribers and impresarios had begun to invite the company to tour abroad. *Power of Darkness* had demonstrated the promise of contemporary foreign theatre and confounded confident declarations of what was and was not a performable play. Equally important, if this theatre was to flourish, Antoine had retained complete control of the repertoire despite pressure from various factions. He had staged naturalist, poetic and comic drama, and new scripts from unknown and established writers were accumulating. His ideas about the theatre, formed by close reading of Diderot, Daudet, Zola and accounts of Wagner's experiments at Bayreuth and by observation of the Comédie-Française, had been developed and modified by a period of intensive practical experience. What he now looked for was the stimulus of seeing other innovative theatre work.

In July 1888 he went, as did Claretie, the director of the Comédie-Française, to see the Saxe-Meiningen Company, on tour in Brussels. Although the company differed from his own in being a financially secure court theatre and although, despite their *huis clos* production of *Ghosts*, the normal repertoire of this sophisticated and well-disciplined troupe consisted mainly of Shakespeare and German classics, Antoine found vindication and extension of many of his own ideas in the Saxe-Meiningen staging. He saw ensemble acting of a more thorough-going kind than anything he had himself yet achieved, coherent staging and costumes which looked authentic to their period. All the actors from principals to extras played in character, submitting themselves entirely to the dramatic action, never attempting to upstage each other or seize the dominant position on stage. They never looked knowingly out into the audience and they turned their backs unself-consciously when the logic of the action demanded. Unlike Claretie, who found the work uninteresting, Antoine went repeatedly to their productions

(*Winter's Tale, Twelfth Night* and Schiller's *William Tell*) and spent hours talking to their actors.

The opportunity to compare other work with his own stiffened his ideas and, when Sarcey publicized some dismissive comments by Claretie, he countered with a long letter explaining the importance of the Meininger. Then, in February 1889, invited to give a series of matinees at the Royalty in London, he seized the opportunity to investigate Wyndham's work at the Criterion and Irving's at the Lyceum. Although unimpressed by the melodramatic acting which seemed like a less fiery version of the Taillade he had seen in his youth, he found experiments in lighting and the *mise en scène* that seemed far in advance of anything happening in Paris.[1]

Antoine's response to each visit was that of someone teeming with ideas about theatre. What he saw was brought to bear directly on the scripts on which he was currently working. His Meiningen letter, besides being one of the most telling accounts of that company's work, demonstrates in its discussion of specific details the extent to which aspects of his own forthcoming productions were present in his mind. Each of his few, carefully observed, criticisms concerned failures of detail which interfered with the illusion and which were evidently to be corrected in his own work. The mountain people, for instance, were dressed in costumes which accurately reflected their place and time but not the texture of their lives, for the costumes were neither worn nor grubby and their hands and legs shone as distractingly white as those at the Opéra Comique. A realistic rain effect was turned off with distracting abruptness when no longer needed; a brilliant shaft of light, highlighting a principal, lacked motivation; the magnificently drilled extras seemed stilted because they spoke in exact unison or fell silent immediately one of the principals spoke. All these examples of incomplete realism distracted audience attention from the action to the imperfect artifice of its presentation.

Antoine's discussion of the Meininger and London work is evidently geared towards particular problems in forthcoming productions of his own. His recognition that extensively rehearsed artifice is essential to the creation of the illusion of reality is everywhere apparent. What he had learned seemed particularly appropriate for two attempts at naturalist history plays on whose staging he was working. Both Hennique's *La Mort du Duc d'Enghien* and the Goncourt *La Patrie en danger* had been politically unacceptable to the second empire when offered some fifteen years previously. The central character of one had been summarily killed as a royalist traitor by order of Napoleon I and the other included scenes of revolutionary uprising that were offensive in the aftermath of the commune. They had, anyway, been dramatically unacceptable to the subsidized theatre. Episodic, they eschewed the well-made plot and used documentary material of the period as the basis of both action and dialogue. Such works were exactly to Antoine's liking. Unplayable, he could play them. Tedious, he could make them gripping.

In attempting to re-create that impression of random noise and of unity within chaos that a great crowd gives, he could aim for a more complex and better-disciplined artifice even than that of the Meininger. As one example of how this might be achieved, he suggested that the extras playing a crowd should be divided into groups with an actor leading each, as at the Meininger, but that each group should have a specific but not uniform movement plan and the utterance of a communal cry – 'Vive Gambetta' was his example – should be staggered, one group beginning, 'Vive', a second joining in on the second syllable, 'Gam', and so on. Whilst not at all what would happen in reality, the effect would be of many voices responding together in a spontaneous, not a regimented, way. Although needing more intensive rehearsal it would seem wilder and more unrehearsed in performance.

La Mort du Duc d'Enghien (10 Dec. 1888)

The Death of the Duke of Enghien played a significant part in the debate about what might properly constitute drama. Hennique's three scenes picture the reception by his dutiful generals of Napoleon's high-handed order that they cross the Rhine and arrest the emigré Duke on neutral territory; the arrest when the citizen army intrudes on the Duke, his newly wedded wife and friends at table, and, finally, the hole-and-corner trial and execution. Virtually all the critics declared roundly that it was not a play but, in Faguet's words, 'nothing more than an encyclopaedia extract', although with a contradiction frequently evident in response to Antoine's theatre, most admitted to having been deeply moved by its action and, even, to having found it written in a 'strong and vibrant style, sharp, rapid and lively' (Annales).

Hennique's play was a remarkable portent of the future. It is hardly the coldly encyclopaedic documentation that contemporary accounts claim, although it does incorporate transcript material from the trial into the dialogue and rejects the familar well-made-play pattern of slowly accumulating clues leading to climax and denouement. An early version of the drama-documentary, developed subsequently by Shaw in St Joan (1923) and Dreyer in La Passion de Jeanne d'Arc (1928) and rediscovered by post-Second World War television scriptwriters, it confronted its audience with the thrill of knowing that the dialogue had once really been spoken and the conundrum of considering how the shaping imagination of the dramatist might have transformed that reality. A dramatic form both feeding and cheating our society's longings for the reassurance of fact, the drama-documentary is the theatre's equivalent of the century's new bastard art form, photography, both in the seeming displacement of the artist by the reality that is there and in the control the artist wields over the audience's perception of what that reality is.

Strict documentation was, in fact, modified by Hennique in the interests of dramatic power, for example, in the unhistorical entry of the Duke's wife into the prison for a final parting. And Antoine himself responded at least as much to the 'interesting problems of *mise en scène*' raised by the play as to its value as 'an experiment in the renewal of historical drama'. Hennique had located his scenes carefully, including details of the time of day and the state of the weather in his stage directions. The settings within which the three climactic moments of the progress towards the death of the title are staged are equally carefully varied scene by scene from a general's study, dominated by a life-size portrait of Napoleon, via the intimacy of a domestic interior, to a cell in Vincennes prison. The quiet ordinariness of the conversation between the army officers in the first scene, besides announcing its difference from the grandiloquent Romantic history play, offered a chilling impression of the reality of power as the perfectly polite generals stretched their feet to warm at the fender and discussed Napoleon's order that they break international territorial law. Indeed, as the otherwise hostile critic Hector Pessard recognized, 'with skill and remarkable dramatic sense [Hennique] found precisely the form' appropriate to the action. Like *Sœur Philomène* and Hennique's earlier *Jacques Damour*, it was a play entirely appropriate to Antoine's interests and ideas.[2]

The Théâtre Libre production emphasized the understatement and seeming lack of structural contrivance of Hennique's play whilst carefully underscoring its dramatic moments. The footlights were suppressed — as usually in Antoine's productions from this point onwards — and the lighting arranged so that it appeared to flow from natural sources: windows, doors or domestic lamps. Antoine used an off-stage rain effect throughout the first scene. Far from stopping with distracting suddenness as had the Saxe-Meiningen rain, Antoine's rain effect swelled and faded. First heard by the audience during the casual pauses in the quiet opening exchange, its continuing sound served as a dull background to the scene in which the enormity of Napoleon's order becomes clear, increasing in intensity as the silences become longer and more pregnant until, filling the silence at the end of the scene, it marks the impassivity of natural forces in the face of the changeableness of human affairs. In the second scene, with more evident irony, the day brightens through the windows at the back as the Duke's fortunes darken, an effect Antoine would use again at the end of *Ghosts*.

He had also paid particular attention to the details of domestic intimacy. The propriety of the table setting, the smooth ordering of the attentions of the waiting servants, the easy conviviality of the meal, all helped to create belief in and enjoyment of the regularity of the lives about to be shattered. That the audience registered both the accurate observation and the dramatic irony of the scene was demonstrated by their loud applause when the Abbé pronounced the grace before the meal. Antoine timed the first note of the anticipated arrest to sound at the very moment when the Duke toasts Louis XVIII and the political world intrudes on the domestic. Trumpets and voices were heard off stage before servants rushed in, sounding the alarm. Still off stage, the tumult sounded nearer and the words that could be distinguished were military orders and revolutionary modes of address, such as 'citizen commandant'. The intrusion of one world on another was startlingly but succintly evinced.

But Antoine reserved his strongest effects for the final scene, the trial and death. First, following the lead of Bayreuth and the Meininger, he plunged the auditorium into darkness. The darkening of the house is a significant gesture in the creation of illusionist theatre, establishing once and for all the claims of the stage over the auditorium as the centre of attention. Whilst house lights in Paris had been dimmed they had not been completely extinguished before, even by Antoine, and the immediate result was an outburst of catcalls and the sound of loud kissing on the backs of hands (an old railway-tunnel joke according to Sarcey) from the habitual troublemakers in the audience, at least one of whom had his ears boxed by Henri Bauer. Bauer's response endorsed the claim Antoine was making. Each member of the audience had the right not to be disturbed by any other. The stage might elicit shared laughter, shared applause from the otherwise silent audience for what happened there, but individual effusions which disturbed concentration and community of response were properly quashed. More importantly, on this occasion, the disturbance was quelled by the powerful effect of the final scene.

A table was placed at an angle to the audience behind which sat the generals whilst Enghien stood in front, turned sideways into the stage. At the back of the stage a couple of guards stood immobile. The whole scene, indeed, was very still, dominated by the words the audience knew had once in reality been spoken. The only lighting came from lanterns, so placed on the table that their light caught the faces of the judges and the Duke. Henry James, who saw the production in London in February 1889, had his character Dorriforth describe this as 'a closer night effect than is usually attempted, with a few guttering candles, which threw high shadows over the bare walls'. Only after the trial had ended and the prisoner been taken away did the stage grow light with a dawn effect that filtered through the windows at the back of the stage as the order and shots of the execution were heard off stage. Dorriforth

found a strong impression in it — an impression of the hurried, extemporised cross-examination, by night, of an impatient and mystified prisoner, whose dreadful fate had been determined in advance, who was to be shot, high-handedly in the dismal dawn. The arrangement didn't worry and distract me: it was simplifying, intensifying. It gave what a judicious mise en scène should always do, the essence of the matter, and left the embroidery to the actors.[3]

This first real exploration by Antoine of the possibilities of stage lighting made a deep impact, generally, despite provoking the first of many complaints from Sarcey that besides not being able to hear, he now couldn't *see* at the Théâtre Libre. The critic of the London *Star* found the 'horror' and 'pathos' of the scene 'indescribable', adding that he, 'would not have believed that so great a tragic effect could be produced with such matter of fact material — such rigid economy of means' (25 Feb. 1889).

That what William Archer named, 'unvarnished simplicity', 'a diminution of artifice' had been judiciously arranged, geared to the fine persuasion of the audience's imagination, is evident from Archer's own comment that, 'the picture is so perfect . . . we see the actors' faces only fitfully, as the candlelight happens to fall on them quite enough' and James' more astute remark that 'the *contrivance* was perfectly simple'.[4]

One of those small intensifications of the given text of the kind first introduced in *Jacques Damour* is found at the end of this play. In the final sequence, after the Duke has been taken out to execution, his wife and her friend enter into the now empty prison cell. Whilst the words of the dialogue are not altered, the ordering is slightly changed, so that whereas in Hennique's ending the off-stage sounds only become distinct when the women, having opened the window, fall silent to hear the reading of the sentence, the Duke's last words and the report of the firing squad's guns, in Antoine's the off-stage sounds of preparation for the execution, including the reading of the sentence, provide an ironic background to the on-stage speeches of the Princess. The silence into which she lapses is the more poignant because she has not at first registered what was happening, whereas the audience has.[5]

Although we now tend to associate realist theatre with the over-furnished stage, this was anything but the impression Antoine's early work made on his contemporaries. Defending the 'shabbiness' of the Théâtre Libre which 'had only what was indispensable in the way of dress and scenery', James' character Amicia noted that, 'the imagination in certain cases is more finely persuaded by the little than the much.' Although the 'little' was in part a matter of necessity, Antoine, who opposed the contemporary tendency to subdue the play to its decoration, claimed in his 1887–90 manifesto that his slender resources forced him to concentrate on essentials and did not prevent the achieving of the 'idea'. For all some of his early sets were rough or unfinished his very privations gave a kind of liberty:

> To make worthwhile experiments it isn't necessary to have resources greater than those of the Théâtre Libre. It is above all a question of willingness, care and attention. Many of these experiments could not be done on the big stages because it is difficult to risk a huge affair for improvements that are still unsure and even debatable.   (p. 34)

In this production, properties and furniture were chosen as indicators of time, place, condition, relationship. The function of the staging was to make the text live.

The public announcement of the Théâtre Libre's London tour (February 1889), which Mayer of the Royalty Theatre funded on condition that no detail of the staging was altered, stressed the claims to simplicity and authenticity. Not only did 'Antoine's genius as stage manager . . . not run in the direction of costly display', but the costumes were 'not fancy ball-dresses but actual costumes of the period, made and worn in the year 1804 or thereabouts'.

This notion of using 'actual costumes of the year 1804' is worth pausing over. It was in keeping that Antoine should use scenic means in realizing the period of a play. Russian artefacts had helped establish a sense of place in *Power* and his own domestic furniture had given a social context to *Jacques Damour*. Now, Hennique having pointed out J.P. Laurens' painting of the Duke's trial that hung in the Luxembourg, Antoine had tracked down the costumier who hired out Napoleonic garments for historical tableau paintings then fashionable with the Academy. Antoine was not alone in his interest in attempting an accurate reproduction of the period in which a play was set. Such attention had been a feature of Charles Kean's Shakespeare productions at the Princess's Theatre in the 1850s and had made an impact on both the Duke of Saxe-Meiningen and Irving, through whose productions it would be a shaping influence on Antoine's own ideas about Shakespeare in the future. But there is an added element in Antoine's attempt here. Whereas these directors, like the academy painters, glamorized the costumes, emphasizing style and decorative detail, he used the tired, faded quality of the actual clothes to demonstrate the straitened circumstances as well as the historical period of his aristocrats in exile.

Although there might be a particular thrill in using what were once real clothes, what is at issue is less whether the genuine article is used than how completely it gives the impression of being the real thing. So the Théâtre

Antoine actor Saverne recalled actors being sent off to make themselves look dusty or to muddy boots that were supposed to have suffered a journey through a storm. One might compare the effect of the observed detail in a Visconti film with the *laissez-faire* of those Hollywood excursions into different times or places in which the heroine endures privation with a perfect modern coiffure and unchipped nail varnish. A different kind of demand is being made on the critical faculties of the audience.

The credibility of the plot is a hazard to staging that asks the audience to suspend disbelief in the artifice of the action on stage. A further risk is that if the contrivance is not *perfectly* simple, if the control over the various elements is incomplete, the audience will be distracted from its imaginative acceptance of the illusion by the difficulties of the real people engaged in promoting it, will find itself attending more to the imperfect artifice of the various on-stage activities than to the action. Something of both these hazards is evident in Antoine's first fully-fledged attempt at staging a crowd scene.

La Patrie en danger (19 Mar. 1889)

The Goncourts' play about the French Revolution, *The Motherland in Danger*, is an uneasy mixture of Naturalism and melodrama, both more ambitious and less well achieved than Hennique's play or, indeed than the Byl and Vidal adaptation of *Sœur Philomène*. It tells in a series of episodes of the early years of the Revolution from the storming of the Bastille (14 July 1789), to Danton's Jacobin attack on the Tuileries (10 August 1792). As with *La Mort*, documentary evidence and transcripts of letters and speeches are incorporated into the dialogue but, whereas the Goncourts' novels are genuinely innovative in structure, 'deliberately dispens[ing] with unity', as Arthur Symons put it, 'in order to give the sense of the passing of life, the heat and form of its moments as they pass',[6] their plays are more influenced by those of the fashionable theatres they frequented than they or their contemporary critics acknowledged.

In the case of *La Patrie* there is, underlying and connecting the episodes, the story of the journey to the guillotine of a proud aristocrat, Count Valjuzan, who has stayed to fight for his king with pen and sword rather than become an *emigré*, and of his valet who, having risen after the Revolution to become a Republican general, is doomed with him when his attempt to rescue the Count and Valjuzan's daughter, whom he had always secretly loved, is discovered. It is the very stuff of historical romance although it lacks the lucid exposition of events of such plays. The conservative critics, pronouncing its monologues and its failure to explain the connections between the scenes, 'the surest means of producing maximum boredom in a theatre' (Faguet) lamented the lost drama whose features they could discern through the episodic structure, and one can see that the audience may well have been confused by such developments as the unexplained reappearance in Act IV of Perrin whose death had been announced at the end of Act III with the cry, 'The Governor of Verdun will not capitulate. He is dead.'

Whereas the Théâtre Libre *habitués* had been sceptical of the wisdom of taking on such a large-scale work when it was read to them, Antoine predicted that his crowd scenes would prove sensational (19 Feb. 1889) as, indeed, they did, although they probably also made the flaws in the play more apparent. Although again retaining all of the authors' dialogue, the staging shifted the interest of the performance from the events of the plot to the underlying concern with mobs and leaders, the forces of history and the climate of the times. The quiet exchanges of Perrin (Mévisto) and his childhood sweetheart before they went to the guillotine in the last act were delicately done and proved moving, but it was the Verdun town-hall scene of Act III that won over an audience that had been restless in the lengthy monologues of the first two acts. Mévisto's monologues here were uttered against the rising and falling tide of an encompassing mob. More evidently than in any previous staging of Antoine's, the director rather than the author was the dominant imaginative presence. The play had become a vehicle for an experiment in staging; a recreation of his memories of the turmoil and excitement of the 1870 commune, and a representation, for its first centenary, of his idea of the Revolution.

Antoine had been impressed by the Meininger policy that actors who happened not to have a speaking role in any given play should participate in its crowd scenes regardless of their status, and that this had been taken so seriously that one leading actress had been dismissed for refusing. He had himself seen Mlle Lindner, one of their stars, wholly absorbed in miming a woman of the people in *The Winter's Tale* one night and playing Hermione the next. He recognized the contribution of such a practice to the creation of the ensemble effect he needed and at once planned to incorporate it, writing to Goncourt of his plans for *La Patrie*:

As for extras, I want in the first place the whole Théâtre Libre company, without exception. Then I will recruit some fifty individuals who will rehearse together some ten or fifteen times. We will fill the depth of the stage with a multitude. This way, I believe we'll have a great sensation of life and movement. It is essential that the auditorium should be gripped.[7]

But company politics and resources played a part in the effectiveness of the Meininger crowd scenes. Whilst the Duke's company enjoyed the luxury of seventy permanent paid actors, Antoine had to compromise on the basis of his tiny core of unpaid regulars and the realities of the French methods of employing extras. Although Antoine himself often took tiny parts, he rarely asked his leading actors to do so.

In common with the leading French companies, and with far more precarious finances, he had to draw his extras, his *figurants*, from street people and students who would perform at short notice for a pittance, as he and Mévisto had done at the Comédie-Française in his clerking days. Whereas the mainstream theatres picked up such people as day labourers, costuming them and telling them where to stand just before the performance, Antoine had the ambitious notion of creating from such resources a Saxe-Meininger crowd whose individual members acted believably and responded to the main action. This meant a colossal investment of energy and money in rehearsals so that enough of the *figurants* shared knowledge of and belief in what they were doing to carry the rest with them in performance. Goncourt, appalled, commented on the vicious, coarse faces of the pimps, sellers of obscene pictures and other riff-raff that collected at the theatre; on the complaisant way Antoine said he would ask if any cared to make their proper debut with him, and on the way he remarked to his actresses, 'Ladies, keep your money and your jewels in your pockets; you see you have here a hundred cut-throats and your dresser seems to have just come out of prison. I take no responsibility.'[8]

Despite the grim jokes, Antoine very evidently did take responsibility, rehearsing intensively from early afternoon until well after midnight for a month with the leading actors, Mévisto, Barny, Deneuilly and whatever of the crowd he could muster. The scale was quite different from anything he had handled previously. He was no longer dealing in representative crowds of fifteen or twenty extras. We are discussing very large numbers indeed, here: the theatrical equivalent of D.W. Griffith's cast for *Intolerance*. His own recollection of 'nearly 500' is an exaggeration, although he did use this number in 1891 for the Rosny Brothers' Salvation Army play, *Nell Horn*. The throng – he usually rehearsed with some eighty people with up to two hundred appearing in the actual performances – was divided into small groups of about a dozen led, as at the Meininger, by one of his own actors and directed by him vocally with much cursing until, according to Goncourt, his bronchial tubes seemed torn to shreds. He used a foreman's whistle to train the crowd to quick responses, at one point unexpectedly simulating a loud pistol shot to demonstrate how a seemingly disparate rabble would respond as one to a sudden sound.

Antoine experimented with different effects to give the impression of a vast uncontrolled mass. He reproduced the Meininger idea of overloading the crowd area until some figures were only partly on stage and some had to remain in the wings in order to imply that the stage life was flowing in and out from the real world. Sounds of marching footsteps, drums, shots were tried in the foyer and in the corridors back-stage to create an impression of distant turmoil and an advancing mob. Groups were placed off stage at three increasingly removed points to simulate the effect of a large and widespread crowd whilst, on stage, small groups were detailed to interrupt the central action with bursts of whispering. In the Verdun scene he had all of the extras filter through a single door into the town-hall chamber setting, at first slowly, then with rising speed and pressure until, like a rising tide, they submerged everything, climbing on to furniture and surging around the leading actors. The most effective versions of each of these ideas were retained in performance. Although the conservative critic Faguet characterized such effects drily, writing, 'alarm, gunshots, drum-rolls. These things happen in the corridors. On the stage - nothing',[9] the more common response was that expressed by the critic of *Petite république française*: 'the crowd is the success of the evening . . . it pushes forward, fills the stage grumbling, threatening, impossible to restrain or control . . . this ferocious multitude . . . never has the life of a crowd been created thus.'

The crowd scenes were made still more striking by the way the seething masses were lit. The chiaroscuro of the last scene of *La Mort* was developed with added insights picked up from Irving's *Macbeth* at the Lyceum the previous month. Irving had taken to darkening the auditorium and aiming for settings of greater historical authenticity after his own encounter with the Meininger in their 1881 London tour. He had also remodelled his stage, replacing wings and painted decor with steps, platforms and columns that varied the stage spaces and levels of the action. Hawes Craven's decor for *Macbeth* ran to seventeen different tableaux and used lighting in a powerfully suggestive way. Many of the scenes were dimly lit, but with spotlights to pick up figures in the gloom or accentuate faces at dramatic moments. The witches revelled by moonlight, Banquo's ghost appeared in a particularly eerie light in the banquet scene, which deeply impressed Antoine, and a magnificent beam of light streamed from the windowless wall of the practicable gallery to illuminate the centre of the stage after the discovery of Duncan's murder. As Antoine recalled later, 'in Irving's production a shaft of moonlight or sun would always appear on the face of the leading character, one hardly knew how or why, but it was very fine all the same'.[10] He wanted as expressive a lighting plan as Irving's, but one whose causes and sources were realistically motivated (cf. figs. 38 and 39).

Irving's device of the shaft of light was used to directly reverse effect by Antoine. The leading actor was not spotlit. Instead, audience attention was demanded momentarily by individual ravaged faces in the grumbling, anonymous mass as they were highlighted by the shafts of light which fell at

13 Goya lithograph, *Dibasion de España*. Not only the bulls and toreadors but the faces of groups and individuals in the crowd are illuminated.

waist or face height, as if from open doors and windows. This occasional lighting-up of a face or small group in a patch of light in the otherwise dense shadow reminded Goncourt of Goya's bullfight lithographs (c. 1820). The analogy is telling because the chiaroscuro in the lithographs is striking but also disturbing (fig. 13). As Gwyn Williams has written of Goya's later work:

These crowds have *faces*. Exactly how Goya achieved this effect it is difficult to say, but even among the collectivities one is conscious of the individuality of these little figures. A few touches bring a man or woman to individual life in a manner which is quite surprising, given the role in comment that he has assigned them. It is in his personalised treatment of these faces in a crowd that Goya, paradoxically, breaks out of his own prison of the first person singular.[11]

The Goncourt play is locked in an old formula. Despite its episodic structure and documentary substance, history in it is taken primarily as the exploits of unusual individuals. The Verdun scene, as played by Antoine, altered this focus. Similarly, whereas all the extras in the Saxe-Meiningen production directed their attention to the words and actions of the principals, the unusual individuals, falling silent as soon as one of them spoke, Antoine had Perrin fight with the crowd for a hearing, attracting the attention of first one small group, then another. Like the gradually slowing rainfall effect, this served the interests of realism, being truer to what happens in life, but political feeling also plays a part here. A Gas Company clerk may very well see the response of crowds to great men differently from the way a duke, or even a member of the minor French aristocracy, sees it. Whereas in the play the Goncourts wrote the crowd was an anonymous mass, in the Antoine production of it there was a disturbing sense of its being composed of people with their own concerns and identities.

Goncourt was present at virtually all the rehearsals in the two final weeks and his journal charts the progress of the production and of his own belief in it. Having stated at the beginning of February that Mévisto was not suitable for Perrin but should take Boussanel, he conceded the part to him on 20 Feb., after the actor had visited him with Antoine to plead for the role. (This was something of a charade, since Mévisto was already rehearsing the part and Antoine had cast himself in the smaller part of Boussanel to allow time to work with the extras.) At first sceptical, then patronizingly amused by the rehearsal activity, by 11 March Goncourt was praising the 'handsome design' of a sequence in Act I in which the wounded Perrin, supported by two citizens, gasped out his story of the taking of the Bastille and recording that, 'the stirrings of the crowd that they begin to attempt promise, it seems to me, great effects'. Three days later, he noted that Antoine had a remarkable feel for mass movement and had introduced numerous ingenious touches which recreated 'this tumultuous life on the narrow field of the stage'. On 16 March, Antoine commented that Goncourt was, 'happy as a child beside me, seeming ready to applaud in the dark of the auditorium. And as the Verdun act was finishing, he said to me, "Oh, if the swine don't find this good, it is surely their own fault".'

Despite the power of the crowd scenes, there were evident problems that the production did not resolve. It was not only that, even in a company riding as high as Antoine's, the financial expense was crippling so that it was some time before he could attempt such effects again; there were also important lessons to be learned about the dangers of anticlimax and the necessary limits of realism in the theatre. Although the hostile elements in the audience had been gripped by the Verdun scene, there had been further barracking in the quieter fourth act of the play and, as Sarcey gleefully pointed out, Mévisto, straining against the crowd, lost his voice and certainly could not have sustained a month's run of the play. Antoine was learning through experience about the artifice of theatre, that what he needed was the impression of reality, not reality itself. Just as a convincing death scene derives not from the wholesale slaughter of actors but from the quality of the words spoken and the actors' skilled imitation of death, so in a scene like the Verdun one, greater artifice was needed to enable the audience to pick up the words of the dialogue and to preserve intact the actor's crucial tool, his voice.

The work with light and crowds here and in subsequent productions was an important element in Antoine's eventual recognition that, 'in the theatre, truth is relative';[12] that imaginative reality lies in seeming, not being. Whilst the *Patrie* script had neither the coherence nor sustained interest in the complexities of crowd psychology to supply the necessary density of texture to Antoine's theatrical invention, it provided a practice ground for the play that did. For all the achievement of the naturalist novelists their inadequacy as dramatists compared with Tolstoi, Ibsen and Hauptmann was increasingly apparent to Antoine. 'It is necessary to recognize that no French dramatist is capable of painting a fresco of this amplitude and power', he wrote when he discovered in *The Weavers* a play commensurate with the energy and commitment of his production. And even Sarcey was compelled to comment that, 'The subject-matter is not very tempting, nor is the action which accompanies it. But the effect is thrilling all the same . . . It is art, of an inferior kind if you like, but incontestably it is art.'[13]

The Weavers (29 May 1893)

Hauptmann's play was the first major reciprocal offering from a theatre founded on the model of the Théâtre Libre. Staged by Otto Brahm at the Freie Bühne in February 1893 and by Antoine three months later, *The Weavers* shared the *grand refusé* status of *The Power of Darkness* and *Ghosts*, having been banned as subversive by Wilhelm II. Presenting the rising of the Silesian weavers against the new machinery that had alterd the structure of work and cut the price of labour whilst increasing profits for the masters, it is a Luddite play, although the cause of the discontent is only spoken directly in the statement in the last act, 'they're going to smash up the power looms. For it is them that is ruining the hand-loom weaver.'

Set in the 1840s and informed both by Hauptmann's talks with veterans of the 1844 weavers' revolt and his experience of famine conditions after the failure of the harvest in Silesia in 1890, it is a history play but one that is more genuinely episodic than the Goncourts'. Its coherence and its idea of history derive not from the succession of events in the life of one heroic individual, but from the way historical and economic circumstances shape numerous different lives, connected by their domestic or employment relationships. With forty named characters amongst the *dramatis personae*, it is a chorus- not a hero-play. The protagonist, in so far as there is one at all, is the common people. Even Sarcey, in the long article he devoted to the production, agreed

14 Antoine in *L'Inquiétude* by Jules Perrin and Claude Couturier, 26 Dec. 1893. One of several lithographs of Antoine in performance by Toulouse-Lautrec. The lamp held by the old woman (Saville) casts light on the couple's faces in the gloom. (*L'Escarmouche*, 14 Jan. 1894. Phot.Bibl.Nat., Paris)

that, despite its failure to observe the classical unities, 'the juxtaposition of scenes created a unity of impression'.

The Power of Darkness stands as a high point at the beginning of Antoine's work at the Théâtre Libre; *The Weavers* occupies a similar position at its end. Where the demands of Tolstoi's play prompted Antoine to new and more ambitious ideas of staging, *The Weavers* gave him the opportunity to match the most developed of his ideas to a worthy script. In each case, a major work made a tremendous impact on its audience. From the dim flickering lighting of the first act, through crowd scenes that had the whole orchestra stalls on their feet with excitement, to his own low-key but moving performance as an obstinate old peasant, holding himself aloof from the crowd, and meeting an accidental death in the final scene, Antoine's signature is evident throughout his production of *The Weavers*.

The opening scene, set on pay-day in the master's house, in which the masters undervalue the men and their work and revolution begins to stir, provides a clear demonstration of the selective authenticity of Antoine's realism. Huge bales of linen and broadcloth carried in by the weavers and stacked up on the stage signified the place and the work; the dim light emphasized the depressed state of the weavers, described by Sarcey as 'shadows gesticulating to shadows', but, as Sarcey also saw, atmosphere was more important than verisimilitude here since an overseer would, in reality, have used a bright light to inspect cloth whose quality he was assessing. The climax of the scene was carefully prepared. The master, refusing to hear the protests of the weaver, Bäcker, flings his money on the ground, at which the weaver demands his pay in his hand. Antoine had the actors hold a tense silence before the master, ordering another weaver to pick up the money, summarily dismissed Bäcker. The silence, creating a momentary doubt as to the master's response, emphasized the power of one, the defiance of the other. At this point, Antoine modified Hauptmann's text. The song that will become the leitmotif of the play is merely mentioned in the author's script, but in Antoine's production the other workers, having grouped themselves into a loose circle at the back of the stage, intent on the action at the front, begin a low threatening singing as Bäcker exits.

The next act shifts to the house of an old weaver, Baumert (Gémier). At its centre, as in so many realist plays, is the family meal and the table at mid-stage around which the characters sit. This family, near starvation, has killed the dog to provide a rare meat stew. Jäger (Arquillière), a disaffected soldier home on leave, provides *eau de vie* for the feast. In the third act Baumert and Jäger in that other recurrent realist setting, a public bar, join with Bäcker of Act I, now unemployed and become a popular orator, and talk revolution. In these two acts the song recurs and swells. Sung solo by Baumert at first, other characters take a part until Act II ends with everyone on stage joining in the chorus, whilst in Act III the crowd of drinking weavers, placed now at the front of the stage, sing the song at full strength to the faces of the gendarmes come to restore order. In Act IV the weavers invade the master's space.

At the outset, the frightened family and guests listen in Dreissiger's (Pons Arles) sitting-room to the singing and footsteps of the approaching crowd. Simulating the advance of large numbers from a great distance, a small group of extras advanced from the corridors deep in the theatre, joined by increasing numbers who had been standing silently in position nearer and nearer the stage area waiting their cue to add their voices, on the 'Vive Gambetta' model of the *Patrie mise en scène*. On stage, Pastor Kittelhaus, with the futility common to clerical figures from Pastor Manders on, offers to reason with the crowd but joins the panicking family in their back-door retreat. Antoine left the stage empty momentarily, as if projecting the threat of the advancing rioters as much at the audience as at the masters, until the very fabric of the set gave way, doors and windows seeming to collapse under pressure from the entrance from every direction of the drunken, angry weavers. For all it was a mob that invaded the stage, its members had individuality. They mimed their characters so that, as Antoine said of the Meininger, wherever the audience looked it, 'glimpse[d] some little detail of situation or character'. Each group within the crowd engaged in prearranged activity. Some shouted and smashed, some attempted to restrain, some climbed on to furniture, some played like monkeys with the objects in the room.

As with the Verdun scene in *La Patrie*, this wild crowd scene thrilled the audience, many of whom stood spell-bound to watch, and it was this scene in particular which led the minister to ban public performance of the play. When rehearsing it for the Théâtre Antoine revival, in 1898, Antoine instructed his company to tone the scene down drastically for the censor's inspection visit. Although, when public performance was finally approved in May 1898, it did not have the political consequences the authorities feared, it did provoke 'very lively demonstrations' and stimulate fierce emotion so that 'certain evenings those in the upper galleries, very agitated, shake their fists at the stalls'. In Austria, the ban on public performance was maintained until 1903, in Russia until 1904 whilst, in Germany, the battle against censorship had to be fought repeatedly city by city after the imperial family had given up its box at the Deutsches Theater in protest at the lifting of the Berlin ban in 1894.[14]

The power of the fifth act is of a rather different kind. There is no sense of the anticlimax that marred the Goncourts' play. Hilse (Antoine), an old weaver who has not previously figured in the action, preaches faith, resignation and selfless work to his children and his half-deaf and blind wife

(Barny) who sits immobile throughout the scene. As the sounds of the riot are heard in the distance, his angry daughter-in-law, Luise (Nau) rushes out with curses to join it. The main body of the crowd seems to approach the house and then pass by off stage, the song swelling and diminishing with it, but a part of the crowd enters the room to call Hilse to join the rising. Since it was important that the dialogue be heard here, Antoine arranged the crowd behind Bäcker, Baumert and Jäger and had them fall silent when their leaders spoke. As he had said in defence of the Meininger practice in his letter to Sarcey:

If the crowd listens and looks at the actor instead of looking at the audience, or, as at the Comédie-Française, at the stars with silent but visible deference, it will be found quite natural that a crowd of 200 persons should be silent together, listening in rapt attention to a character who interests everybody.

In the unnatural silence, Hilse tells of his resolve to trust in God and continue the work he has laboured at for fifty years. A military air played on a fife and the disciplined footsteps of soldiers marching sounding again from off stage draws the crowd away. The audience hears the sound of guns fired at the crowd but sees the old man return doggedly to his weaving by the window as if Hauptmann would endorse Hilse's resignation at the end of the play. But in a final volley the window is shattered and Old Hilse, caught by the stray bullet, falls dead at his loom. Antoine's response to and elaboration of Hauptmann's opposed sound and silence, contrary attitudes, on- and off-stage action maintains the tension of the scene up to the startling death at the end. The chance nature of the death and its unexpectedness for the audience prevents any suggestion of bathos in a scene which, in Sarcey's words, 'overwhelms the imagination and grips the heart'.

Antoine's introduction of the song into Act I, the swelling volume of Act II and the dominant positioning of the singers in Act III were in keeping with his decision to substitute a song that had been taken as a call to action by the Young Germany movement, Heine and Schneckend's *Die schlesischen Weber* (The Silesian Weaver), for the cry of anger and despair of the weavers' song, the *Weberlied*, that Hauptmann had used in his play. Jean Jullien found the substitution dishonest, saying that 'It is the socialism of Young Germany, of Heine, not the cry of pity and despair of the Weavers. It makes a very strong effect on the public but it is obtained by means incompatible with a work of truth.' Certainly, it seems to contradict Antoine's claims to authenticity, for the truth was that the *Weberlied* had played a vital part in the 1844 rising. As one of Hauptmann's chief sources, the historian Zimmermann, had written in 1892:

In its largely musical lines in regular metre a threatening despair finds expression, a wild hatred and fury especially against the fourth businesshouse, the first to be attacked, which was seen to be openly blossoming forth in ever greater wealth and splendour alongside the mounting distress . . . the song sped from house to house like a summons; it fell like fuel upon minds in ferment.[15]

Whether or not he was aware that Hauptmann's song derived from the rising, Antoine held to his substitution on the grounds that it intensified the effect of the play. When, in the autumn following his own production, he saw the German version of the play in Berlin he commented that, 'the play isn't performed here with the great gust of anger and revolt it has with us; I told Hauptmann that he would be very surprised to see it in Paris' (Nov. 1893) and, much later, wrote that he didn't find the German cinematic version had 'as much power and grandeur' as his production had had and added that 'the German *metteur en scène* should have got the [Schneckend/Heine] from us'.

The poster Ibels designed for the play, a magnificent composition in orange and black, emphasized, by a curious slip, the kind of shift in tone that Antoine had effected. It showed a worker bent nearly double slaving not over a weaving-loom in his room but over a chain of coal trucks in front of a slag-heap. The scenes of mass action, confused emotion, the wildness of desperate people that Antoine was recreating in rehearsal had evidently interacted in Ibels's visual imagination with another set of verbal images. This is part of the opening sequence of Zola's *Germinal*:

To his right there was a fence, a sort of walk of heavy baulks of timber shutting off a railway track, while to his left there rose a grass bank with some sort of roofs on top, like a village with low gables all the same size . . . the lights reappeared quite close, yet still he could not make out why they were burning high up in the dark sky, like smoky moons. But his eye was caught by something else at ground level; it was the solid mass of a block of low buildings, surmounted by the silhouette of a factory chimney . . . three coal fires were burning in buckets to give light and warmth to the workers. The rippers must have worked late for the waste was still being brought up. He could now hear the labourers pushing their trains along the trestles and pick out moving shadows emptying the tubs near each of the fires.[16]

It is exactly this that the poster reproduces and is a more subtle form of adaptation to the demands of a time and place than the rewriting of dialogue, shaping of plot or introduction of spectacular effects characteristic of nineteenth-century theatre. The words of the play are respected but the *metteur en scène* interprets, even alters, the tone of the piece. It is a procedure wholly recognizable in the present. One would be hard put to think of any outstanding directors since Antoine who had not engaged in this kind of adaptation. Such interpretation of mood and presentation of environment are taken as functions of the imaginative, stage-conscious director who listens to and interprets the play for the actors and audience today, but are at variance with Antoine's declared aim of being wholly subservient to the text.

In Zola's formulation, 'art is life seen through a temperament'. The director's temperament here overlays the author's and one is back with the dilemma, not resolved by Antoine and not resolved today, of whether it is possible to determine, except by individual intuitive response, when truth to the imaginative conception of the author has become untruth. Theatrical achievement turns on a director's capacity to create a consistent and original version of the play which nevertheless convinces its audience that it is responsive to the spirit of the original.

The Weavers was the last large inventive achievement of the Théâtre Libre. It drew on the lessons of the earlier exploratory work with crowds and was, in its turn, a source for Antoine's *Julius Caesar* which would be his first major production at the Odéon (fig. 41). It is clear that its massive demands exhausted Antoine personally as well as financially. The cost and the casual employment of extras would remain a trial to Antoine even at the Odéon, where he again used crowds of 200 persons for some productions, but could not keep such numbers on the payroll for a full season. In response to the acclaim his crowd scenes received in *Julius Caesar*, he would write:

In a work like *Julius Caesar* the crowd occupies the first place and that was one of the great problems to resolve. Abroad, in the centres where one finds the great stages, the job of being one of the crowd is a profession in itself. Parisian theatres, alas, have not this resource and it is necessary to recruit them from day to day from a group of temporary unemployed, tramps or professional prowlers. Dangerous people when circumstances gather 200–300 together in a restricted space.[17]

It is a sign of the courage and temerity of the man that he persisted in the face of such odds in his attempt to realize 'the sensation of multitude' not in a circus ring or an arena but within the confines of the picture-frame stage.

5   Playwrights' theatre

The Théâtre Libre was conceived as a playwrights' theatre. Antoine's first manifesto, published in 1887, offered young authors 'the possibility of being played' and he held to this idea throughout the life of the theatre. As well as giving the French première of plays by Verga, Ibsen, Strindberg, Hauptmann and Björnson he performed 112 new plays between March 1887 and May 1894, including work from sixty-nine authors who had never previously had a play performed. However this achievement might be qualified, either because many of the authors were already known through fiction, poetry or journalism or because some of the plays were tedious, some gratuitously horrible, a few hardly different from mainstream staple fare, it remains remarkable and was perceived as such by Antoine's contemporaries of all persuasions.

Brieux, dedicating *Blanchette* to Antoine, wrote:

> For ten years I took manuscripts to all the Parisian theatres; most often they returned them without reading them. Thanks to you, thanks to the Théâtre Libre, I was at last able to learn my trade as a dramatic author. And here within two years is the second play of mine you have produced.   (1892)

These are not empty compliments: the recognition of the Théâtre Libre as significantly enabling, not just because it gave serious and inventive writers the hope of performance, but because the playwrights could learn from the experiences of those performances is corroborated in numerous other prefaces and dedications. Both François de Curel and Brieux claimed to have learned about dramatic construction from watching Antoine rehearse[1] and others, including Courteline, Ancey and Jules Renard, found Antoine's productions of their work revelatory. The sense of mutual learning and development that I will investigate in this chapter is a matter of crucial importance for dramatists now. The reciprocity between play script and performing agency has occurred, rarely but always vitally, in the theatre since, when companies have existed in which writers have been able to work closely with the performers of their plays.

The importance of the author to the Théâtre Libre was registered publicly. Although Antoine did not otherwise permit outsiders to sit in on rehearsals, the dramatist was free to attend and bring with him whatever friends he pleased. Most authors did so and even the most world-weary, like Goncourt

15 Poster for François de Curel's *Les Fossiles*, Théâtre Libre, 1892. One of a
set of eight poster-programmes commissioned by Antoine from the then
unknown Ibels for the 1892–3 Théâtre Libre season. Antoine was a patron
of the visual arts, in so far as it was financially possible. Besides Lautrec and
Ibels, Signac, Forain, Willette, Steinlen, Rivière, Vuillard, Raffaelli and
Charpentier figure among designers of his poster-programmes.

at the rehearsals for *La Patrie*, found themselves not only enchanted by the
energy and insight Antoine brought to their plays but alerted to previously
unexplored possibilities of words in action. The company's offices in rue
Blanche included a smoking-room, available for use by authors, many of
whom took to using it as a private club and it became, for a while, an
important meeting-place for writers. The writers, it should be noted, were
virtually all men although many of their most interesting characters were
women – fallen women like the Goncourts' Fille Elisa or new women facing
the implications of independence on inadequate means, like Brieux's
Blanchette. The women who frequented rue Blanche were actresses or
patronesses.

Each prospective new work was read to the full company by its author or
by Antoine in what was soon a sufficiently important social occasion for the
literary *cognoscenti* to warrant a full-scale oil painting, although one of the
kind that Antoine, who gave free hanging space to contemporary post-

16 *Playreading at the Théâtre Libre*, painting by Dillon, 1890. Antoine stands at the table reading a play. Geffroy sits opposite with Mévisto standing, leaning towards him. Mlle Barny stands by the doorway and the writers Ancey, Jullien, Alexis, Hennique (with the cane) and Darzens sit along the back. Also in the picture and variously identified are Descaves, Arquillière, Vidal, Mlle France, Mlle Dorsy and Salandri. Antoine could not afford to buy the painting. (Photo Harlingue-Viollet)

impressionists, could not afford to buy (fig. 16). Curel, noting that Antoine's 'least judgements were religiously heard', recalled such an occasion:

I am seated on a chair, a manuscript in my hand, and before me thirty or forty people, authors, actors, actresses, awaiting feverishly the reading of *L'Envers d'une sainte* which, according to custom, I am going to give to my future interpreters before rehearsal. For two months Antoine has told anyone willing to listen that he has discovered a dramatist of genius and all those with any right of access to the Théâtre Libre haved hurried to take the measure of this great man . . . [The author reads in a monotone.] Then Antoine comes to me, takes the book from my hands saying, 'the author does not know how to read, I am going to continue in his place'.
(Vol. II, p. 9)

The tickets, with what *Figaro* described as a 'nuance which demonstrates the great originality of this eccentric little stage' (12 Oct. 1887) read as an invitation from the dramatists (see fig. 7) and Antoine repeatedly reminded his actors that their function was to re-create the author's imagined world and to speak the dialogue exactly as written, with no concessions to individual whim or fashionable expectations. He called cuts *tripatouillages*

Application du Cercle Chromatique de M^r Ch. Henry.

P. Signac

17 A multi-coloured pointilliste logo designed by Paul Signac and used as
poster and programme-card for the season 1888–9. (Photo Villa)

(tamperings) and was vocal against the liberties taken with texts in the
Théâtre Français. Although he did himself sometimes make alterations
which, as I have already indicated, altered the tone or intensity of a sequence,
these seem to have been thoroughly condoned by the dramatists as
developments of stageworthiness arising from rehearsal. There is no record
of a dramatist objecting to the kind of alterations Antoine introduced and,
indeed, they were usually incorporated into subsequent printings of the play.

The Théâtre Libre's policy of taking new scripts and performing them
essentially as written drew the attention of regular theatres to previously
unknown writers, but it also served to strengthen authors' defence of their
scripts in those theatres. Antoine was always ready to stir up opinion on
behalf of such Théâtre Libre writers as Curel, Hennique or Courteline when
their plays were taken by regular houses, leading vociferous applause and
even publishing an open letter when the Comédie-Française wanted Curel to
modify the text of *L'Amour brode*. But the existence of his theatre encouraged
more established dramatists too. Jean Aicard was able to transfer his four-act

18 Toulouse-Lautrec's 'La Loge au Mascaron Doré' (The Box with the Gilded Mask), designed as a poster for Antoine's last Théâtre Libre production, *Le Missionnaire* (24 Apr. 1894). Lautrec also designed posters for *Une Faillite* (Nov. 1893), *L'Argent* (May 1894) and for *La Gitane* at the Théâtre Antoine. (Photo Villa)

19 Poster for *Le Devoir*, lithograph by H.G. Ibels, showing corner café setting. (Photo Villa)

verse play *Le Père Lebonnard* to Antoine rather than submit to the rewriting demanded by the Comédie-Française where the standing agreement, as Sarcey pointed out, was 'that the author will consent to such suppressions, corrections and accommodation' as the work makes evident are needed'.[2] In *Dans le Guignol*, the short satire on Théâtre Français rehearsals Aicard wrote as prologue to the Théâtre Libre production of *Le Père Lebonnard* (October 1889), the playwright-character declares, 'I am leaving artists who have become functionaries and going to seek the spirit of Molière with the free actors and free public.'

Whilst Antoine's belief in some of his writers might look naïve now – Bergerat, for one, relished being treated as if he were Shakespeare – the sense of discovery was crucial to the energy that powered the Théâtre Libre, to the confidence of its writers in their freedom to experiment and to the urgency of its productions. As Curel later recalled:

I have never truly believed in myself, except in that enthusiastic milieu, and I never look back without stopping with tenderness and recognition on those who were my interpreters, remarkable by the sheer strength of their sincerity.   (Vol. I, p. xx)

Gaston Salandri recorded finding, 'this time again the same welcome and the same zeal' when Antoine accepted a second play of his, *Simone*, and Edmond de Goncourt suggested that the lack of 'an Antoine and a Théâtre Libre' in his own young days was 'the real reason why the whole group of writers [he, his brother and their friends Gautier and Flaubert] never attempted anything in the way of serious dramatic writing'.[3]

However, there is, inevitably, another side to the fêting of the dramatist in Antoine's theatres and one which shows him more evidently the forerunner of the twentieth-century theatre director. Antoine saw the director's task as being the interpretation of the script for the stage without deliberate distortion or self-projection and the dramatist had to be prepared to trust that interpretation. Acceptance of Antoine's mastery in his own sphere of the *mise en scène* was part of the bargain. He consulted his authors, welcomed them at rehearsal, was open to suggestions about casting, but, although in most cases there was evidently a genuine working partnership between director and playwright, in the last resort, as we have already seen in relation to the casting of *Power of Darkness* and *La Patrie en danger*, he was tenacious of his own idea. Few of his writers did try to interfere because Antoine's care and expertise in his own field were so apparent. Moreover, whilst the writer's play was central to its production, it was still only a part of the director's season in which realist prose plays were paired with verse dramas, one act with three-act pieces and plays by unknowns with those by the already famous or notorious.

In choosing to perform interesting new writing, Antoine also assumed responsibility for identifying it. Archer in England would lament that there were 'no writers of unconventional talent' to be found; Grein at the Independent Theatre in London would fall back on Théâtre Libre plays to make up his repertoire, while Copeau, opening his theatre in 1913, would declare that 'we do not imagine that there exists today in France an entire army of neglected young talent that deserves to be brought to light and that, as from tomorrow, will respond to our call'. Antoine searched plays out. He advertised; he appealed through the columns of the leading dramatic critics for new writers to save the Théâtre Libre from becoming the home of famous people instead of 'a refuge for the young, an experimental laboratory'; he braved Sarcey's derision at the prospect of the countless bad scripts that would rain down on him 'from all corners of France' and he instigated projects such as the Byl and Vidal adaptation of *Sœur Philomène* or the Méténier *Frères Zemganno*. In the early years of the theatre, he spent the better part of his summers reading scripts in retreat in Brittany – some 500 in 1891.[4]

The assumption of total control over programming and artistic policy gave Antoine power as the major producer of new work. Although he widened the basis of judgement, choices about dramatic quality still had to be made and, whilst he accepted advice from such supporters as Zola and Mendès, he was the final arbiter, necessarily rejecting many more plays than he accepted even at the risk, as with his rejection of a play by Henri Bauer of *Echo de Paris*, of the loss of a major paper's goodwill. One of the fortunate authors, Henri Bernstein, later recalled:

Our generation had Antoine and only Antoine. He judged without appeal. If he accepted your manuscript, you were saved, you would be believed in; if he refused or ignored it then years of emptiness or black anxiety stretched ahead. Antoine over a long period was shown worthy of this magistracy, without equal. Honour to him, honour to his example as much as to his work.   (*Comœdia*, 19 June 1921)

Particularly initially, Antoine was remarkably eclectic. Curel, for one, having been warned by the reader at the Comédie that he was 'the prisoner of a little clique of naturalist writers', discovered that 'it was impossible to be more completely wrong about Antoine's attitude' when three of his own non-naturalist plays, submitted by him under three different pseudonyms, were picked by Antoine as the best of the batch of the summer of 1891. More verse plays, including work by Banville and Villiers de l'Isle Adam, were performed by the Théâtre Libre in its first two years than by the other Parisian theatres combined. In Mendès's words, the Théâtre Libre was 'at the same time the consolation of the old Romantics and the hope of the young naturalists', whilst Faguet wrote of the December 1888 programme:

Three plays; three genres, three schools, three rules of nature; one comedy in the manner of Musset, one fantasy in the manner of Banville and one drama in the manner of 1610. Something for all tastes. The Théâtre Libre is the free tribune of the theatre. No one welcomes it more than me. They are accused of being monopolized by a very closed, imperious and intolerant school . . . I am pleased to see it is nothing of the kind.

And, in 1892, Antoine invited new work via an interview in *Le Courrier français*, saying, 'just as at first I opened my door wide to the naturalist theatre, now I open it as wide to the symbolist theatre'.[5]

As the warnings and accusations referred to here demonstrate, however, despite Antoine's eclecticism, his was known as a realist theatre from the outset and has retained this reputation despite the factual evidence. Indeed, the appeal to symbolist writers did not bring in plays in the way the 1887 call had, for, by the time symbolism was making its impact, Antoine was firmly identified with the first avant-garde and Paul Fort and Lugné-Poë were ready to found theatres in direct opposition to Antoine's.

Despite arguments to the contrary by Antoine's playwright son, André Paul, it is perhaps not so surprising that this should have been the case. Realist plays, with their claim to go to root experiences and address the real rather than an ideal or glamorized world, spoke most directly to the contemporary audience, as is evident from accounts of the reception given to various parts of combined programmes. Equally, as ideas and issues quickened into action on the stage, they caught the attention of critics and provided stimulating copy. Focusing attention on the poor and the everyday, the lower-middle and working classes virtually ignored by mainstream French theatre, realist plays could claim to extend the boundaries of what was admitted on the stage, expose the conflict of the inner self with the public self and refuse sentiment whilst demanding intensity of feeling. They brought to the stage a way of seeing the present, already apparent in fiction and painting. Baudelaire had suggested in 1860 that the painter of modern life goes in 'quest of the ephemeral, the fleeting forms of beauty in the life of our day ... Often bizarre, violent, excessive', creating, as Tim Clark has more recently suggested, 'a myth of modernity' in which the modern equalled the marginal. That Théâtre Libre writers nourished, like Antoine, on Zola's writing and Manet's painting repeatedly figure the marginal and the excessive, the counter-clerk, the criminal and, particularly, the prostitute, helps to confirm the existence of such a myth of modernity and to explain why the plays galvanized attention in the way they did.[6]

The form of the plays was as notable, as modern, as their content. The polished language and ingenious plots of mainstream drama were replaced by colloquial prose dialogue and episodic structure which made the drama seem 'un lambeau [a shred] d'existence' or, in Jean Jullien's more familiar echo of Zola's phrase, 'une tranche de vie' (a slice of life), the theatrical analogue of the impressionist paintings which were, in Zola's words, 'bathed in the real light of the sun, and not in the false day of the studio'. The claim is to moral as well as theatrical truth, as it would be again in later periods of theatrical rebirth, in Greenwich Village in the second decade of this century, for example, or in London in the late 1950s.[7]

La Casserole

Méténier's one-act play La Casserole that filled the last half hour of the final programme of the 1888–9 season, provides an excellent example of the first phase of French realist plays in the Théâtre Libre. Méténier, who had drawn on his experience as sometime secretary to the police commissioner for En famille, in 1887, and had introduced Parisian street slang into his version of The Power of Darkness, brought these elements together in what he claimed was a 'very violent but very accurate picture of the Parisian lower depths'. The play, whose title is the slang term for a police informer, is set amongst pimps, prostitutes and petty criminals in a wine bar in the grossly overcrowded and dangerous quarter of La Roquette.[8]

Of the founding company, besides Antoine (Père Chabot, an old alcoholic) and Mévisto (Merlan, a pimp), the cast included Pinsard (le patron) and Tinbot (a republican guard), two of Antoine's few remaining genuine amateurs, as well as the loyal Mme France as an old whore and Mlle Fleury as a young one who encroaches on the others' territory and is accused of being an informer. Lugné-Poë appeared briefly for the second time with Antoine as a young spiv., ejected by the café's bouncer in the first moments of the play. To play the bouncer, la Terreur de la Maube, Antoine brought in Leo Will, an underworld friend of Méténier's from his police days and one of the strongest men in Paris, who provided the shock of 'the thing itself' intruding on the imitation of the thing with a show-stopping sequence of weight-lifting that astonished the on- and off-stage audience alike.

Antoine took the Chateau Rouge bar in the Maubert as the model for his set and sent Pinsard to study the gestures and walk of Père Trolier, patron of the Chateau Rouge. The particularity of the bar was registered in the big double door leading to a dance-hall at the back of the stage, through which the shapes of passing dancers could be seen, the off-stage sound of the dance-band and the various notices posted about the stage: 'Entrance to the dance, 20c', 'Here, you pay when you are served', 'No drinks less than 15c'. The basic organization of the stage space, however, was one that recurred in Antoine's theatres. Within a box set, with doors rather than old-style flats for exits, was, to the left, a zinc counter in front of a shelf loaded with bottles and, to the right, the shop-front and a glass door opening to the street. There were cheap colour prints on the walls and two tables, of bare white wood, surrounded by benches and stools, were placed at opposite sides of the stage.

The organization of the stage was beautifully balanced and flexible. Within it, the characters smoked, drank and played cards, moved to and from the bar, the dance-hall or the street. In some sequences, the two tables formed parallel centres of interest, the audience's attention taken by first one and then the other, to be diverted from both when an eruption into the central space became briefly the single focus of attention. Besides the virtuoso weight-lifting, the action at stage centre included the striking of a liaison between one of the prostitutes and the half-drunk, comparatively rich, old Père Chabot, a fight between Carcasse and La Rouquine, the two young prostitutes, around which the other characters formed a tight and excited semicircle and, at the end of the play, the stabbing to death of Carcasse by Merlan and Merlan's arrest.

The world of the play is lively but unsentimentalized. Although the crowd scenes had none of the scale of *La Patrie* earlier in the same season, there was a continual movement between the street, the bar and the dance-hall of clients, prostitutes, dancers, musicians and police, played by extras that included, with sardonic Théâtre Libre humour, several of Méténier's criminal acquaintances. The absence of sentiment is evident in the cold way the old whore Lisa is made to set up Carcasse in revenge for the younger woman's poaching of her client; in the casual picking of Chabot's pockets, and in Merlin's egocentric attitudes: his concern for La Rouquine's money rather than her affection, his failure to stand by her when the Patron throws her out, his willingness that she should take the blame for the theft he has committed and his casually vicious language, littered with obscenities and abusive slang terms for women and the police in lines like: 'More flics (*fliques*) passing by. What a filthy area. You can't take a step without crashing up against cops (*sans se foutre dans de la rousse*).'

Once Antoine had adopted the idea of a theatre devoted to new and refused plays he was dependent on what authors chose to bring him, and in the late 1880s this was the new realism. The programme in which Méténier's play was presented demonstrates the breadth and variety of tone for which Antoine always aimed. *La Casserole* began at half-past midnight. The evening had opened with a one-act prose version of Poe's 'The Tell-Tale Heart', one of the *Tales of Mystery and Imagination* so admired by Baudelaire and his followers. The main show was *Le Comte Witold*, an undistinguished three-act idealist piece by Count Rzewuski, a subscriber from the opening of the theatre and a frequenter of rue Blanche, one of those encouraged to turn dramatist by attendance at a writers' theatre.

Antoine combined the known and the unknown in his programmes, the idealist *Le Comte Witold* with the realist *La Casserole*, and looked for the appropriate staging for each. He used dance movements for Banville's fairy play, *Le Baiser* and *tableaux vivants* and pantomime in the Descaves and Bonnetain *La Pelote*; constructed a decor of black curtaining and a single metal bedstead for Margueritte's mime play, *Pierrot l'assassin de sa femme*, whose atmospheric musical accompaniment included both 'Au clair de la lune' and the 'Dies Irae' (fig. 20), and put himself into considerable debt to stage Mendès' *La Reine Fiammette* with splendid Renaissance-inspired hangings and costumes. But despite this genuine openness he was clearly more inclined by his own temperament and culture to perceive stage truth in a mimetic and substantial way.

Antoine was fundamentally literal-minded. Even as he flirted with it, he declared that, 'theatrical symbolism consists in making tangible a philosophic or moral idea by means of a fact or material object' (*Voltaire*, Jan. 1893). The costumes for Mendès' play were historically accurate and Bergerat's fanciful garden, in *La Nuit Bergamasque*, was furnished with real plants. Although delighted to use *commedia dell'arte* gesture for that play, to investigate the use made of shadow effects in the Chat Noir's cabaret and to use black curtains, green light on phosphorescent apparitions and whispering voices reiterating

20 Drawings by Langlois for *Pierrot assassin de sa femme*, the bare stage and the fire are indicated (*La Vie moderne* 1888, p.200. Phot.Bibl.Nat., Paris)

the word 'assassin' in *Hannele Mattern*, Antoine's major and continual area of experimentation was, nevertheless, into ways of creating the illusion of social and psychological reality on stage. Theatre for him was relationship, his work a continual probing of the enigmatic immediacy of drama that derived from the living presence of human beings moving about on the stage and using the writer's words as if they were their own.

The majority of Théâtre Libre plays exposed private lives to the audience, showing the inner self of the characters in conflict with the public self. Many were set amongst small shopkeepers, artisans, army regulars or peasants if the setting was rural, in what was often an unheroic and invariably an unidealized world. The structure tended to be episodic and the language direct, often introducing areas of experience which, if referred to at all on the stage previously, had been modified by euphemism. *En famille* included a long description of an execution, *Sœur Philomène* realistic medical language. The minister responsible for banning public performance of *La Fille Elisa* justified his action on grounds of its excessive authenticity, saying, 'without opening one of these houses [a brothel] on the very stage, I do not see how it would be possible to enter one more completely. In these circumstances I do not see how it would be possible to give the authorization demanded.'[9]

An off-shoot of plays of psychological realism and social enquiry that became particularly associated with the Théâtre Libre was *comédie rosse* – drama, of which *La Casserole* is an example, noted for its *rosserie* or gratuitous nastiness. Its world view derived from Zola's *Thérèse Raquin* and its tone from Becque's *Les Corbeaux* which, incidentally, after failing at the Comédie-Française in 1882, had become something of a cult text, but was not revived on stage until performed by Antoine in 1897. *Comédie rosse* parodied the strong plots, the sexual triangles and aristocratic milieu of social-problem melodrama by presenting characters engaged in petty swindling or squalid adulteries. The glamorous if tubercular courtesans of Dumas fils' writing, the sentimentalized fallen women, self-denying and redeemed by death, were replaced by common prostitutes, brutalized by ignorance and poverty, 'slaves', like those Baudelaire identified as subjects for the painter of modern life:

> confined in those hovels, often enough decorated like cafes; unfortunate creatures these, subjected to the most avaricious tutelage, with nothing they can call their own, not even the eccentric adornments that act as condiment to their beauty . . . whilst behind a counter laden with liqueur bottles lolls a fat shrew, her hair tied up in a dirty silk scarf, which throws on the wall the shadow of its satanic points, thus convincing us that everything dedicated to evil must be condemned to have horns.
>
> ('The Painter of Modern Life', pp. 431–3)

With mordant wit, *comédie rosse* demonstrated how the fittest survive in the contemporary world, indicting society with scenes in which characters used violence for self-gratification or self-protection. The endings, mocking the artifice of the conventional happy ending, were sardonic rather than sad with dilemmas resolved by a sexual or financial accommodation. The dialogue of *comédie rosse* often included low colloquial expressions, criminal jargon and phrases which defied verbal taboos, particularly with reference to sexual activity. The title of Méténier's play *La Casserole* used the criminal-slang term for an informer, whilst Sarcey was deeply offended that a character in *Lucie Pellegrin* should have cried out 'these pigs of men' when another character told of a crime committed against her (25 June 1889).

Although *En famille* is of the type, the genre was distinguished first with Jean Jullien's *La Sérénade* (Dec. 1887). Briefly, a wealthy shopkeeper discovers that his son's tutor, whose presence is a symbol of his own social aspirations, is having an affair with his wife. Prepared to turn a blind eye to this, he then discovers that his daughter is pregnant by the same man. The play ends with the whole family sitting down to drink together. Paul Alexis' play, *La Fin de Lucie Pellegrin* (June 1888) has as heroine a woman who was both lesbian and prostitute – lesbian because of the harshness she had suffered as prostitute. In Ancey's *L'École des veufs* (Nov. 1889) a son becomes the lover of his bourgeois father's young mistress and, needing money, moves in on the ménage rather than take the girl away. The father, slave to physical passion, comes to accept his humiliation. The play ends with the son granting the father one night with Margueritte but departing on the exit line, 'à demain' ('till tomorrow'). In Jullien's *Le Maître* (Mar. 1890), the heirs of a miserly peasant count out his goods as the old man clings to life. Such plays, combining anger and comic relish, introduce a tone not previously encountered on the stage – or, at least, not since the Jacobean period in England.

With his usual sense of occasion, Antoine wrote to *Le Temps* (Aug. 1887) to announce that *La Sérénade* would cause a sensation. It did: press commentators found it scabrous, some quoted examples of its crude language, and others claimed to be too shocked to bring themselves to do so, but *Le Petit Moniteur*, finding the occasion a gross buffoonery, regretted having 'to protest against the enthusiasm of the public'. Referring to the play subsequently, Verlaine wrote to Jullien, 'Salut . . . / A vous . . . qui punissez / L'ordre bourgeois, Jean, mon confrère' and Jullien himself subsequently defined the genre as including, 'bitter *rosserie* with hatred of the bourgeois and an obligatory cruel denouement'.[10]

Linert's *Conte de noël* (28 Dec. 1890) is perhaps the extreme version of *rosserie* and, unlike most others, did upset the audience. In it, the child of an adulterous union is murdered so that the guilty wife can continue her respectable existence in the marital home. The infanticide and the central relationship in which a busily practical older woman advises the young mother are evidently derived from *The Power of Darkness*. In the first scene, in the peasant's house, Rosa sets up her Christmas-tree and the crib beside which children will come to sing the 'Venite Adoremus' and goes through the procedure of mulling wine with which to offer the Christmas drink to the dead. The audience is made to feel anxiety for Rosa and pity for her unsuspecting husband as she confides her adulterous pregnancy to Mère Raminot. From time to time in the second scene, set in a courtyard surrounded by the brightly lit windows of neighbouring houses, children's voices are heard singing carols. In the final sequence, the older woman re-enters as the bells for the midnight Christmas mass ring out and the following dialogue ensues:

MÈRE RAMINOT:	It's done.
ROSA:	I want my baby, where is my baby?
MÈRE RAMINOT:	Chut, it's finished, he's already cold. I've thrown him to the pigs.
VOICES (*singing*):	Venite adoremus.

The peasant calls his wife into the warm, saying, as the door closes on them, 'Come and drink to the dead, that will warm you up.'

The play subverts audience complaisance by demonstrating that the shock is felt less in response to the murder itself than to the manner of disposing of the body, a technique that anticipates the use Edward Bond will make of violence a century later. To some, the horror the play produced seemed wholly characteristic of 'style Théâtre Libre'. Romain Rolland, surveying the cultural scene some years later, would write, 'they continue to feed children to the pigs at the Théâtre Libre, when they don't crush them under the floorboards', although Antoine was, in fact, scrupulous about rejecting plays that he found needlessly horrific. He had returned Linert's first play, *La Mort*, saying:

I won't conceal that I found the first page of your manuscript rather chilling. You know that I don't recoil before any harshness or violence when I believe that there is 'literature' in it. But I distrusted your play because many authors, confounding *liberty* with *licence*, send me filth which I return to them with a firm expression of distaste. Well, sir, without being carried away, I confirm that your play is one of the most curious and the most interesting that I have found among the manuscripts that I receive.

Whilst he was not prepared to play *La Mort*, he was willing to look at other plays the young author might write.[11]

Throughout the life of the theatre, conservative critics threatened not to return if Antoine persisted in showing such plays. Hector Pessard complained that 'for them, all skies are grey and all chimneys smoke irremediably. All that is not wicked is naive. Of two ways of expressing the same idea, they choose the most brutal.' Noël and Stoullig wrote, 'M. Paul Alexis has not been afraid to take us to Lesbos ... Who will show us Sodom?' and summed up their sense of the Théâtre Libre in a sardonic description of the programme devoted to the authors of the anti-Zola *Manifeste des Cinq*:

Let us recap. In the first play, M. Antoine plays the role of a man who dies of lung disease, partnering an old woman who is going to die paralyzed. In the third, M. Antoine, coughing and spitting blood, plays the role of a young man who dies of consumption. In the second, he doesn't die but he represents a skeleton bringing to the cemetery a Pierrot who tells us he has killed his wife and will kill himself next. In the fourth, the same M. Antoine is at the bedside of his mother who is about to die. Ah. So this is the theatre of the future.

Sarcey was appalled that 'the funereal and macabre' was allowed to infect even 'joyous pantomime' in Paul Margueritte's Pierrot play, and Ganderax

21 *Rosserie*: 'States of a soul.' Cartoon by Eugène Rapp depicting the conservative critic Sarcey's growing horror as he watches Gramont's *Rolande* (after Balzac). Rolande, warned by her dying mother, becomes aware that her father (Baron Hulot) continually seduces young girls and has to pay his blackmailer. (*La Vie moderne*, 1888, p.712. Phot.Bibl.Nat., Paris)

regretted that poetic plays were pulled in the same direction, that Pierrot 'is Pierrot murderer of his wife'. Faguet declared that:

All their art, in fact, all their wisdom and hardiness of spirit consists in having discovered that man is a filthy beast. They have been so perfectly charmed with this unexpected discovery that they proclaim it with energy every evening.[12]

Although, as is already evident, by no means the majority of the plays Antoine produced could be labelled *comédie rosse* and very few that could were taken on tour or retained in repertory when Antoine opened the Théâtre Antoine, reports of the plots of plays like *Conte de noël* or *Lucie Pellegrin* established the theatre's reputation with those who had never attended it. Indeed, in October 1891, one Chirac caused an outcry by staging three short and cynically obscene plays at his newly formed Théâtre Realiste in rue Rochechouart. Chirac was arrested, but Antoine recorded that the 'abominable scandal' had 'probably delayed for some years our contact with the public at large' (20 Dec. 1891), a prediction reinforced when accounts of Chirac's 15-month jail sentence appeared in the press in Brussels and the provinces under the headline, 'The Affair of the Théâtre Libre' (15 Jan. 1892). That there were other abuses of the name and fame of the Théâtre Libre is evidenced in a collection of obscene plays called *Le Théâtre naturaliste* which, dealing in rape, flagellation and lesbianism with none of the bitter wit or moral fire of true *comédie rosse*, was printed in Amsterdam in 1889.

The assumption that Antoine's repertoire did include what he labelled 'ces ordures' occurs not uncommonly in provincial and foreign press accounts. Before the London tour, *The Times*, for example, described the Théâtre Libre as 'the happy hunting ground of the ultra realistic or fin de siècle dramatist who specially affects the horrible and revolting' (5 Feb. 1889) although the more liberal *Pall Mall Gazette* had the grace to point out that whilst some of the theatre's productions were 'scandalous and repulsive', others were 'unconventional without impropriety' and that the plays to be performed in London were of this kind (6 Feb. 1889).

There is evident ignorance and prejudice here, but it is undeniable that, as so often, literary revolution did produce a new orthodoxy in many of its followers. Four years after *La Sérénade* had shown the way, Jean Jullien wrote of Pierre Wolff's *Les Maris de leurs filles*:

Antoine has taken a role which suits him marvellously, that of an old bourgeois father, obstinate and grumpy, who loves a lively, sentimental, slightly stuck-up young woman, played by the exquisite actress, Mlle Meuris. M. Grande, as usual, takes the egoist, the husband-fooler, crass, insolent . . . All these characters the audience of the Théâtre Libre knows by heart. It has applauded them in *La Meule, L'Honneur, Tante Léontine, La Dupe* and so forth.   (*Le Théâtre vivant*, vol. II, p. 206)

Although Jullien still claimed to find this 'neo-vaudeville' much better than the vaudeville of other theatres, he pointed out that young writers, becoming aware of what appealed to Antoine, tended to adapt their style accordingly.

Antoine himself seems to have wearied of the thin texture of much *comédie rosse*. He had always particularly cared for plays whose central characters, not merely the victims of circumstance, experienced significant conflict, like *Jacques Damour* and *Sœur Philomène*, and such plays increasingly took his attention, as if his response to dramatic texture developed with his experience of it. As he said in an interview in 1893:

The influence of Ibsen gives, it seems to me, larger ideas to young authors, a more ambitious design; they will be led to be more concerned with psychology; they won't restrict themselves only to the study of characters. What's more, in broadening their design, they will include something of the ideal with the real which doesn't occur amongst our current realists who are dry and hard in their psychology.

(*Voltaire*, Jan. 1893)

This sense of 'larger ideas' is perhaps most clearly seen in the depiction of female characters in the plays Antoine increasingly valued. Characters like Carcasse and La Rouquine in *La Casserole*, like Lucie Pellegrin and Fille Elisa might be thought of as first-phase Théâtre Libre heroines. Zolaesque street-walkers, they are naturalistic in that their perceptions and actions, their life chances, are demonstrably shaped by their environment. But, for all that, although no hero rescues these betrayed village girls and the warm-hearted courtesans have been replaced by rapacious or bewildered whores, these characters retain relationship with the Marguerittes and Denises of second empire drama because they are, in essence, stereotypes, figures whose acknowledged function is to service the erotic needs and fantasies of men.

Ibsen's *A Doll's House* was more truly revolutionary than is often allowed because, whilst it would be a long time still before a woman dramatist found a valid dramatic voice, that play makes a powerful claim for complexity in female characterization and asks awkward questions about a woman's role in contemporary society. It also demonstrates the potential dramatic interest of the generality of women – those not normally classified as prostitutes.

Blanchette (1 Feb. 1892)

The February 1892 programme included two such plays. Besides providing an example of Antoine's staging in the later years of the Théâtre Libre, the occasion presented Antoine with a testing challenge to his claims for the authority of the dramatist and allows an insight into the kind of concessions he would find necessary when he moved from the independent into the commercial theatre.

Blanchette, the second of Brieux's plays that Antoine had performed, was played with François de Curel's first, *L'Envers d'une sainte*. It was not a happy pairing and the fate of the two plays, each of which turns on the dilemma facing an aspiring woman, was remarkably different. In Brieux's play, the daughter of a café-owner who has gained her teacher's certificate becomes frustrated with the demands and possibilities of the parental home and leaves to make her way in Paris. In Curel's, a middle-aged nun who has returned to secular life after many ascetic years tries to befriend the daughter of the lover whose betrayal had led to her taking the veil. Whilst Curel's play was booed, Brieux's was such a success that Antoine was able to boost his finances by touring it in Belgium, Holland and Italy as well as the French provinces. With

22 *Boubouroche*, Act I, by Courteline: 1897 revival for the opening of the
Théâtre Antoine. The photograph shows a characteristic café scene.
Practicable glass at the back enables the audience to see characters in the
street outside. (From stage r.: Pons Arles; Arquillière; Desfontaines; Beaulieu;
Verse; cashier (name not recorded); Antoine. (Photo-programme illustré)

those two other staples, *Jacques Damour* and *The Power of Darkness*, *Blanchette*
was taken on at the Eden Theatre in December 1893 and then at the Porte
Saint-Martin for a month's run to boost that theatre's failing finances.

    The most characteristic Théâtre Libre sets were the humble domestic
interiors of *Jacques Damour* and *En famille*, and the corner cafés of plays like
Boubouroche or *Le Devoir*, where people stood or sat at plain wood tables for
their pastis or coffee (figs. 19 and 22). Such unglamorous interiors were
recreated as the normal and necessary surroundings of a life experience
different from that usually shown on the stage. As such, they embodied the
claim of realist drama to new authenticity in their very plainness and sparsity.
They had that immediacy for the audience, too, that comes from the sudden
recognition of something familiar transposed into the artificial world of the
stage that, intelligently done, grips as nothing else can and make us cry, 'it
was so real'.

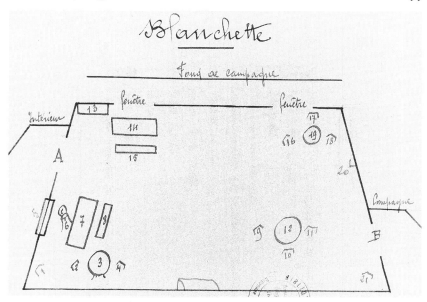

23 *Blanchette* stage plan: photograph of the prompt copy for the 1897
Théâtre Antoine revival. The stage furniture is numberd in the prompt book
to facilitate stage setting and blocking record. (Photo Villa)

The prompt copy for *Blanchette* includes stage plans for each act, on which
each item of stage furniture is numbered for clarity in positioning props or
directing actors' movements, and the photographs of the revival at the
Théâtre Antoine in 1897 show how these were realized in performance (figs.
23 and 24). As commonly at Antoine's theatres, a box set including a stage
ceiling is used, and there are two practicable entrances clearly marked so that
actors know if they are entering from the street or the house. A corridor
accessible to the actors is made between the back-cloth, on which is painted a
view of the countryside, and the supposed back wall of the cafe, in which are
set practicable windows. The on-stage world is presumed to continue
beyond the confines of the stage. The house lights are, of course, off, denying
the existence of the auditorium; the stage lighting, which comes from in front
and above, simulates daylight. The stage furnishings, wooden bread-rack,
round tables and stools, have a rustic solidity to them; the decorative
features, lace curtains, prints and a plain-faced clock above the bar, are
carefully observed and the bar, towards the front right of the stage, is
equipped with bottles and glasses appropriate to a small country bar. The
impact of Antoine's bar settings on the contemporary audience can to a
degree be realized from the photograph (fig. 25) of the Comédie-Française,

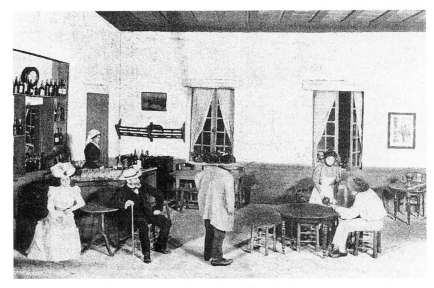

24 *Blanchette*, Act II. Blanchette is forced by Père Rousset to wait on the lorry driver.
(From stage r.: Lucie Galoux (Clem), Mère Rousset (Barny), Galoux (Marsay), Rousset (Antoine), Blanchette (Mellot), Bonenfant (Gémier). This is one of the few photographs to show Antoine's back. (Photo-programme illustré)

1903 production of the play, which is modelled remarkably closely to Antoine's own set.

The thoroughness with which Antoine worked out what movable properties were necessary and where they must be positioned is evident in the opening notes to the prompt copy. Such care was crucial to the solidity and to the smooth running of the play. The opening notes read:

5 – diverse bottles
counter – diverse bottles; empty glasses; a bottle of *eau de vie*; doz. little glasses; 3 coffee cups with saucers and spoons; sugar bowl with sugar; account book; ink; pen; box of dominoes; a book; dish cloth; a diploma

Act I	Act II
table 3 – basket of veg.	counter – 10-centime piece
on counter – crochet work	cupboard 13 – blue apron
Rousset – money, pipe, matches and	Rousset – stick, piece of wood, knife
pouch	left corridor – apron, square of wood,
Morillon – coin	broken glass
George – hunting gun	off right — packet with 6 books; lamp
Blanchette – little box to hold some rice	with v. long stem in pieces in a box
Lucie – crochet work	with straw

25 *Blanchette* at the Comédie-Française, 1903: The domino match. The remarkable resemblance of the setting to that at the Théâtre Antoine demonstrates the extent to which Antoine's conception of a realist setting was taken to be definitive. (*Le Théâtre* 116, Oct 1903. Phot.Bibl.Nat., Paris)

Left corridor – 2 drawings of Romulus
  coffee percolator with coffee

Act III
in cupboard – plate with cheese; knife
on cupboard 13 – blue apron
Rousset – knife; a chignon comb
left corridor – coffee pot with coffee; a glass (to break); a dish cloth
off right – a bundle of linen and clothes
1 2 4 9 11 16 17 18 21 – straw stools
3 – little round table   5 – shelves   6 – tall chair
7 – counter   5/15 – wooden benches   12 – big round table
13 – little cupboard   14 – table   19 – round table
20 – nail for hanging the diploma

The detailed annotation of the prompt copy also shows how carefully the actors' movements were orchestrated. The accompanying gesture or movement of each phrase of dialogue is noted by the relevant dialogue or on pages interleaved with it, the exact moment identified by a series of underlinings and superscript numbers. And small marginal sketches of stage positions at crucial moments of the action appear beside the relevant piece of dialogue.

Towards the end of Act I, Morillon asks Rousset for Blanchette's hand for his son Auguste whilst Auguste and Blanchette state their love for each other. The front part of the stage is divided between the two pairs as a small marginal sketch makes clear:

26 *Blanchette*: the domino match Act I. Reproduction of a prompt copy sketch showing positions (the numbers reflect those of the stage plan, fig.23)

Antoine, having discovered that there is deep fascination for an audience in seeing an ordinary activity accurately played out, often used his discovery, most notably at crucial moments of the action. When his characters play cards, they do so according to recognizable rules, artisans engage in their craft with skill, waiters wipe glasses and arrange covers just as they would if a real patron were overseeing their work and, here, the two old men are engaged in a convincing game of dominoes as they discuss the fates of their children. The placing, the commentary on the game, its tense silences, help shape the audience response to the request and Rousset's refusal. One of his actors recorded that, as each new actor took on Morillon's part in successive Théâtre Antoine revivals, Antoine's direction of the scene would go like this:

'Why are you waiting to place a domino? – Not like that, Sir – what are you doing? – You have played twice in succession – Haven't you ever played dominoes? – No, too quickly, you speak without thinking. – That says nothing, you're singing.' Then coldly, 'It is not possible, sir, to perform the play with you.'

The scene, beautifully paced in performance, always gripped the audience and drew great (and illusion-breaking?) applause. It is, indeed, this scene which is registered in the Comédie-Française photograph.[13]

The front table (12 on the plan, fig. 23) and the space between that and the counter (7) were the crucial playing-places. Early in Act II, the affections and tensions within the family are absorbed by the audience as, in common with his wife and daughter, they watch old Rousset assemble his present, the lamp, from its constituent pieces. The climax of the act is a battle of wills between Blanchette and her father. In the moment caught in the photograph here (fig. 24), two nouveau-riche customers, timid mother behind the bar and dominant father (Antoine, with back turned to audience) concentrate attention on Blanchette who, weeping with humiliation, stands behind the table and waits on the coarse workman.

Brieux evidently benefited from working in a playwrights' theatre and from sitting in on rehearsals, as he was the first to acknowledge. Just as Louise France's remarkable début as the old concierge in *La Pelote* in March 1888 led to the appearance of a horrible old woman in numerous subsequent Théâtre Libre plays, so the part of an old peasant that Antoine took in Jullien's *Maître*, with which Brieux's first play *Ménage d'artistes* had shared a bill (21 Mar. 1890), was the basis for the more fully observed Père Rousset, the curmudgeonly old father of *Blanchette*, Brieux's next play, much as the plot of *Ghosts* was clearly the model for Brieux's *Monsieur de Reboral*. Hauptmann in his turn developed his idea of Drayman Henschel from Brieux's Père Rousset.

Brieux's drama, lacking the harsh realism of Jullien and the complexity of Ibsen, is nevertheless partly shaped by their inspiration, although it is in reality closer to the work of Pinero or Henry Arthur Jones. Whilst his drama cannot support the claim Shaw made in 1909 that 'after the death of Ibsen, Brieux confronted Europe as the most important dramatist west of Russia', the problems he posed were of the moment and the parts were a delight for character actors. Barny's presentation of the 'furtive endearments' of Mère Rousset towards her brusque husband was very convincing, and Père Rousset (fig. 27) became one of Antoine's most celebrated, and most polished, parts in which, according to Charles Mosnier, 'all the humour, all the craftiness, all the wicked spite of the old peasant flourished before us without seeming artifice'.[14]

Very little in the way of a direct record of the staging of *L'Envers d'une sainte* survives. Antoine had difficulty casting the play, trying some twenty-three actresses in the part of Julie before finally fixing on Nancy Vernet, and rehearsals were long and fraught. Antoine remained unsatisfied that his actors had entered sufficiently into their roles either in this or in Curel's next play *Les Fossiles*. With the ferocity he characteristically demonstrated on behalf of a play he strongly believed in, he attributed the failure of *L'Envers d'une sainte* both to the flippant attitude of 'a crowd of young fools' among his subscribers who 'care nothing for the regeneration of dramatic art' and wanted only to amuse themselves, whilst Curel offered them *Bérénice*, and to his company's inadequacy before 'a theatre of such novelty, wholly interiorized, that it is extremely difficult to interpret' as contrasted with the self-admitted brilliance of the performance in *Blanchette* (2 Feb. 1892).

But whilst the production of *Blanchette* was a success, it faced Antoine with the dilemma of where trust and authority lie when the dramatist reneges on his own play. In the Théâtre Libre version, the last act opens with Rousset's business evidently in decline. Blanchette returns in expensive clothes accompanied by a rich lover. Rousset's bitter attack on his daughter's immorality turns to joy when she offers him the money to put his affairs in order. The evident *comédie rosse* of the ending offended several critics. Whilst

27 Antoine painted by Louis Malteste as Père Rousset, one of his most celebrated roles, showing characteristic peasant clogs and rough clothes. (Photo Harlingue-Viollet)

Antoine admitted to some slackening of audience enthusiasm in Act III, he recorded that the huge success of the piece would cut the ground from under the feet of the Théâtre Libre's adversaries and on 17 February gave a public performance at the vast Théâtre des Arts at Rouen which was a triumph and made 4,000 francs. Brieux, however, had been disturbed by Sarcey's review. Although he replied, 'but is it the truth?' to Sarcey's suggestion that Elise (Blanchette) should return and marry her peasant lover because 'the public loves to see the people in whom it is interested happy', he nevertheless gave Antoine a revised last act. That champion of the author's claims avoided the issue for the moment by being too preoccupied in rehearsal to take on the new version. When Antoine toured the play to Brussels in March, Brieux published a letter in the Belgian press rejecting the final act. Antoine's response was to cut the third act altogether and use neither of Brieux's versions, so that the play ended with Elise leaving the paternal home in defiance, her future, like that of Nora in A Doll's House, open to speculation. Antoine toured the play's two acts in Holland and in Italy in December 1893, but he turned down Brieux's next play on the grounds that it was too similar to one he had just accepted from a newcomer, Barres, and recorded tersely, 'Brieux has taken his play to the Cercle des Escholiers which is going to stage it, so all is for the best.'

Despite the coolness Brieux's open letter had occasioned, Antoine revived Blanchette in August 1897 for the opening programme of his professional repertory theatre, and included Brieux's revised third act. This time Blanchette, having returned to her roots, passionately denounces the city as a dirty and deceitful place where men want her only for their sexual satisfaction. She finds that she still loves Auguste, a philosopher in clogs. A chastened Père Rousset agrees to the marriage he previously forbade and she now accepts the apron she bitterly rejected in Act II and gaily proceeds to serve the road-worker.

Whether Antoine's respect for the dramatist's inspiration or his anxiety for the success of his new enterprise most influenced his judgement in acceding to Brieux's demand is open to question. What is clear is that the ending completely changed the thrust of the play and that it has been the basis of at least one subsequent suggestion that Antoine was compelled to compromise his values when he entered commercial competition. What had previously seemed an examination of the dilemma facing someone frustrated by the limitations of her peasant world, and an indictment of a society which had no place for an educated girl without means, became a morality tract against the foolishness of educating a girl beyond her sex and station, a lesson in humility and a reinforcing of the old adage that true love will conquer all.

Sarcey willingly claimed the credit for Brieux's Sardouesque ending and there was an ironic justice, if no conscious irony in La Quinzaine dramatique's evocation of the memory of the old regime's leading actor to support its claim that, whilst the interpretation by 'this homogeneous and earnest company' was perfect, Antoine himself raised the tone of the stage to the sublime so that:

One doesn't recall in vain the memory of M. Got in speaking of Antoine whose creation of Père Rousset is an absolute masterwork of dramatic composition. Notably at the end of the second act, in the bitter revolt of the old peasant, each reply flushes up his anger and the dull menace grinds out between his clenched teeth.

The revised ending was no more completely satisfactory to Brieux than to Antoine. He tried yet another, less conventionally happy ending for the Comédie-Française revival. Blanchette, overcome by misery and hunger, returns to beg food from her father and is glad to be allowed to work in the café again. As one critic put it, 'its nails have been cut and polished since it was performed at the Théâtre Libre'. But at least without the love plot, something of the original tone had been restored.[15]

Conclusion

At least one critic has been sceptical of Antoine's importance as the initiator of the new drama, pointing out that Zola and Goncourt plays were also performed at large theatres and that the playwrights who were Antoine's 'so-called discoveries' only achieved large audiences when their work reached the Vaudeville, the Odéon or the Porte Sainte-Martin. But this is to misjudge the influence of the studio audience in the late 1880s and, particularly, of the kind of guests invited to the press review of each programme. These included, besides dramatists and journalists, the actors and entrepreneurs of such theatres as the Porte Saint-Martin and the Odéon who were eager to take up work for which an appetite had been created, and the press undoubtedly stimulated that appetite. Albert Carré, who produced the subsequent work of many of Antoine's discoveries at the Vaudeville and staged the first French *Hedda Gabler*, recorded in his memoirs that his interest in realism was a direct result of his attendance at the Théâtre Libre.[16] Other theatres felt the pressure on them to extend their programme and alter their performance styles in the face of comments like the one in the magazine *Le Tintemarre*: whilst 'Becque, Bergerat and Banville [had] played to empty houses or hawked work around without success, Antoine fill[ed] his house with just such writing' (26 Sept. 1889). As Courteline, who had become one of the leading French dramatists by the turn of the century, put it, 'if you want to get to fundamentals, you must recognize that Antoine would have got on well without me whereas, without him, I would have found an ephemeral success in Montmartre'.

In a period of widespread new literacy and a burgeoning urban white-collar class of clerks and shop-workers, theatre critics were important purveyors of information and arbiters of taste. News of what was new in Paris, the cultural centre of Europe, travelled quickly both within the city and out to people ready for change in the theatre elsewhere. It is clear that large audiences for such drama were achieved elsewhere *because* of the excitement centring on the Théâtre Libre.

The stir caused in the press by Antoine's two opening experimental evenings was such that all the Parisian papers published his programme for the 1887–8 season and, from September 1887 onwards, reviewed all his work. As Becque, writing in *Figaro*, put it tersely at the opening of the second season, 'there was no dramatic life last winter except in that house' (13 Oct. 1888) and Faguet, defending himself against complaints about the space he devoted to the Théâtre Libre, wrote:

Is it my fault that the Salon des refusés shows me pictures whilst the Salon shows hardly any? The Théâtre Libre has this great, this inestimable superiority over the others, that it gives plays as if that was what theatre was made for. (3 Feb. 1889)

The variety and excitement of the monthly premières provided such excellent copy that there were more than 12,000 newspaper articles about the Théâtre Libre in France alone during its first three years. Even hostile critics frequently began their regular surveys with the Théâtre Libre and two columns was not an unusual length for the report. In some papers, including *Le Soleil*, *Figaro* and *Le Temps*, the Théâtre Libre would be mentioned two or three times a week and even when its plays and production styles were under attack its immediacy and energy had to be admitted. The most influential critic of them all, Sarcey, not only gave column space in *Le Temps* to the open letters Antoine frequently fired off to him, but regularly included such contradictory comments as, 'I have not ceased to harass M. Antoine; at bottom he knows well, there is not in all the press a man more sympathetic to his efforts' (23 July 1888) and, 'I am a declared adversary of the theories on the base of which the Théâtre Libre was founded; but I am enchanted that it exists. I pay all justice to the man who organized it and maintains its persistent success' (4 May 1891). And foreign papers followed suit. The London *Times*, usually scandalized by its productions, was compelled to admit of *Le Père Lebonnard*:

The whole performance showed that the foundation of the Théâtre Libre, due to the indefatigable efforts of M. Antoine, is deserving of the encouragement of all those who desire that there should be a tribunal to decide between authors and the tyranny of the theatrical administration. The representation of yesterday has decided a case in favour of the author, and has definitively justified the existence of the Théâtre Libre.

(22 Oct. 1889)

The reading public was further informed because Théâtre Libre plays that were in any way successful were published by Charpentier or Tresse and Stock as soon as they had been discussed in the press. Strindberg, for one, although unable to attend performances in Paris, followed accounts of the Théâtre Libre in copies of *Figaro* and *Gil Blas* supplied by Edvard Brandes, who also sent him editions of new plays, until in November 1888 Strindberg announced his 'intention in the near future to establish a Scandinavian Experimental Theatre modelled on the French Théâtre Libre' in Copenhagen and was writing *Pariah,* on the pattern of the *quarts d'heure* plays, and *Lady Julie* for performance there.[17]

In London, to take an example of how information was disseminated in the English-speaking theatre, the audiences for Antoine's tour were disappointing, but they included Henry James, J.T. Grein, George Moore and William Archer, all of whom published lengthy articles about the work. Moore, after seeing *Ghosts* in Paris, wrote of the production as 'opening the theatrical ways hitherto so strictly barred, to literature, and towards freeing the drama from the fetters of convention and prejudice'. He asked, 'Why have not we a Théâtre Libre?', and was particularly interested in the subscription list and the fact that Antoine ran his theatre on a shoe-string budget. Grein, after reporting the first season of the Théâtre Libre for the *Dramatic Quarterly,* asked, 'Is a British Théâtre Libre, a theatre free from the shackles of the censor, free from the fetters of convention, unhampered by financial consideration — is not such a theatre possible?' and used Antoine's programme as the basis of his Independent Theatre, which opened with *Ghosts,* included *Le Baiser* and *Sœur Philomène* in the repertoire and eventually offered Brieux's *Blanchette* as the final production in 1898. Shaw, outlining the importance of the Independent Theatre, wrote:

Everything followed from that: the production of *Arms and the Man* by Miss Horniman and Florence Farr at the Avenue Theatre, Miss Horniman's establishment of Repertory Theatres in Dublin and Manchester, the Stage Society, H. Granville Barker's tentative matinees of *Candida* at the Court Theatre, the full-blown management of Vedrenne and Barker, Edie Craig's Pioneers and the final relegation of nineteenth century London Theatre to the dustbin by Barrie.

Certainly, both Yeats and Synge had attended Théâtre Libre productions in Paris and William Fay, founder member and leading actor with the Irish Players, noted on various occasions, 'we got the idea from Antoine'; 'it was Antoine's courage in the face of what seemed hopeless odds to carry out his ideas that inspired my brother and I to try it', and 'from Archer we had news of Antoine's revolt against the Parisian theatre ... Antoine's example proved of great service and inspiration to us.'[18]

There is no doubting the genuineness of Antoine's commitment to freedom of expression in the theatre, but it is equally clear that he relished the attention gained for his theatre by public demonstration of such commit-ment. Like Sarah Bernhardt and Henry Irving, he was a skilful manipulator of the publicity machine. Inspired by the example of Manet, he tended to measure success by the heat generated in the house and in the press concerning the matter, the structure and even the language of the play and was not averse to contributing to the heat. He told George Moore that the writer's 'business is to write the play, mine to have it acted. If the public like it, so much the better; if they don't they hiss or leave the theatre', but he perceived that those who cared enough to hiss invariably came back. He wrote in anticipation of one production that 'the fuss will begin again better than ever with *Rolande*' (fig. 21) and, after the Goncourt *Germinie Lacerteux* had been booed at the Odéon, added to the furore by sending a telegram to the one critic who praised the play describing the audience as 'gueux imbeciles' (crazy beggars) and announcing that he was putting *Patrie en danger* into immediate rehearsal. (Which goes some way to explaining the barracking and orchestrated hostility against *La Patrie en danger*). Even more mischievously, when the banning of a public performance of *La Fille Elisa* on the grounds of obscenity coincided with a ban on Sardou's *Thermidor* on political grounds, Antoine wrote an open letter to Sardou, saying:

At this time I judge that it is our duty to remind you, you too, of the existence of the Théâtre Libre . . . If you wish, then, *Thermidor* will be performed in a month at the Théâtre Libre; we will call on all the young actors who love their art, and I will put all the money I have into it . . . I only ask one favour: that I may have, if you judge me worthy of it, the role of the gendarme who kills Marais and so I will be certain that the pistol shot of the denouement will not miss its mark.

The false naive tone and the sting in the tail ensured that the letter was reprinted with relish throughout the press. Whilst such events inevitably made enemies, they guaranteed that the theatre remained in the public eye.[19]

That coupling of a willingness to provoke public discussion with a belief that lively theatre necessarily challenged orthodox attitudes is evident in the advance press warning Antoine issued before each of the final programmes of the 1888 and 1889 seasons that members of the audience might find the last play of the evening offensive and prefer to leave early. The result was that, although Méténier's *La Casserole* (1 June 89) was not staged until after midnight, the theatre doors had to be left open so that the crowd in the foyer could hear. As with *La Fin de Lucie Pellegrin*, Paul Alexis' play about the reminiscences of a dying lesbian and prostitute the previous year, the excitement generated by the play had the practical effect of stimulating the audience to take out subscriptions for the following season.

There were disasters and miscalculations, some at least owing to Antoine's jealousy of his enterprise. He rebuffed Mévisto's attempt to share the organization of the new theatre at the outset and so soon lost his leading actor. Lugné-Poë, summarily dismissed as régisseur after his success in the Conservatoire competition, nursed his resentment of Antoine for the rest of his life. After three successful trips to Brussels Antoine, hearing that a Belgian Théâtre Libre was to open, hastily booked the Théâtre Molière in May 1888 with the idea of eclipsing a rival. His publicity failed beside the prospect of a new play by Camille Lemonnier and the result was a loss of 1,500 francs and a telegram to Mévisto, 'Break down. Affair a disaster. Send me all the money you can find. Counting on you. Letter follows but it's urgent. Go and see Chastenet.'

It is evident that Antoine's eye for what would make an event led to occasional works which were Grand Guignol in their horror, works whose 'sinister form of so-called realism', Daudet claimed, led to 'the equally untrue idealist reaction' of the theatres of Paul Fort and Lugné-Poë.[20] And, indeed, the emphasis on the new carried with it the necessary eventual decline of the theatre. On the one hand, it led to the inclusion on the subscribers' list of people drawn only for the excitement of the public event, ready to barrack or cheer at anything that seemed politically or sexually risqué and, on the other, as Daudet saw, it invited the rivalry of a newer new that would draw to itself the prime attention of the avant-garde members of the audience and, before long, of the press too.

Although Antoine lavished both faith and money on Hauptmann's symbolist *Assumption of Hannele Mattern* and had an extraordinary set of posters designed by Toulouse-Lautrec, among others, for the 1893–4 season, he had evidently lost his position as the leading theatrical innovator. He always worked to a very tight budget. He could meet his normal running costs, including the hire of the Théâtre des Menus Plaisirs, from subscriptions, but it took longer to recoup the expense of elaborate projects such as *La Patrie en danger*, *Nell Horn* or *The Weavers*. In April 1894, deeply in debt, he knew he must resign as director of the Théâtre Libre. After his final performance as the narrator in Luguet's *Le Missionnaire*, for which Toulouse-Lautrec made his famous poster 'La Loge au Masceron Doré', Antoine noted in his diary:

I took the difficult role of the reader and all evening was exposed to the pleasantries of the audience. It happened that at one moment in the midst of the noise a handful of sous hit me in the face; it is extremely symbolic. This brutal gesture decided me on the instant to abandon the Théâtre Libre. The wretches don't know and if I had dared interrupt the performance and suddenly revealed the true state of things to them, it is probable that they would have been ashamed.   (*Souvenirs*, 25 Apr. 1894)

Whereas in the optimism of the opening years Antoine could override the catcalls of the boulevardiers and negotiate with entrepreneurs for public performances to raise money, now, exhausted and dispirited, he was ready to cancel and pass on.

But for all that, the Théâtre Libre had survived for some seven years. As well as demonstrating by example that a theatre devoted to new writing could flourish, Antoine created an awareness of the importance of new writing to the life of the theatre at large, an awareness that has re-emerged as a stimulus in successive twentieth-century theatres. Somewhat as with the English Royal Court or Theatre Workshop writing of the 1950s and 1960s, the theatrical activity itself, the dramatizing of questions of moment for their audiences, gave the theatre cultural significance. The various presentations of cruelties, crimes, abuse, offered their largely radical middle-class audiences an occasion for investigating the darker areas of social and family life with its mutual destructiveness, guilt and recrimination. Few of the writers were individually outstanding but, between them, they developed a remarkable language of guilt, fear and hypocrisy. Copeau differentiated his own project from Antoine's largely on the grounds of the works to be performed. Where 'they unwittingly committed the folly of limiting their field of action to a narrow revolutionary programme', the basis of the Vieux Colombier's repertoire would be 'established works'. It is telling, then, that amongst the 'established works' presented by Copeau are Renard's *Le Pain de ménage* and *Poil de Carotte*, Curel's *La Nouvelle Idole*, Porto-Riche's *La Chance de Françoise*, Courteline's *Boubouroche* and Brieux's *Blanchette*: all part of that same 'narrow revolutionary programme' and previously performed at either the Théâtre Libre or the Théâtre Antoine.[21]

6 Director's theatre: 'A hundred plays a year'

When, despite predictions to the contrary, the Théâtre Libre not only survived its first season but was seen to flourish, conservative critics and writers declared that such success was possible only because, ignoring the real world and the interests of *la grande publique*, it addressed itself to the rarefied world of the intelligentsia and the literary avant-garde. Sarcey had begun it by claiming that 'transported to a true theatre *Sœur Philomène* would be a lamentable fiasco' (12 Nov. 1887) and the Director of the Théâtre Française, Claretie, had described independent theatres as, 'dangerous because they put [young artists] face to face not with the true public which judges without bias but with a special public which applauds rather than criticizes and acclaims rather than teaches'.[1]

Given the beginnings in Montmartre, the prestigious subscription list and the loud behaviour of groups of boulevardiers in the audience in the later years of the Théâtre Libre, there would seem to be some foundation for such attitudes. Antoine supported his counter-claim that the general public, never given the chance to learn, had been cheated of a lively culture by the complacencies of commercialism and the protectionism of vested interests, by citing the success that greeted the 'unperformable' *Power of Darkness*, the 'obscure' *Wild Duck*, the 'deeply offensive' or 'badly structured', plays of Hennique, Méténier, Brieux or Curel whenever they were taken on tour or given public performances in Paris. The Théâtre Antoine, the professional theatre Antoine opened in 1897, after his brief and thwarted appointment as co-director of the Odéon, to revive Théâtre Libre plays and to produce comparable new work in competition with Boulevard theatres was an attempt to demonstrate the truth of his claim.

Against the idea that the avant-garde artist is part of a privileged elite, engaged in often self-indulgent experiment, detached from the mainstream and hardly relevant to the needs of a complex industrialized society, Antoine advanced the claim that such artists are the unacknowledged centre, the mainstream of a culture all but destroyed by bourgeois philistinism and popular ignorance. In common with many subsequent innovators in the theatre he believed in opening the centre to the mass, both because theatre is the most public of all the arts and needs the response of a wide and various audience to flourish and because the popular audience for demanding and expressive drama, having once existed for the theatre of Shakespeare, Molière, Lope de Vega, might be recreated.

Within a year of founding the Théâtre Libre, whose amateur actors played at monthly intervals in a borrowed house, Antoine had had plans to establish Théâtre Libre principles in 'a true theatre which will play every evening before a paying public' (*La Nation*, 17 Aug. 1888) and in October 1889 Goncourt had recorded that Antoine was always, 'living in hope of this theatre which would enable him to produce a hundred plays a year'. Antoine's May 1890 manifesto, a declaration of intent, had been, essentially, an appeal for state or private funds to allow him to open a theatre which would offer 'new plays, a comfortable auditorium, moderate prices and ensemble acting' instead of the 'uninteresting plays in deplorably fitted theatres, at exorbitant prices, with an uncohesive company' currently available (p. 72).

Opened in 1897, the Théâtre Antoine set itself against the current tendency to long runs of a single play. It was determinedly a repertory theatre, performing some fifty plays a year. There were evident differences from the Théâtre Libre. Although he made some attempts, symbolism, the newest area of theatrical experiment, was alien to Antoine's idea of theatre and the Théâtre d'Œuvre had by 1895 taken over as the home of stylistic innovation. Antoine continued to produce new plays – far more than any other contemporary – but this was no longer his exclusive aim and few of the new plays he produced were ground-breaking in the way so much of the Théâtre Libre work had been. Rather, he consciously turned from revolution to consolidation and systematically revived his Théâtre Libre productions, determined to make the new work that had appeared in the independent theatre available to the general public at prices affordable by the lower middle and working classes. Even the biographical sketches of actors and writers included in the theatre programmes were polemical, with the history of the Théâtre Libre very much in evidence. Gémier, for example, had been, it was noted, 'refused twice at the Conservatoire' and Arquillière, having made his debut with the Théâtre Libre in 1888, had been 'in all the sensational premières, all the literary battles, *La Mort du Duc d'Enghien*, *Le Canard sauvage*, *Les Fossiles*, *Les Revenants*, *Les Tisserands*'.

In 1897–8, amongst the fifty plays offered at the Théâtre Antoine, audiences could see, besides the opening programme of *Blanchette* and *Boubouroche*, *Sœur Philomène*, *Jacques Damour*, Ancey's *Ecole des veufs* and Courteline's *Lidoire*, as well as *Ghosts* and the famous *Weavers* that had, until now, been banned from public performance. Both *Ghosts* and *The Weavers* were sufficiently successful to enable Antoine to keep them in the repertoire. Perseverance in bringing into the public domain supposedly coterie plays

THÉÂTRE ANTOINE

Mⁿ ANTOINE & Cⁱᵉ

TRADE MARK

ARTICLES ABSOLUMENT
IRREPROCHABLES

PRIX MODÉRÉS

LA MAISON N'A PAS DE SUCCURSALES

ENVOI FRANCO DU CATALOGUE

Dessin de Bershll

Maison de confiance.

28 Cartoon of Antoine as honest and, by 1905, wholly self-confident, shopkeeper. Note the comment that 'The establishment has no branches'. (*Le Cri de Paris*, 22 Oct. 1905)

and performance styles, coupled with success in attracting and holding a near-capacity audience in so doing, is the real achievement of the Théâtre Antoine. It was an achievement frequently celebrated by observant contemporary commentators and, not least, by cartoonists (fig. 28).

One of the reasons for establishing the Théâtre Libre as a theatre club had been to avoid the continual subjection of work to theatrical censorship. The Théâtre Libre had been able to play whatever it chose and its very existence had shifted contemporary perception of what was acceptable. The outcry when much-praised Théâtre Libre productions were denied a public showing; the questions asked in the Senate about the banning of *La Fille Elisa*; the selling out of the 300,000 print-run of that play which, 'deafened Paris under the cries of the street hawkers for many days'; the absurdity that *The Power of Darkness* was considered too horrible by the London censors but was acceptable to the French ones had all helped to undermine the authority of state censorship by the late 1890s. In his new theatre, Antoine would reapply persistently until the ban on a performance at the Théâtre Antoine was lifted, and was quite unscrupulous in doing so, to the extent that the actors learned to tone down certain elements – like the scenes of workers' anger or the portrayal of a bullying policeman in *The Weavers* – for the benefit of the visiting censorship commissioners.[2]

The struggle came to a head in 1901, when Brieux's play about venereal disease, *Les Avariés* (*Damaged Goods* in England), was denied public showing. Antoine, extending his Théâtre Libre practice of reading new plays to the company, held a reading of the play on the stage of the Théâtre Antoine. The ensuing public discussion, drawing attention yet again to the vagaries and restrictions of censorship, was instrumental in the decision taken within two years to abolish theatrical censorship in France, some sixty-six years before England.

Whilst it is the case that there was no longer the consistent shock and excitement, the sense of living at the cutting-edge of the new, common in Théâtre Libre days, the old spirit was frequently evident, although content rather than form usually provided the excitement. The crowd scenes in *The Weavers*, for example, had the gallery audience on their feet, cheering and hurling insults at the orchestra stalls and many of the new plays stimulated comparably fierce reactions. For example, Brieux's play *Maternity* (1903), which, concerned with conjugal rights, illegitimacy and a trial for criminal abortion ends with the court in uproar and the conclusion left to the audience, was given a 'singularly vibrant and warm reception', creating an effect of a political meeting rather than a theatre. In the third act, in which the abortionist is prosecuted, cries from the gallery transformed the theatre into a tribune as the audience responded to such comments from the characters as, 'And all the men that seduced the girls I saved – have you punished them?' and wildly cheered the opinions they approved.[3] On occasion it was less the play than the author that was the source of excitement. Antoine's staging of an adaptation of Zola's *La Terre* which had been refused by Coquelin in the aftermath of the Dreyfus case was a polemical act and one that divided its audience sharply.

The one-act play, rediscovered as a lively form at the Théâtre Libre, figured prominently at the Antoine. Courteline provided a new one virtually every year and Jules Renard produced some brilliant examples of the short form. There were also new full-length plays by Brieux, Curel, Renard and Jullien and numerous other, now forgotten, contemporary French dramatists, some, like Donnay and Descaves, who had figured at the Théâtre Libre and some newcomers, like Trarieux. Now that he no longer limited himself entirely to new work, Antoine was able to give Becque's *La Parisienne* the satisfactory production it had so far lacked and to begin to contemplate the classics. He started with a tentative and not very well received attempt on Racine (1898) and ended with a revelatory *King Lear* (1904) that guaranteed his appointment to the Odéon in 1906.

The Théâtre Libre audience had been provided with various written communications. At the Théâtre Antoine and then at the Odéon introductory talks by enthusiastic specialists were offered before particularly interesting or inaccessible plays. Like the open letters to the press, the Preface to *Miss Julie* and the five editions of the house magazine, *Le Théâtre Libre*, distributed to Théâtre Libre subscribers, the talks before a performance were a gesture of intimacy towards the audience and an indication of the distance between Antoine's theatre and commercial entertainment, between the seriousness he assumed in his audience and the philistinism assumed by commercial managers.

This combination of concern for and instruction of the audience is in keeping with the mixture of democratization and autocracy evident at all levels of Antoine's interaction with his audience and, indeed, with his actors in his professional theatres. His concern both in the 1890 manifesto and at the Théâtre Antoine is with the democratization of the auditorium – all shall equal see – but also, as is apparent in the lowered house lights and the fourth-wall staging, that the audience must be subject to the stage. It is significant that in describing his ideal theatre, Antoine reproduced the view *from* not *of* Wagner's stage at Bayreuth. Having made the picture-frame stage so much his own, he never questioned it, unlike the next generation of designers and directors, Appia, Craig and Reinhardt.

Antoine's ideal theatre retained the fourth-wall stage but altered the seating in the auditorium so that all seats would have an equally good view, being steeply raked and all placed front-on to the stage, rather than some set at an angle, as in the common horseshoe theatre. Amongst the seats he removed in remodelling the Odéon in 1906 were those in boxes designed to give a view of and to the house rather than the stage (see fig. 29). One small contribution to the campaign to direct audience attention from itself and on to the stage emphasizes the paradoxical nature of the undertaking. In remaking the proscenium arch at the Menus Plaisirs in 1901–2, Antoine had a clock put above the arch so that the audience could measure the promptness

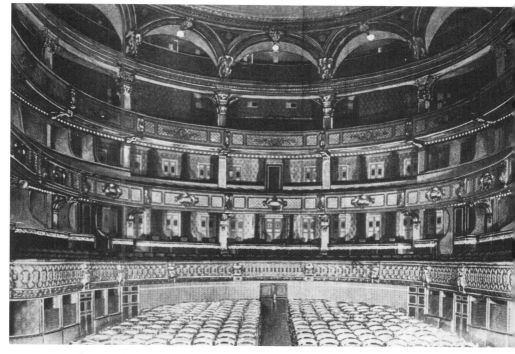

29 The remodelled Odéon, 1906, showing that angled seats in stalls and boxes have been removed to give good sightlines. The remodelling was startling enough to warrant pictures and comment throughout the press. (Phot.Bibl.Nat., Paris)

of curtain up and the brevity of the intervals – and presumably learn to avoid interrupting the performance by being late. But a clock so evidently measuring real time must surely have threatened the illusion of fictional time on the stage below.

I can best indicate how Antoine's repertory theatre functioned by giving an account of the pattern of daily activity which seems to have been largely consistent throughout the life of the theatre. By contrast with the Théâtre Libre, Antoine, in his own theatre and with a professional company, albeit one that included actors and stage crew who had previously worked with him without pay, was in a position to organize the hours of his company and did so, often reminding them that the unpaid Théâtre Libre actors had rehearsed at the end of a full day's work elsewhere.

The life of the company centred on rehearsal. Those members not in a particular production were encouraged to watch from the auditorium and learn from their colleagues' work. In the morning, one or more of the régisseurs, of whom he employed three and, later, four in addition to Christian, his stage manager, would prepare the stage, call the actors and run through the coming evening's play, working closely from Antoine's detailed sketches of the lay out of the stage and the *mise en scène* of the original production, in the prompt book. The rehearsal of a Théâtre Libre play, and subsequently of Théâtre Antoine plays already in the repertory, being an act of retrieval, Théâtre Libre actors still with the company played their original roles and new actors, instructed by the régisseurs, were incorporated into the production.

An observer at the Odéon, where much the same rehearsal pattern was maintained, described how Antoine, watching silently from the darkened auditorium and, missing nothing, would suddenly appear on the stage, his voice 'sharp, mordant, authoritative: the voice of a master', to demonstrate his idea or to replay a sequence:

and always the emphasis is on perfection in every role. With him there were no minor roles. Every detail is shaped, advised, all in a torrent of picturesque words, and always with a cigarette drooping from his lip.[4]

Even more than at the Théâtre Libre, Antoine demanded scenic intelligence from his professional actors. Each was responsible for all aspects of his or her stage appearance and had to be physically as well as vocally in character whether speaking or not. His actors, besides fading their hair and skin, had to suggest old age by giving greater heaviness to their body movements and assuming the slowness or trembling of age. The heavy stage make-up of the day, red lips, heavy black eyeliner, was rejected; the black lines of crows' feet and forehead wrinkles replaced by light face contouring with a little burnt umber mixed with white applied with the finger. Those playing peasants had to darken their hands and arms with a mixture of glycerine and red ochre.[5]

In the afternoon, rehearsals of scenes from other plays in the repertory would follow on the stage or in the foyer. A schedule might run like this:

On stage

12 hrs	*Les Tisserands*
1 hr	*La Retour de l'aigle*
$2\frac{1}{4}$ hr	*Herakléa*
$4\frac{1}{2}$ hr	*Blanchette*
$5\frac{1}{2}$ hr	auditions

In foyer

12 hrs	*En Paix*
$2\frac{1}{4}$ hrs	*Rolande*
4 hrs	*L'Ecole des veufs*

The actors who, at any given time, might be performing one role in the evening, carrying another for the next evening, rehearsing a new play during the day and retrieving an old Théâtre Libre role would, as in the seventeenth-century theatre, carry the dialogue and moves of dozens of parts in their heads.

The work was intense. That no prompt was needed by any of the twenty-three actors in any of the forty-five plays in the 1903 South American tour is a measure of the standard of accuracy achieved. It is also the case, however, that the early Théâtre Libre emphasis on virtuosity in acting was no longer evident. The pressures of time and accuracy at the Théâtre Antoine meant that Antoine usually cast to type, as he had increasingly done in the later years at the Théâtre Libre, to the extent that older actors took the parts of elderly characters, younger actors of young ones. Although in his May 1890 manifesto and later in his journalism Antoine proposed classes in enunciation, movement and dramatic history, there can have been little time for this. The evidence suggests that all rehearsals were directed towards particular plays and that actors learned to enter into and to project their characters through observation, detailed criticism and experience.

Later in the afternoon, having let the actors go, Antoine would audition or work on technical matters of staging with the stage crew and the régisseurs, spending hours perfecting the set and lighting. Although the Théâtre Libre had had access to the stores of the Montparnasse and the old Menus Plaisirs, Antoine's emphasis on precise environment necessitated attention to set and he had increasingly put his scanty resources into this. For *La Reine Fiamette*, he had 'passed around sixty-two consecutive hours overseeing the *mise en scène* and the set, rehearsing through the night and working during the day, sawing the wood himself helped by Catulle Mendès until two in the morning' (*Gil Blas*, 17 Jan. 1889) and to Brieux's suggestion that an old set might be made over for one of his plays, he had explained, 'it's only the cost of some scenery, I have my idea'. Now, with his own workshops and having had all the electrical equipment modernized when he took over the Menus Plaisirs, Antoine was able to achieve for every production the kind of decor the play seemed to demand. Besides Max, his electrician, Antoine employed full time on monthly contracts a chief technician, a prompter, a wardrobe mistress and a properties chief, all of whom stayed with him for many years. In addition, for each performance, some twenty technicians and twelve stagehands were hired on a casual basis. The hay, the real animals in the solidly built Beauce interior and the magnificent painted back-cloth and planted grassy verges of the outdoor scene of *La Terre* demonstrate how far he was able to go in creating a realistic environment (cf. figs 33 and 34).

After the evening performance, the rest of the company would join those who had been in the show to hear a reading of a prospective play or to work on one that was to be newly brought into the repertoire. Saverne's first rehearsal call was for midnight and he actually performed at 1.00 am. Daily posted call-sheets would inform the company who was called for what, but it was regarded as an essential part of the ensemble work that the whole company should attend readings of new plays.

Antoine had declared in his 1890 manifesto that his proposed company of thirty-five artists would be subject to rigorous discipline and all would be treated equally, and his practice at the Antoine came very close to this. With no stars to take the best rewards and no actor named separately on the poster, profits were much more equitably shared at the Antoine than elsewhere. Whilst Molière's company was claimed as the model, some ideas – that no actor would have the right to refuse a role and the rejection of the star system, for example – evidently derived from the Meininger. Although Antoine wrote enviously of the discipline of the Moscow Art Theatre Company when he saw them in 1922, the Théâtre Antoine also had a reputation for discipline and intensive rehearsal. Jacques Copeau, founding his own company in 1913, acknowledged the inspiration of the May 1890 manifesto and of Antoine's practice.

As will be apparent from this account, although democratic in its politics, and although Antoine worked closely with actors, designers and writers, the fundamental structure of the Théâtre Antoine was despotic. He was its creative centre and all major policy decisions derived from and returned to the man called *le patron*, as Brecht would later be called 'the boss'. No actor contradicted his interventions and the story was that when he called for a stagehand, six would appear instantly. Like subsequent innovative directors, Antoine held his position by force of personal commitment.

Antoine's reputation for turning amateurs into outstanding actors meant that, despite the long hours, intense work and tales of despotism there was a continual stream of applicants for audition, many of whom returned repeatedly if unsuccessful. He recorded details of each applicant in a register: 'pretentious'; 'impossible – never see again'; 'natural but poor voice, hear again in a year', and seems not only to have had a good memory of people he had auditioned but would recall an actor who had interested him if an appropriate part cropped up subsequently. A burly bus driver, for example, turned down brusquely when he auditioned for *La Mort du Duc d'Enghien* at the Antoine, was recalled for a quite different part after the move to the Odéon. Charles Mosnier, who became a valuable member of the company and took over Antoine's parts after the move to the Odéon, had written to ten directors when he wanted to move to Paris, but only Antoine, who remembered having seen him act in Marseilles, replied. Possible candidates were asked to return a week later with two further audition pieces and, if the decision was then favourable, would be offered a part in a specific play. Some would gradually be absorbed into the permanent company of little more than twenty persons. That the permanent company at any one time had virtually equal numbers of men and women was an effect of playing a modern repertoire.

Georges Saverne's is a telling case-history. Although an actor of some years' standing, he regarded the Théâtre Antoine as a hothouse for actors which he was determined to enter, but, having found himself among some twenty others at audition, fled in terror when faced with Antoine. After receiving an invitation to re-audition, he was offered the part of Pilate in Trarieux's *Joseph of Arimathea*, a play that was taken off after three performances. Recalled, in the course of the next year, for occasional bit-parts Saverne, like others joining a production whose *mise en scène* was already fixed, had to perform after only two or three rehearsals, learning on the job, by observation and imitation and suffering fierce criticism for insanity or stupidity whenever he went wrong. The manner in which he was finally offered a contract in February 1899 is indicative of the way Antoine interacted with his company. Furious at having been given a role in the *Weavers* revival at only two days' notice and determined to reply in kind when Antoine began his attack, he was disarmed when Antoine publicly shook his hand saying, 'Thank you, my old Saverne, it is very good. Come tomorrow and sign your engagement.' The appreciation as much as the contract wiped out 'the rebuffs, the bitterness, the miseries'. He stayed with Antoine for ten years.

There were still five ex-Théâtre Libre members (Grand, Michelez, Verse, Marley and Luce Colas) amongst the twenty-three on the 1903 tour and many of the others had been with Antoine for years. But Antoine was single-minded about building up his company and whilst the mutual loyalty was real, there were also harsh splits. Gémier, disaffected by the introduction into the company of certain Conservatoire-trained actors, notably de Max, Dumeny and Signoret, left Antoine for the Gymnase in 1901, taking Janvier and Arquillière with him. The newcomers eventually moved with Antoine to the Odéon as, indeed, did most of the company, including Saverne.

Antoine relished making flamboyantly generous gestures which, whilst strengthening his troupe, demonstrated its supremacy. He engaged Le Bargy, the actor who had gained a place at the Conservatoire the year he had been rejected, offered a role in *Birds of Passage* to the currently unemployed Chelles, one of the leaders of the revolt against him at the Odéon in 1896, 'which completely stupefied him, because he was not able to conceive that I would be able to sacrifice my little susceptibilities to artistic talent' (15 Dec.

1903), and accepted Lugné-Poë's wife, Suzanne Després, when Poë announced that despite his personal hostility towards Antoine, she would get the best training with him. Not only did Després become his leading actress, making her name as Poil de Carotte (Carrot-head), the red-haired boy hero of Jules Renard's bitter autobiographical play, but she was re-engaged by him at the Odéon, despite a rift that followed a legal battle with her and Lugné-Poë over a contract dispute in 1904. When he moved to the Odéon, he nominated the disaffected Gémier as his successor at the Théâtre Antoine. Quite apart from the personal foibles involved in these acts, the additions to the troupe provide important markers of a change in perception, an acceptance of realist acting, that had been brought about by Antoine's work at the Théâtre Libre and the Antoine.

If the *mise en scène* at the Théâtre Antoine, once developed, remained fixed, the work on a new *mise en scène* was thorough and collaborative, although always with Antoine as the obsessive centre. After the initial reading, he would work alone with the text, visualizing the play, sketching numerous plans, working out entrances and exits and imagining the lay-out of the surroundings within which the scenes visible on stage would exist. He would then discuss his plans with a designer, working out colour and materials and the exact kind and positioning of doors and windows and other practicable furnishings, and the designer would be given a week to realize the ideals in a model.

Poil de Carotte (2 Mar. 1900)

Renard's one-act play, *Poil de Carotte*, a painfully humorous account of his childhood relationship with his embittered and malicious mother and his tentative alliance with his father (M. Lepic, played by Antoine) was a quintessential Théâtre Antoine production.

The single setting, a garden scene, as shown in the stage plan (fig. 30), is placed well within the confines of the stage which are marked by a painted landscape at the back and skyscapes high at either side. Between the set and the painted scenery were secondary playing spaces, a country road, the interior of the house, the black depths of the granary. Properly visible to the audience only when gate, doors or windows were open, these allowed simultaneous playing, drawn-out entrances or exits and, notably in this play, when the shutters remain determinedly closed over the windows, a potent demonstration of the cruelly neurotic mother's hostility to husband and son.

The following props, with characteristic attention to detail, are noted as present on stage at the beginning of the play: a scythe (not too heavy); a wheelbarrow; a large bundle of wood; a basket with peas (not shelled), a bowl

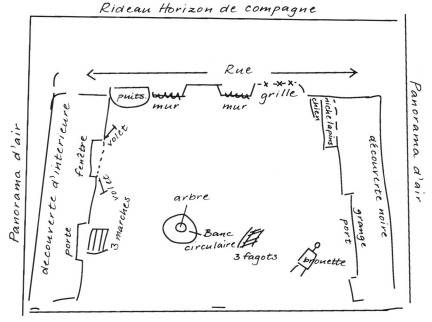

30 *Poil de Carotte*. The sketch and annotation, taken from Antoine's prompt copy of the play, shows his use of areas (the road, the house interior, the dark inside of the barn) that can be looked into from the basic set, and of back- and side-cloths beyond which allow glimpses of countryside or sky through the gates and above the walls and buildings.

and a well-rope, tied to a bucket full of water, whilst off stage, ready for use, must be a newspaper; tobacco in a screw of paper, cigarette paper and matches; a basket; a bowl to be broken on stage, and a game-bag and gun.

In preparing a play Antoine would try the effect of setting acts at different times of the day. Although he notes on another *Poil de Carotte* sketch that there is 'daylight throughout', his passion, since Irving's *Macbeth* and his own *La Mort du Duc d'Enghien*, was for shades of moonlight and for preternaturally calm or tormented faces caught by a shaft of light from a candle or lantern. Paul Mounet-Sully, always for Antoine the greatest of the Comédie-Française actors, wrote after *Judith Renaudin*:

Do not listen to those people who reproach you for darkening the auditorium and lighting the stage. In the sacristy, there is a ray of sunlight, and in the scene on the deserted shore, a ray of moonlight, which have a thrilling effect, unlike any other lighting. The garden in that gentle evening twilight is charming, charming, and I thank you again most warmly for the great pleasure that I owe to you. I hope that it is not the last.

(*Souvenirs*, 5 Nov. 1898)

He was also something of a colorist, using toning and sober fabrics in peasant plays, brilliantly coloured turbans and scarves for oriental or gypsy settings. As soon as costumes or properties were available, they were used in rehearsal, so that the actors learned to live in and with them. As at the Théâtre Libre, none of the carefully listed properties was arbitrary clutter. That Poil de Carotte is dressed in his brother's cast-off clothes is indicative of the neglect he suffers, and many of his actions, cutting grass to feed the rabbits, joining Annette in shelling peas, are poignant signifiers of his grasping at affection.

Albeit the illusion in Antoine's theatres was of real life continuing behind the transparent fourth wall, the stage picture, as we have seen in chapter 2, was organized as real life never is. It is not just that Antoine composed with colour and shape, although he did. He so arranged his actors on the stage that audience attention was directed to the intense, conflicting or alien ways of feeling and being with which the play was concerned.

Following Antoine's own study of the text, the next and crucial stage of a Théâtre Antoine or Odéon production was intensive work with the actors. Antoine worked on stage at first, playing one role then another, continually changing his position. His script of Renard's play contains a multitude of rough sketches in which the quick movements about the stage of Poil de Carotte and, particularly, his changes of manner, 'low and malicious', 'very bright', 'coming forward very self-importantly', 'lively, light', are charted. As soon as the atmosphere and basic blocking was established, he emphasized the fact of performance by locating himself in the auditorium whilst a stand-in took his role. The actors stayed within the frame and Antoine would continually change his seat, to ensure that the composition of the picture was right, the sightlines clear from every part of the house, a practice that in his abortive first direction of the Odéon in 1896 had disconcerted the established actors, who were accustomed to play to the stalls. The final *mise en scène* was established and written up by the régisseurs for subsequent use, only in the last two or three days of rehearsal when all furnishings and costumes were complete. The training the régisseurs received, incidentally, paid dividends, as Rostand, remembering Lugné-Poë, remarked on the appointment of Firmin Gémier to the directorship of the Théâtre Antoine in 1906: 'all his lieutenants have become generals'.[6]

Antoine's priorities for the stage image are evident in his criticism of the work of other directors in the articles he wrote for *Comœdia* in the 1920s. He described a *mise en scène* at the Opéra as being sumptuous but 'insecure and without a directing idea' (10 Nov. 1922), and attacked productions which had misunderstood the seeming informality of naturalist acting, writing of one that:

the important scenes were played in the corners of the sets, invisible to a part of the auditorium; the actors masked each other, sitting on tables and speaking with their backs to each other without even looking at each other.   (8 Dec. 1922)

The directing idea, discipline and thorough rehearsal, attention to the stage image as seen from all parts of the auditorium, attention to stance, gesture and eye-contact as ways of demonstrating relationship between characters, behaviour that would indicate the state of mind of the individual – all these are crucial in his own productions at the Antoine and the Odéon.

Although Renard thought Antoine moved with immoderate speed from first rehearsal to performance, *Poil de Carotte* was a tremendous success. As well as giving it 125 times in Paris in its first year, Antoine sent it on tour with a second cast to the provinces, Belgium and Switzerland. After he revived it at the Odéon in 1909 it was taken into the Comédie-Française repertoire (1912). Copeau included it in his 1917–19 New York Vieux Colombier season and it was filmed by Julien Duvivier (1926 and 1932) and by Paul Mesnier (1951). Antoine produced Renard's next play, *Monsieur Vernet* (1903) and, although they had subsequently quarrelled, it was to Antoine, too, that Renard took *La Bigote*, in 1909.

La Bonne Espérance (December 1902)

Recurrent aspects of an Antoine *mise en scène* are evident in the picture of Act II of Heijermans's *La Bonne Espérance* (fig. 31) in which Gérard, arm raised, breaks into a revolutionary song. In realist, as in any other theatre, certain patterns emerge as time and use prove their worth. As we have seen, Antoine habitually used a box set and frequently set the box considerably within the confines of the stage and sometimes at an angle to the audience, a practice begun with the boudoir scene of *La Nuit Bergamasque*, revived for *Rolande* and developed for Strindberg's *Miss Julie* and Ancey's *L'Ecole des veufs* where, because the salon of the old cuckold Mirelet was set on the bias, Antoine could intensify the bitter farce by using the view into the various rooms that led off at angles.

In *La Bonne Espérance*, he used the door opening on to the quay and the clear view of the hearth given by the exaggerated angle of vision. The photograph shows how the practicable door and window and the space between them and the back-cloth worked. The different inner and outer spaces could be juxtaposed, entrances anticipated and exits registered, whilst the figures, who passed by in the extra acting space but did not enter the room, contributed to the illusion that the stage space was continuous with the life beyond it. The action here, as repeatedly in Antoine's productions,

31 *La Bonne Espérance*, Act II: Gérard, standing, sings a revolutionary song. The firm back wall of the Dutch interior has usable door and window and practicable area outside between the wall and a back-cloth painted with a harbour scene. The set is angled. Antoine's productions were frequently enlivened with on-stage music as, here, the fiddler. Designer Cornil. From stage r.: Jacques (Berthier); fiddler (Gilles); Mariette; Sarah (Luce Colas); Michel (Pillot); Gérard (Kemm); Denizot (Tunc); Jeanne (Barny). (*L'Art du théâtre*, Sept. 1903)

centres on the hearth and the table, those important signifiers of domestic life.

Much as the Elizabethan property man knew how to set out a throne or a court-room scene in any play in the fast-changing Elizabethan repertory, so, in the Théâtre Antoine, the table and the hearth, like the bar, shelves of bottles and cash-register in café scenes had their accustomed places. And, as in that earlier theatre, the chosen disposition, practical as it was for movement and sightlines, also instanced place to the audience, in this case 'home' or 'café'. The Théâtre Française, as we have seen, found it appropriate to mirror Antoine's set when it produced *Blanchette*.

Heijermans's play, translated from the Dutch, had first been performed in

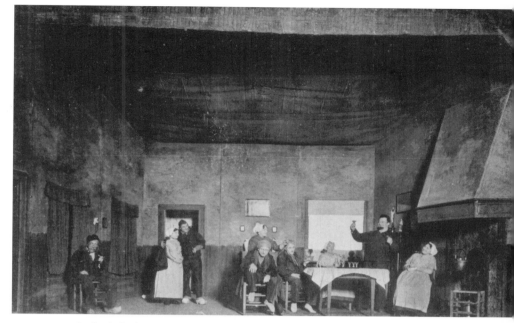

32 *La Bonne Espérance*: Amsterdam production of the same scene as in
fig 31. (*L'Art du théâtre*, Sept. 1903)

1901 by the amateur Dutch Society of Amsterdam. A photograph of the
same moment of Act II of that production (fig. 32) demonstrates Antoine's
influence but also brings home the imaginative quality of his *mise en scène*: the
postures, the distribution and interaction of the figures, the variations in
height, the use of the door space as a frame, create an image notably more
natural-seeming although in fact more studied. The author had evidently
learned from Antoine's tours to Amsterdam of the power of accurately
observed peasant life as a subject for drama.

I have not been able to discover whether Synge saw the production on his
visit to Paris in 1903, but the third act in which the fisherwomen, gathered
around the fireplace whilst the storm rages outside, count over their men lost
at sea and a terrible cortège of grieving widows and orphans assembles at the
news that a body has been washed ashore, is very suggestive of the
lamentation scene of *Riders to the Sea*. Although Heijermans's play pales beside
the stark force of Synge's, it made a tremendous impact on its audience that
derived not just from the intensity of the acting and the seeming authenticity
of the Dutch peasant world but from the rapid succession of scenes and, most
notably, the storm scene in which gusts of wind briefly drowned the talk and

dimmed the lights whilst the characters waited for news of the men at sea.

The portrayal of the hazards of fishing life brought a further element to Antoine's sense of the importance of environment. Much later, his film version of Hugo's *Les Travailleurs de la mer* (a copy of which has recently been found), would break new ground with its scenes of men working at the boats, ships facing the elements and its use of the Breton coast and real fishermen as set and extras.

The costumes were, as usual, based on reality. The bonnets, skirts and culottes were bought in Holland and their accurate re-creation of a Dutch peasant world impressed the French audience. The question of stage authenticity, though, is nicely posed by the author's complaint that Antoine had made a grave error in clothing his actors in the costumes of the Volendam when the play was set in a village by the Zuider Zee and that, compared with the accuracy and simplicity of the Dutch production, the sophistication of Antoine's set and effects blurred recognition that the action was happening in a poor little village.[7]

Although we might seem to have come full circle from the hand-cart of furniture pushed across Paris for *Jacques Damour*, the complaint demonstrates how fully Antoine's example had altered expectations since his rejection, in staging *The Power of Darkness* in 1888, of the then prevailing Opéra Comique exoticism. It suggests too, since the audience were so thoroughly convinced and the author, despite his complaints, admitted that the play was more powerful in Antoine's production, that Antoine, far from being the intransigent literalist of legend, was rather an imaginative realist offering an emotive interpretation of reality.

The complaint about sophistication, even excess, in staging should not be ignored, however. Although he never acquired the revolving stage he longed for, Antoine did seize on improvements to lighting and stage effects wherever he could and relished the effects his workshop could achieve. There is a risk of delight in pattern and detail for their own sake in, for example, the tiling of the walls of the *Bonne Espérance* interior. In the last years at the Odéon Antoine's attention to the picture, the detail, the show, did get out of proportion to the work it decorated and this possibility lurks in some of the more elaborate productions of the Théâtre Antoine.

This revives the lurking problem of theatrical realism that surfaced with the fountain of *Chevalerie rustique* and did not lessen when Antoine achieved the capacity to create sets that imaged the real world with ever greater accuracy. Beyond a certain point, the more convincingly places and objects are reproduced on stage, the more conscious the audience becomes of the artifice of the stage itself. Curiosity or wonder at the verisimilitude can interfere with the capacity or the wish to suspend disbelief, as the pictures of *La Terre* reproduced here suggest.

33 *La Terre*, Théâtre Antoine, 1902 (interior) Act II. The barn. Note the
solidity of the set, the lighting from candles, the real hay and implements
and the distribution of the large number of characters: the interactions seem
natural but the leading figures are visible and carefully balanced. Designer
Menessier.
From stage r.: Buteau (Signoret); Lise (Fleury, hidden); Fouan (Antoine);
Delhomme (Leubas); Jean (Kemm); Françoise (Becker); La Grande (Marie
Laurent, mostly hidden); Fanny (Andrée); Jesus Christ (Degeorge); Bécu
(Matral) plus various children and extras and two distractingly real hens.
(*Le Théâtre*, vol. 90. Sept. 1902. Phot.Bibl.Nat., Paris)

La Terre (21 Jan. 1902)

Antoine's own sense of the play, in the staging of which he had invested
enormous energy and resources, was that the adaptation had little of the
power of Zola's novel except in the last act. The problem lay particularly in
the third act, the village fête, where he concluded, 'the picturesque *mise en
scène* could not disguise the thinness of the text'. Staging could not make
good a weak text and may have emphasized the weakness. Cornil designed
an impressive interior for Act IV, Menessier designed Act II, the barn scene
shown here (fig. 33), which Stoullig called 'a triumph of Naturalist *mise en
scène*', whilst Amable was responsible for Act V, a panoramic series of scenes
in the course of which eight different back-cloths depicting the changing
countryside through which Old Fouan roamed in his desperate journey to his

34 *La Terre*, Théâtre Antoine, 1902, Act V. Soulas (Desfontaines) finds Fouan, rejected by his children, collapsed by the roadside. The back-cloth is the last of a series of magnificent landscapes, after Millet, used in quick succession as Fouan wanders across the countryside. The stage is floored with earth and grass hummocks and a planting of real hay is stretched across the stage at the point where the back-cloth meets the stage floor. Designer Amable. (*Le Théâtre*, vol. 90. Sept. 1902. Phot.Bibl.Nat., Paris)

death, 'ravished our eyes' (fig. 34). The skill and detail are remarkable. The completeness of the barn-dwelling set is arresting: the candles in bottles lighting the barn, the hay-lined upper sleeping-place, the solid heavy-beamed roof, the big doors, the agricultural implements. Antoine noted that the last act, with its changing landscapes, 'created a sensation'.[8]

The photographs are impressive. The staging was magnificent but to what end? Albeit this is 'true to life', scenery has overwhelmed language as fully as in any nineteenth-century commercial spectacular. We wonder that such a life-like room has been transported rather than find ourselves transported into such a room. We may be transfixed less by the dialogue than by the full-size trees and the stooks of real wheat, less by the meaningful gestures of the actors than by the arbitrary wanderings of the real hens. As Renard commented of the decision not to use real rabbits in *Poil de Carotte* two years later, 'a rabbit with twitching ears could undercut the emotion'.[9]

The adaptation of *La Terre* that Antoine played was not a great success and was never published. In five acts and ten scenes, it seems to have been modelled on the pre-Théâtre Libre adaptations of naturalist novels. Its authors Saint-Arroman and Hugot had offered it to Antoine only after Coquelin had refused it, and they did not like Antoine's production. Antoine preferred the scenes on which Zola had advised and wanted him to make further alterations after his return from his post-Dreyfus exile. When Antoine made his film version of *La Terre*, twenty years later, the farm buildings and the open fields of the Beauce starred legitimately, because the location filming compelled audience belief that they had before them not the brilliant subterfuge of a stage set but the real thing, an unmediated image of the places of Zola's novel.

Praise for the way the actors lived their roles at the Théâtre Antoine recurs throughout the period. Extracts from a long article in *Figaro* are typical:

If the action of the play you are watching takes place among peasants you see with what perfection all the actors become countryfolk. Before performing this play, these people evidently cultivated potatoes or wheat ... They had to join the theatre after some years of drought ... Next time, you're transported into the room of humble fishermen. Indubitably, you think that these actors, to incarnate these sea-folk so truthfully, must have abandoned their boats and nets on finding that the prompter hissed (*souffleur soufflait*) less dangerously than the storm.   (30 Nov. 1904)

But it is not surprising if years of unremitting work did take some tolls. A letter from Shaw to Granville Barker, sent after he had seen the much-praised 1906 *Wild Duck*, could have more to it than the deflating of a rival reputation:

The garret scene was admirable; but there would not be room for it at the Court. It was played at great speed and raced at the end of every act to get a curtain. Gregers described by Relling as an expectorator of phrases, went full steam ahead all through. There was no character in Gina or in old Ekdal – indeed there was no character in the acting at all as we understand it, but it was a bustling piece of work (to conceal Ibsen's deficiencies no doubt); and Relling brought down the house at the end when he rounded on the Expectorator. Hjalmar enjoyed himself enormously, and was amusing and convincing. Hedvig's voice was the voice of experienced and authoritative maturity; but she pulled off her pathos with professional efficiency. Stage management ad lib.; Gregers and his father walked ten miles in the first act if they walked a foot.
                                                                     (*Letters*, 7 May, 1906)

Even allowing for an element of Shavian mischief, there is an implication of something routine about the event and even of playing to the audience that is a far cry from the early performances where it was the remarkable innocence and simplicity of Hedwig, the startling individuality of Old Ekdal and the subtlety and control of gestures and silence that drew comment. Both company and director at the Théâtre Antoine engaged for a decade in a continual round of performance and rehearsal that left little time to take stock, to refresh ideas of theatre and even to absorb with any degree of seriousness the changes and innovations in writing and the *mise en scène* that might be happening elsewhere.

Possibly the acting in its later years had developed mannerisms unperceived by regular audiences but evident to the sceptical outsider. Perhaps theatre people such as Shaw, Frank Fay and Harley Granville Barker had developed an idea of naturalistic acting that was distinct from Antoine's. Certainly, the troublesome counternotes come particularly from the English — and Irish — avant-garde. Frank Fay, leading actor of the Irish Players, and previously an admirer of Antoine's enterprise, commented in 1904:

I had a royal time in London. I saw Antoine twice and was somewhat disappointed. Curiously Archer's impressions in this week's *World* agree with mine. He says Antoine had no facial expression, of that I could not judge, being too far away. I could not see anything vitally different in his method from the others, except that once or twice he spoke more quietly than the others with little or no regard for the necessities of a theatre and though the effect was very 'natural' in an everyday sense it was, I think, the sort of naturalness that, like the Duse's Italian company is of doubtful value. His intonation (a vital thing after all) did not strike me, whereas I think Rejane's tones would strike anyone from anywhere as being absolutely real. Antoine is very restless, moves about and fidgets with his tie and collar.[10]

Antoine's actors were aware that, absorbed in creation of the *mise en scène*, he often improvised the words of his own insufficiently rehearsed role, or had insecure bits of dialogue arranged where he could quietly consult them amongst papers or in books. Whilst often casting himself in walk-on parts — he played a *gendarme* in *La Bonne Espérance* — he did still frequently take leading roles. The work on the *mise en scène* for *La Terre* was so intense that the actors had assumed the stand-in would have to play Antoine's part of Père Fouan. He memorized its 1,200 lines successfully the night before the first performance.

Acting in virtually every production, taking responsibility for selecting and staging plays, hiring, casting and training actors, employing stage hands and ensuring their competence as well as having ultimate financial responsibility for the whole enterprise, Antoine stood poised between the old-style actor-manager and the new director. And, indeed, after the Théâtre Libre a number of actor-directors had opened their own theatres in Paris. In addition to the enterprise of Lugné-Poë in 1893 and Coquelin in 1897, the Théâtre Bernhardt was opened in 1898, the Théâtre Réjane in 1910, whilst in 1901 Claretie had fought to transfer the right to select plays from *sociétaires* (contract actors) at the Théâtre Français to the director.[11]

That the Théâtre Antoine attracted a regular near-capacity audience was due to the quality of the productions, to the frequently changing programme and also to Antoine's insistence on maintaining reasonable seat prices. His was, as the cartoonist implied, a 'Maison de confiance'. As *Le Théâtre* commented in 1904:

> If you want to know the reason for the fashion of the Théâtre Antoine, it is easy to tell you: variety of shows, well-made *mise en scène*, excellent acting, and finally, as is witnessed by the most important category of the public, those who form the majority of theatre lovers: moderation of prices, because it is unnecessary to conceal the fact that theatre is expensive and it is a difficult pleasure for small incomes.   (no. 138, p. 2)

But for all the theatrical and financial success of his nine years at the Théâtre Antoine, the tensions deriving from the need to combine the two kinds of responsibility of actor and director were destructive as well as creative. His appointment to the directorship of the Odéon in 1906 where, by contract, he was not allowed to be both actor and administrator, to a degree resolved the dilemma and meant that for eight years he had the time and scope to develop his ideas about the *mise en scène* and about the function of a national theatre.

7   Staging the classics

King Lear (29 Nov. 1904)

The late nineteenth-century realist stage with its specifically localized set and its theatre language, in which the sub-text is communicated to the attentive audience by subtleties of body language and vocal expression, is probably the extreme remove from the bare stage, fluid action and verbal fire of the Elizabethan theatre. Interesting, then, that it was Antoine who demonstrated to early twentieth-century French audiences and critics that Shakespeare was a dramatist for their own time and place.[1]

Antoine staged five Shakespeare plays. His 1904 *King Lear* was the production that propelled him from the Antoine to the Odéon where *Julius Caesar* was his first major production (Dec. 1906). *Coriolanus* (Apr. 1910), *Romeo and Juliet* (Dec. 1910) and *Troilus and Cressida* (Mar. 1912) followed. His was the first ever French production of *Troilus and Cressida* and the first *Lear* in France with Fool, Shakespearean scene order and tragic ending. Indeed, it was only the fourth French production of *Lear*, the first having been in 1783. When last performed in Paris, in 1868, in a translation by Lacroix, barely half of Shakespeare's text had survived. The Gloucester sub-plot was removed and Cordelia, played by the young Bernhardt, lived to become queen in Nahum Tate style. There had been an attempt to play a fuller text in 1837, at the Théâtre Imperial du Cirque after Macready's restorations in England had shown the way, but it had failed dismally and reinforced the tendency to play Shakespeare as historical romance.

It would be hard to overestimate the significance for French theatre of Antoine's productions. They demonstrated his claim that 'it would be possible to stage the whole play, without the cuts, adaptations and transpositions with which we have so profoundly distorted the work of great Will for a century and a half' (5 Dec. 1904). Further, his attention to the theatrical demands of the text, notably to its speed and fluidity of action, and the claims he asserted both in his productions and in his later critical articles to the coherence of Shakespearean design had an importance beyond the specific occasion. His claim that Shakespeare's juxtaposition of the metaphysical with the insignificant and his use of seemingly trivial scenes, such as the opening sequence of *King Lear*, was a crucial part of the greatness of the plays went against the grain of French neo-classic criticism.[2] By demonstrating and celebrating its differences from the traditional French repertoire, Antoine showed how stimulating Shakespearean drama could be for contemporary audiences and for subsequent innovative directors from Copeau to Mnouchkine.

With hindsight, it is possible to mark Antoine's progress towards the point when a Shakespearean production became necessary. Taine's account of English Renaissance drama and the distinctions Diderot made between the acting of Shakespeare and of French Renaissance tragedy had informed his earliest ideas of theatre. Although it was the lighting in Irving's theatre and the quick and noiseless scene changes at the Criterion that particularly impressed him on his first London visit, it was in Shakespearean productions that these were used. *Twelfth Night* and *A Winter's Tale* were amongst the plays he saw in that formative 1888 Meininger season and, whilst he never saw their *Julius Caesar*, he talked at length to members of the company about the production and, on his first, abortive, appointment as director of the Odéon in 1896, he had asked Gramont to prepare a translation of that play.

Antoine's continuing interest in Shakespeare was both intellectual and practical. On the one hand, he had responded to the 'magnificent things' Becque had to say about Shakespeare and Molière in the summer the aging dramatist spent with him on the Breton coast (15 Aug. 1898) and, on the other, he had repeatedly recorded his irritation with French Shakespeare revivals, lamenting the use of grossly adapted texts, as with Prozor's *Romeo and Juliet* (2 Nov. 1890) or Bernhardt's *Hamlet*; of ponderous stage sets, and of activity that had little grounding in the text – like Bernhardt's entry wrapped in a carpet in *Cleopatra* (24 Oct. 1890). His sense of what might be done had been stimulated again by the power and speed of an unabridged *Romeo and Juliet* that he saw directed without intervals by Possart in Munich when he toured with Jean Coquelin in 1897, whilst the possibility that someone else might steal his fire, always a spur to Antoine, had emerged when Lugné-Poë had produced *Measure for Measure* and Ford's *'Tis Pity She's a Whore*, in 1898.

Antoine's first attempt at French Renaissance drama, *Britannicus*, in the second Théâtre Antoine season, had been a failure and he admitted that neither he, his company nor his audience were quite in tune with Racine. By contrast, his revivals of those foreign plays which had generated excitement and sometimes hostility at the Théâtre Libre were very successful. Indeed, his own tours and productions modelled on his by foreign avant-garde theatres, meant that, by the turn of the century, such works as *The Power of Darkness*, *The Weavers*, *Ghosts*, *The Wild Duck* and *Miss Julie* had already begun to assume the status of modern classics: a status confirmed by the productions of Ibsen and Strindberg at the Théâtre d'Œuvre. Shakespeare, the preeminent foreign Renaissance dramatist, therefore presented a sympathetic challenge.

Antoine had announced plans for a production of *King Lear* in his 1898–9 season but, as with *Power* and *Ghosts*, the available translations proved unsatisfactory. The Lacroix theatrical version was hopelessly mangled and the available literary translations by Montegut and by Victor Hugo seemed archaic and flowery: the alexandrine line seemed to stilt the Shakespearean flow of thought. Antoine used a new prose translation for each of his Shakespeare productions. That the matter of an appropriate translation recurred in the production of a 'classic' text is significant. It marks a refusal to be absorbed into the dominant ideology of the accepted version, a recognition that, whilst the dramatist's text endures, a translation of it, like a director's interpretation, is a filter that must change with the times and with assumptions about the drama. Read now, Pierre Loti's translation is disappointing. Although speakable and faithful to the paraphraseable meaning, the language has lost much of Shakespeare's metaphoric texture and, with that, the capacity for sudden and contrasting verbal simplicity at the most deeply felt moments of the play. But it clearly allowed Antoine's audiences to catch much of the excitement and complexity of the play. Its very speakability was, of course, an unconscious appropriation by the modernity of 1903.

Although *King Lear* might appear an over-ambitious choice for a first attempt at Shakespeare, it is not difficult to see its appeal for Antoine. It is the archetypal episodic play. Much richer emotionally and intellectually more challenging, its social, temporal and spatial multiplicity are, nevertheless, of a part with those historical plays (*La Mort du Duc d'Enghien, La Patrie en danger*) to which Antoine had attended so carefully at the Théâtre Libre. And it offered him, personally, the curmudgeonly old-man role to surpass them all.

Antoine identified Elizabethan dramatic rhythm as the most pressing problem in staging Shakespeare on the modern stage. It was precisely this, the rhythm, the shifts in mood, the speed of the action that had been blunted in the ponderous sets and machinery of nineteenth-century staging. Justifying his own version of the play, Lacroix had asked whether there were any admirers of Shakespeare 'intrepid enough' to remain in their seats for the eight hours he estimated it would take to play the full text. Antoine who, never interested in the picturesque as such, had used decor as a means of interpreting the text, relished the problem. 'It is necessary', he was reported to have said in explanation, 'not to hinder the progress of the play.' Instead of the usual five-act piece, which Irving, for example, had played in 1892, he had only two ten-minute intervals and played the full text in two and three-quarter hours. One critic, discussing Lacroix's comment in the light of

Antoine's production, concluded that 'what astonishes about the play is its brevity, its clarity, its speed and its plenitude'.[3]

Antoine gained continuity whilst retaining variety of scene by adapting what he had seen at the Theatre Royal, Munich, and allowing the action to continue immediately on the proscenium stage in front of a curtain bearing a non-figurative design. He wrote:

You see the curtain that frames and hides the stage? It forms the mobile background to a proscenium which is never empty. The actors follow on without pause and the curtain opens simultaneously on decor that will situate and – in the English sense – will illustrate the scene.

And he later claimed that there was scarcely a play which could not be staged in under three hours providing it had an efficient setting.[4]

Shakespearean drama with its brief, often unlocalized but crucial scenes between two or three characters and its large-scale sequences where place is clearly located in the dialogue is rather well served by this device. Of the twenty-eight scenes, Antoine played sixteen with scenery and twelve on the proscenium stage before the curtain (figs. 35–9). A felt carpet laid on the stage enabled the stagehands to set the next scene silently behind the curtain whilst the action was progressing in front of it. A series of thirteen different painted back-cloths that could be dropped quickly into place were used for full scenes. Illusionist, unlike the curtain, these showed interiors, the castles of Lear, Gloucester and Albany whose plain but massive columns and arches were painted to look like stone, and exteriors in which individuals on the heath, Dover cliffs or the battlefield are set before panoramic landscapes.

Although the exterior scenes, particularly the heath, have added realistic detail in the form of hummocks of grass and vegetation, there was minimal stage furniture in the interior scenes where the stage was stripped bare except for the throne, the stocks, a chair, some joint stools, Lear's bed, as indicated in the text. Props were carried on and off by characters in the course of the action. The Fool, notably, sat on the floor, and virtually every scene made telling use of curtains or drapes which at once provided rich colour, the authenticity of tapestry against stone and an opportunity for Shakespearean lurking and overhearing.

The flow of the action is well demonstrated in the first sequence of the play. The brief opening lines between Kent and Gloucester, in which the notion of the division of the kingdom and the existence of Edmund are introduced, were spoken on the apron; then, as a trumpet sounded, the neutral curtain opened, Kent and Gloucester moved to the side of the full stage and Lear entered with his court on to a full set of the throne room, speaking his order, 'Attend the lords of France and Burgundy'. After the

35 *King Lear*, Théâtre Antoine, 1904, Act I, the banishing of Kent. Notice the medieval draped costumes, the stylized Norman arches and the absence of clutter. Designer, Jusseaume.
From stage r.: Cordelia (Méry), Goneril (Lion), Lear (Antoine), Kent (Desfontaines), Regan (Brille). (*L'Art du théâtre*, Dec. 1904)

botched division of the kingdom, the cursing of Cordelia, banishment of Kent and hasty marrying-off of Cordelia to France, Lear speaks his exit lines:

> Thou hast her, France; let her be thine, for we
> Have no such daughter, nor shall ever see
> That face of hers again, therefore be gone
> Without our grace our love our benison.
> Come noble Burgundy.

The neutral curtain closes on the exiting court, leaving Cordelia on the apron to address her sisters who have also been strategically positioned at the front of the stage: 'the jewels of our father, with wash'd eyes / Cordelia leaves you'. By the time they make their exit, the back-curtain scene-change is complete and the curtain can open on a room in Gloucester's castle; Goneril's closing words as she exits stage left, 'We must do something, and i' the heat', can be

36 *King Lear*, Théâtre Antoine, 1904. Lear and the Fool (Signoret) before the curtain on the apron stage: 'Thou should'st not have been old before thou had'st been wise.' (*L'Illustration théâtral*, Dec. 1904)

followed immediately by Edmund coming forward and speaking his opening soliloquy, 'Thou, Nature, art my goddess'.

The impression of fluidity was revelatory, as was the respect Antoine had paid to Shakespeare's dramatic structure. As Léon Blum commented:

Everything of the Shakespearean drama is respected, even what seemed impossible to retain in the theatre: its speed, its mobility, I would almost say its ubiquity, the incessant coming and going of the characters, the interaction of the multiple plots.[5]

37 *King Lear*, Théâtre Antoine, 1904. Gloucester's castle. Regan plucks
Gloucester (Mosnier) by the beard. Gloucester, blinded, will move to the
front of the stage and, the servant having slain Cornwall (Saverne), the
other servant will come to the apron with flax and white of eggs for
Gloucester's eyes, during which the curtain at stage right is drawn to
conceal Cornwall's body and to enable the scene change. (*L'Illustration
théâtral*, Dec. 1904)

Although he would reconsider the problem of Shakespearean structure when
he staged *Coriolanus*, the solution Antoine found for *King Lear* drew praise
from Copeau and was soon adopted by Reinhardt, who saw Antoine's
production.

Antoine cleared the stage space of furniture and clutter and made telling
use of drapes and curtains, but he never considered abandoning decor, as
Copeau would, and allowing the words to create the picture. Place and
environment were too important to his conception of drama to allow that.

38 *King Lear*, Irving's production at the Lyceum, 1892: sketch by Hawes
Craven of the final scene, included in the programme. Characteristic light
effect with setting sun painted on the back-cloth remaining static
throughout the scene while characters are lit by front lighting. (Photo: Villa)

And, although one of his more celebrated experiments at the Odéon was,
Poel-like, to stage Racine as if within a French Renaissance theatre, he located
his Shakespearean production in the time in which the play was set, as did
nineteenth-century English interpreters of Shakespeare, not in the time in
which it was written, as would increasingly be the English practice after
Poel's experiments. The back-cloth for the final scene, set on Dover cliffs, is,
indeed, reminiscent of Irving's 1892 production, although Antoine's staging
looks considerably simpler (figs. 38 and 39).

Although he was one of very few to be so disconcerted, Copeau found a
lack of homogeneity between the conventionality of the curtain and the
painted illusionist scenes, and the photographs suggest that there was some
discontinuity not just between the apron and full set scenes but, as often in
Antoine's realism, between the interior and exterior scenes.

Whilst there was no suggestion that he might move to the baroque
fantasy that would characterize Reinhardt's *Midsummer Night's Dream*
productions, or to the abstraction of Gordon Craig's screens, Antoine's belief

39 *King Lear*, Théâtre Antoine, the final scene. Whilst the back-cloth very clearly echoes Hawes Craven's design, Antoine's staging is much simpler than Irving's.
From stage r.: Edgar (Capellani), Edmund (Vargan), Albany (Marquet). (*L'Art du théâtre*, Dec. 1904.)

in historic authenticity was evidently undergoing some modification at this time. Although he had gained his experience of Shakespeare performance in the theatres of Irving and Saxe-Meiningen, behind whom were Charles Kean's famous evocations of Periclean Athens and ancient Rome, his *Lear* was set in a rather indeterminate ancient period. His brief to Jusseaume and Ibels, who designed the costumes, was that they must aim for an *impression* of a distant past where fabrics were rich and flowing. As the production photographs reproduced here show, the costumes and furnishings are story-book medieval rather than ancient British in feel.

Similarly, the action itself was less constrained by realistic detail than had sometimes been the case. The blinding of Gloucester (fig. 37), which seemed so harrowing to Antoine's audience, was done without blood. Evident both in this production and in Antoine's writing at this period is a new perception that artistic truth is not necessarily achieved by presenting the thing itself on stage. This is a matter that Antoine would return to in his subsequent discussion of the *mise en scène*. In 1922 he would write that 'decor must be conceived in the character of the work and not aspire to photographic truth'.[6]

The decision to stage *King Lear* was, in part, a political one. With a critical triumph evident, *Le Matin* claimed that it would now be impossible to close the door of the Odéon on Antoine as had happened in 1896. Léon Blum, noting that two months into the production its success was undiminished, wrote:

Perhaps he was the only man in Paris able to carry out such a difficult undertaking. But he is angry, nevertheless, that the official theatres, subsidized and furnished with every facility, have left the honour to him. Antoine possesses only limited resources and a tiny stage. What would he not do with greater means and in a bigger theatre?

(*Au théâtre* (1906), p. 258)

The Odéon: *Julius Caesar* (1906)

Antoine's next Shakespeare production, *Julius Caesar*, was big theatre in every way. As his first major production after his appointment to the Odéon in 1906 it was a far more controversial choice than *King Lear* at the Antoine had been. Where *Lear* had introduced a classic play into a contemporary and notably adventurous repertoire, *Julius Caesar* demonstrated that Antoine's attack on the conservatism and narrow nationalism of the French repertoire would be continued from within the National Theatre itself. Explaining the choice in an article on the mechanics of staging the play, Antoine was also announcing that his policy with regard to classics at the Odéon would be as outward-looking as it had been to contemporary writing at the Théâtre Libre. Striking at the heart of French theatrical insularity, he pointed out that Mounet-Sully himself had only reached his peak as an actor when he played Hamlet and that in Germany, Austria, Russia, England and America it was accepted that a man of the theatre, whether an actor or director, had finally to measure himself in Shakespeare.[7]

In the event, the production assumed political importance as the showpiece that demonstrated the justice of Antoine's appointment to doubters in the Arts Ministry, to audiences and, perhaps most importantly, to the company, whose recalcitrance had been one of the major factors in forcing his resignation at his first Odéon appointment ten years previously. It demonstrated, too, that Antoine, unchastened by the earlier experience, would pull out all the stops – and more – at the Odéon's disposal to demonstrate the kind of resources the government ought to be allotting to its national theatre. It was a remarkably successful demonstration in everything but the appeal for an increased subsidy.

The sets, designed as for *King Lear* by Jusseaume after many hours of discussion with Antoine, were organized, as was traditional on the nineteenth-century stage, on different depths of stage to allow elaborate sets to be prepared behind the ongoing action. Radical remodelling of the awkward Odéon stage was necessary to enable this and particularly to enable Antoine to use different levels of staging and flights of stairs that could support some sixty extras in his scene in the senate and to install easily movable architectural pieces for his recreation of the Roman forum, which he believed crucial to the address to the mob after Caesar's death. Antoine had the area at the back of the stage cleared and the foundations hollowed out to permit sets to be raised and lowered. The joists supporting the stage were strengthened and hooks that could support from 2,000 to 2,500 kilos installed. Something of the technical complexity of the staging is evident, despite the dimness of the rehearsal photographs reproduced here (figs. 40 and 41). He used the curtain and apron device again for fluidity of action – the Portia and Lucius scene, for example, is played there. But whereas in *Lear* twelve of the twenty-eight scenes were played on the apron, now only six of seventeen were, and the whole stage was enclosed within a frame of Corinthian columns.[8]

It is clear that Antoine's memories of both Irving and Saxe-Meiningen informed his idea of Shakespeare production and the French critics responded in kind. As Gaston Sorbet wrote:

The numerous sets are, some of them: ample and majestic, others: picturesque, all are rich in colour and evocative power. And it is now to the Odéon that the worshippers of Shakespeare from England and Germany must come to celebrate their cult.[9]

The care with which Ibels, as costume designer, researched historical detail enabled Antoine to make an informed choice about what to use and what to adapt as, indeed, did his own research on ancient Rome; he twice visited Rome in the run-up to the production. He had a detailed study made for him of Rome in 44 BC which ran to some forty-three pages and included maps of the city, detailed plans of the forum and pictures of busts of various characters in the play. It also contained factual and literary information about the feast of Lupercal and the individual conspirators.

Research and practice had given Antoine a better idea than other contemporary directors of what was and what was not anachronistic in dressing and setting the play. So the senators' togas were draped in the authentic Roman manner but, since the visual impact of the forum scene and of the death of Caesar seemed to Antoine to demand an effect of white on white, the togas and setting were made up in white, although Antoine

40 *Julius Caesar*, Odéon, 1906. Antoine noted of these photographs of the
erection of scenery for the forum that the whole could be dismantled in the
15-minute interval. The whole stage area was reconstructed to allow the
hoisting and sinking of flats and the different levels of stage floor during
this scene. (*Je sais tout*, 15 Feb. 1907)

41 *Julius Caesar*, Odéon, 1906. A rare photograph of the play in rehearsal. The crowd, without costume except for the helmets worn by Roman soldiers, arranged for the forum scene. The different levels allow the crowd to mill about without masking the principals. (*Je sais tout*, 15 Feb. 1907)

recognized that a range of colour would actually have been used in ancient Rome. No one asked how togas would have been worn in the Elizabethan theatre.

It was in discussion of the question of selection for this production that Antoine admitted, in his 1907 article, that 'truth in the theatre is relative'. Because *Julius Caesar* seemed to him to be centrally concerned with power and politics, it was essential that this should be reflected in the set even if what was known about the historical context of the play had to be modified. So, for example, he wanted the assassination played before the full senate, although he knew it had not historically been so. He pointed out, further, that since the way any of us sees reality is closely dependent on the way our age sees it:

it is certain that realism, which has its *raison d'être* in its minutiae, is a question of proportion: a drama must first and foremost be mounted in the spirit of the work. A play of Marivaux cannot, so far as the decor is concerned, be put in a frame any more than it can be played as a comedy of Molière or a drama of Victor Hugo. Those who say that we wish to make photographs, misunderstand.

If the work on the classics led him to this new formulation about the 'spirit of the work', the perception itself was not new, as his use of *commedia dell'arte* gesture in Bergerat's *La Nuit Bergamasque* at the Théâtre Libre had shown. The further implication of such a statement, however, that it was in the staging of the play's *own* period that answers to questions about Shakespeare might be found was never taken by Antoine, although this was precisely what he investigated when he turned to French Renaissance drama. Perhaps the English and the Saxe-Meiningen Shakespeare productions were too powerful to admit such a challenge. Perhaps, as Oscar Brockett has suggested, he believed that whilst Corneille and Racine could only be understood as products of their own time, Shakespeare, being more universal, 'should be costumed and set in the historical periods indicated by the action, for this does not conflict with the spirit of the plays and minimizes anachronisms'.[10]

Chiaroscuro, the expressive use of light and shadow, had been essential to the effect of many Théâtre Libre productions whose guttering candles and lantern-shafts had thrilled or appalled their audiences. Access to the Odéon's more sophisticated lighting resources enabled Antoine to demonstrate his belief that lighting was a wonderful source of emotional power. A red-coloured filter was used to cast a bloody glow on the doomed Caesar's head, as if (somewhat anachronistically) from a stained-glass window. Rays of the sun and shafts of moonlight, reminiscent of Irving's *Macbeth*, contributed to the mood. The slowly changing light in the scene in Brutus' garden led Jules Renard to note in his journal, 'It is perhaps the first time that I have felt Shakespeare' (4 Dec. 1906) and the *Temps* critic to write wonderingly that, 'One sees the dawn come, feels the humidity of the morning. One is cold. It is all illusion' (10 Dec. 1906).

As Antoine observed, 'in a work such as *Julius Caesar* the crowd has the primary place', and this production was the culmination of Antoine's work with stage crowds. At the Odéon he had to draw on much the same pool of casual labour as at the Théâtre Libre and the Antoine. The same kind of people whom he used to represent rebellious weavers and the French revolutionary mob had now to be trained to appear as grave senators and as Roman plebeians and, although with public subsidy he could now hire 250 extras, the sensation of multitude still came from Antoine's well-established organization of variety and movement. Each extra was assigned to a group and had to obey instructions for that group in rehearsal. Seven actors functioned as first to seventh plebeian and acted as group leaders. In certain scenes – the opening, the murder of Cinna – only one or two groups were called. For the forum scene, the groups intermingled and, as the photograph

42 *Julius Caesar*, Odéon, 1906. Mark Antony (de Max) addresses the crowd in the forum. (*L'Illustration théâtral* 8 Dec. 1906)

(fig. 42) shows, were set at right-angles to the audience who, therefore, saw them in profile and had the impression of a massive crowd stretching out into the wings beyond the limits of the stage. The prompt copy of the play reveals the care with which the crowd's reactions were tied to the speeches of the characters. As Antony begins his 'Friends, Romans, Countrymen' address, some of the crowd are detailed to quiet others who are talking and coughing. At the first 'Caesar was ambitions', those led by the second plebeian murmur. On the repetition of 'And Brutus is an honorable man', those in the seventh plebeian's group applaud whilst the second's hush them, the balance between the two altering until, at Antony's 'Shall I descend?' those in the first, second and third groups all cry 'Oui, oui' and take the lead in sympathetic response to the 'If you have tears, prepare to shed them now' speech, all sighing as Antony reaches, 'whilst bloody treason flourished over us'. 'Oh, this multiple and surging Shakespearean crowd', wrote Sorbet:

such an uncontrollable monster if one were to listen to old commentators – and even some young ones. Don't believe a word of it. In the action which takes place at the foot of the Capitol, the crowd is a character with a thousand heads, but its role is as nicely written, as strictly controlled as the others'. It is integrated into each change of fortune in a direct and never an idle way.

For all Antoine felt the crowd had 'primary place', then, the lesson of *La Patrie en danger* was well learned. In orchestrating the movements of the crowd, the playing space for the major characters was carefully maintained. Indeed, they were commonly placed at a level above the mass of the crowd, as Antony was in the forum scene or in front of and surrounded by them, as the tribunes were in Act I scene i, which was played on the proscenium.

Saverne (Lepidus), who had moved with Antoine to the Odéon, noted that in the scene in the senate, the orchestrated entrance of senators from the summit of the immense amphitheatre to sit in order on the stone steps and their rising in unison at the fanfare that signalled the arrival of Caesar had a majesty that in itself warranted a trip to the Odéon. But, impressive as the sequence was, it was subordinated to the dramatic requirements of the play, being designed as preparation for the entrance of Caesar.

Shakespeare's dialogue for the scene of Caesar's murder was the kind of writing that delighted Antoine. It includes numerous implicit stage directions around which the attentive director can plot the scene. The changing positions of the Odéon actors were minutely recorded in the rehearsal book (fig. 43). As Caesar swept down to his place in the senate, Trebonius and Antony, who had entered with him, stayed back on the steps, well positioned for Casca's, 'Trebonius knows his time; for, look you, Brutus, / He draws Mark Antony out of the way'. Each stage of the scene planned by Shakespeare – who kneels, who thrusts himself forward and in what order, who presses close to Caesar – is followed by Antoine. The orchestration of the murder itself is at the director's discretion. When Cimber, petitioning, 'throws before [Caesar's] seat / A humble heart', Caesar is evidently seated, but later, by Brutus' account, will lie dead not on his throne but 'on Pompey's base'.

Antoine placed Casca behind Caesar's seat to make the first thrust on, 'Speak hands for me'. Casca then fell back quickly to the senate steps with Cinna, who had also stabbed first, so that they were set apart ready to launch their cries of 'Liberty, Freedom' which follow immediately on the assassination and quell the rising panic of the watching senators. Caesar, meanwhile, risen from his throne, was stabbed by Brutus, centre stage, before lurching forward to die at the foot of Pompey's statue. Antoine used Brutus' insistence that Publius leave as the exit signal for the mass of senators. After

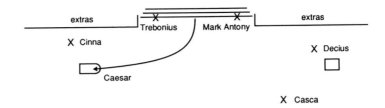

i) Caesar's entrance - all kneeling

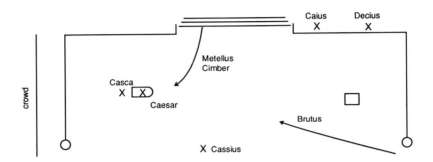

ii) Moving into positions for Cimber's appeal to Caesar

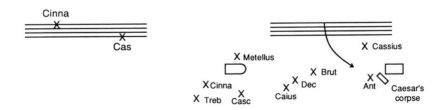

iii) Cinna, on steps, cries,   iv) Antony's entrance
     'Liberté, déliverance'

43 *Julius Caesar*, III.i. Odéon, 1906. Sketches reproducing Antoine's stage
plans for senate and assassination scenes.

      ⬭   Caesar's throne

      ☐   Pompey's statue

44 *Julius Caesar* Odéon, *1906*. The senate, immediately before the
assassination scene (realization of fig.43(ii).
Seated, Caesar (Duquesnes); kneeling Cassius (Garnier), Cimber (Chevelet),
Brutus (Desjardins). (*L'Illustration théâtral* 8 Dec. 1906)

the noise and flurry of this the conspirators, suddenly alone, dominate the
stage as they gather around the corpse to kneel, wash their hands in Caesar's
blood and utter the famously ironic words which, in the French text, read:

> BRUTUS: Que de fois on verra saigner sur un théâtre ce César que voici, plus
> vil que la poussière, étendu le long du piedestal de Pompée.
> CASSIUS: Et chaque fois que l'on jouera ce même drame on dira de notre
> groupe: Voila les hommes qui donnèrent à leur pays la liberté.

But there is one further turn of attention when, before they can withdraw, the
grieving Antony enters alone down the now empty steps to kneel with very
different emotion by Caesar's body. It is remarkably clear direction which
always attends to and allows space for the words and for the implied gestures
and interrelationships of the characters. In keeping with the practice of the
time, the name of the *metteur en scène* was not listed on the programme, but
the audience was clear about whose work it had come to see and Antoine's
name was called repeatedly after this scene as it was again at the end of the
play.

The critical and commercial success of the production was important, since it had stretched the resources of even a subsidized theatre. It was labour-intensive in a way that would be impossible today, even in opera. Twenty carpenters had worked for three months on the sets using some 2,000 metres of planks and 4,500 metres of canvas and twenty painters for two months to decorate them. Twenty-five sempstresses worked from July to September on the costumes and about one hundred more workers of one kind or another were employed in making wigs, shoes and armour, preparing make-up and dressing hair. For the daily performances forty-five actors, two hundred and fifty extras, sixty musicians, seventy machinists and one hundred more dressers, make-up artists, prompters and stagehands were employed. One can well believe that Antoine had, as he said, braved sea-sickness to see Beerbohm Tree's production of the play in London. Despite playing to capacity houses for the thirty nights of its run, the cost was some 4,500 francs a night so that a loss was inevitable. The minister's report at the end of the season: 'the average return for December was 3,975 francs, thanks to the success of *Julius Caesar*, and 1,225 francs in February', gives an idea of the returns possible on a packed Odéon house. Antoine insisted on keeping Odéon prices low, whilst the ministry took what profits were made and never gave a subsidy to match Antoine's plans, so that Antoine's major Odéon productions frequently made a loss despite capacity houses.

The *King Lear* innovations were elaborated in *Julius Caesar*. But then, characteristically, Antoine returned to the initial problem with renewed energy: a new version of the flexible stage was tried in *Coriolanus* and *Romeo and Juliet*. Paul Paquereau designed a set that was essentially fixed but offered playing spaces in different areas and at different levels of the stage and an inner stage within which various scenic back-cloths could be used. Antoine played all twenty-nine scenes of *Coriolanus* in this set, which he claimed to have modelled on the 'mansion' of medieval mystery plays (*L'Information*, 5 May 1910). At the left of the stage stood the gate to Rome with statues of Romulus, Remus and the wolf outlined against the sky, and a passage used as the exit to the countryside; at the right were the ramparts of Corioli. Centre stage were four steps, leading up to a raised dais and curtained Roman portico, within which various scenes – the interior of Coriolanus' house, the Volsci camp – could be set. Similarly, one side of the stage of *Romeo and Juliet* (fig. 45), presented a walled Verona street, the other, the Capulet balcony and garden, whilst the inner stage, the central curtained space, was used for indoor scenes – Friar Lawrence's cell or Juliet's chamber. The duel and the ball were enacted on the open stage at the front and the only complete scene-change was for Juliet's tomb at the end of the play. The lighting was focused on the area of action, the rest of the stage being in darkness.

45 Sketch of three scenes from *Romeo and Juliet* showing the fixed outer
stage and scene changes on the inner stage.
(i)   the Capulet Ball, the first meeting of Romeo and Juliet.
(ii) Juliet's chamber; the balcony at stage left is a permanent fixture.
(iii) Friar Lawrence's cell.
(Drawings by Annette Lenton from photographs of the Odéon production.)

For all Antoine cited medieval sources, commentators were struck by the
modernity of the idea. Copeau, usually hostile to what seemed to him the
over-furnishing of Antoine's stages, liked the grandeur and coherence of
action enabled by such a setting and, particularly, the fact that the continued
presence of Rome and Corioli on the stage allowed the audience to situate
itself with Coriolanus 'between two extremes'. Copeau was stirred, too, by
the impression the acting gave of freedom, vigour and youthfulness and was,
with something of a backhander, grateful that an unaccustomed restraint in

the number of extras enabled him to enjoy the meticulous organization of the crowd and battle scenes. All in all:

the young Odéon troup, exercised and broken in by the constant work that their chief imposes, leave nothing to be desired. There is not a soldier, not a common man, not a senator or an insignificant officer that does not play his role conscientiously.

Although the staging may well look cluttered to later eyes, other commentators proclaimed that in its 'extreme simplicity' it offered 'a modern equivalent' of Shakespeare's theatre.[11]

The effect of the staging was to create a frame within a frame; a fluid fore-stage area and a series of fixed inner-stage tableaux. Although some conservative critics were offended by the comic scenes, which had traditionally been cut in productions of *Romeo and Juliet*, the only real attack on what was otherwise a popular and critical success came from the *Nouvelle revue française*. Having approved *Coriolanus*:

no more excess of props; no more fantastic crowd scenes; no more light rivalling the dawn, twilight and stars all at once. A performance in one location in a single decor,
(no. 3, 1910)

the review found both the incidental music and the setting of *Romeo and Juliet* intrusive and objected, particularly, to the real plants climbing up and, it claimed, falling off Juliet's balcony (no. 5, 1910). Its writers were, of course, closely associated with Copeau who was already developing his own anti-realistic theories of the *mise en scène*, but the extant photographs and the fact that preparation of the decor delayed the opening for three months does suggest a greater elaboration.

The production of *Troilus and Cressida* (Mar. 1912), which emphasized the harshness and irony of the text, was less successful than the others so there is very little discussion of it in the press. But the staging seems to have taken a further step towards stylization. There were four playing areas, the apron and, separated from it by three curtains, playing areas at right, centre and left of the stage. That Pandarus and Cressida, watching the returning army, stood on the apron and looked out into the audience suggests that Antoine was on the verge of breaking the illusion. It is tantalizing that there is not more information about this production.

The innovations of Antoine's successors have taken Shakespearean production into a much fuller scenic simplicity and stylization. Antoine's prime achievement, as so often, was to reveal and enable. His work challenged the preconceptions of audiences and critics and demanded that the French theatre give serious attention to Shakespeare's plays. It also raised questions about the theatrical possibilities of the work for future directors and actors, as Copeau's extended critical discussion of Antoine's experiments demonstrates.

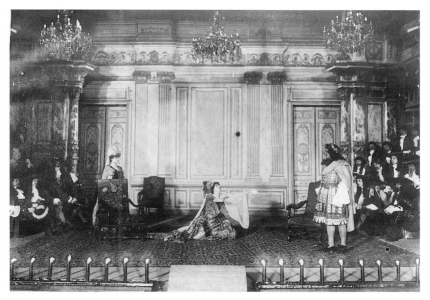

46 *Andromaque* (Odéon, 1909) in seventeenth-century style. Stylized armour is used to signify antiquity. Lighting is from candles across the front and from chandeliers. Andromaque (Albane) kneeling; Pyrrhus (Desjardins)

Racine and Molière

Antoine startled the theatre world in 1909 when he staged two parallel versions of *Andromaque*. One was a revival of his 1906 staging set, Saxe-Meiningen fashion, in ancient Greece, with appropriate costumes and architectural settings. The new production, much more controversially, attempted to reproduce the original Hôtel de Bourgogne staging, since Racine's characters seemed to Antoine to belong not to the Homeric but to the courtly seventeenth-century world. For the 'authentic' production the stage, lit by candles, was set to resemble a large seventeenth-century drawing-room and the small on-stage audience was costumed appropriately. Where previously they had studied the ancient world, Antoine, Ibels and Jusseaume now studied not only the costume of the seventeenth century in the Bibliothèque Nationale, the Musée Carnavalet and the library of the Théâtre Français, but the contemporary music and dance and the courtly style of speech and gesture.

The actors performed in seventeenth-century wigs and costumes with the addition of togas and leather battle skirts to signify the ancient world as they would have done in Racine's day (fig. 46) although paradoxically, as I have found in my own 'authentic' stagings of Handel opera, such signification functions now to make the production more intensely of its own specific time and not at all suggestive of the ancient world as it would have been in the original production. The specificity of time was emphasized for Antoine's audience because the costume and bearing of Pyrrhus were modelled on familar images of Louis XIV. The two *Andromaque* productions were revived each year until 1913.

Once at the Odéon, Antoine had necessarily turned his attention to French Renaissance tragedy. It was probably the most difficult of any work he had ever had to direct. His need to find a distinct style of performance in key with his work in contemporary theatre was intensified by his complicated relationship with this drama. The difference between the contemporary and the classical theatre, where 'character is most frequently just an abstraction, a synthesis without actual life' had been used by him in his Théâtre Libre argument that 'a realistic work must be played realistically just as a classic drama must be declaimed', and he would later maintain that 'Corneille shows us magnificent statues, not a fold in their togas is out of place, but Shakespeare reveals men to us.' But, for all that, his passion for theatre had first been fired by this drama and particularly by the acting of Mounet-Sully who, in *Andromaque*, for example, had 'played Oreste with a rhythm, a lyrical abandon which were for [Antoine] a complete revelation of Racinian luminosity and harmony', and his emphasis on Mounet-Sully's revelation of the dramatist's 'luminosity and harmony' is in keeping with his sense that the central concern of his own work was truth to the dramatist's imagination.[12]

Whereas the foreign classics he produced were strange to French audiences, Antoine needed to cut through the decades of familiarity and performance practice that smothered the much-revived plays of the French Renaissance. Rather as Possart's interval-less *Romeo and Juliet* had been the spur for Antoine's use of the neutral curtain in *King Lear*, so a production of *The Marriage of Figaro* in eighteenth-century costume and settings that he had also seen in Munich in 1897 was suggestive here. Beginning with a fairly crude idea of what constituted authenticity, Antoine's Odéon productions involved him in increasingly rigorous investigations into how to be true to the spirit of the drama of a period different from his own, a drama that he found magnificent but somewhat alien. Already in 1903, when thinking about French Renaissance tragedy, he was exploring the idea, appealing also to directors as different as Poel and Brecht, of setting it in the period in which it was written. He stated that:

research on local colour or historical truth seems to me vain for such masterworks.
I believe firmly that it spoils the meaning of these marvellous tragedies to situate them anywhere but the country and time where they were created.[13]

For his first production of this kind, Corneille's *Le Cid* (1907), he recreated the appearance and social context of the Théâtre du Marais as it would have been in 1636. The stage was given a heavy-beamed wood ceiling from which hung a candelabra and was backed by a single simply painted backcloth. As many as 624 wax candles on the stage and in the theatre were lit and actors in seventeenth-century costume took up their positions as an on-stage audience. Rachel de Ruy from the Opéra sang to a lute accompaniment and then, just as the play was beginning, the actors were interrupted by the entrance of a nobleman bustling in late with his retinue to his place among the on-stage audience. Antoine had made a play-around-the-play using the arrogant nobleman, a tutor with his two pupils, fops teasing the actresses and an assortment of dressers, stagehands and candle-snuffers, busy at their tasks.

Whereas Antoine's staging of the classics increasingly drew the fury of traditional critics, this production, which was a great popular success, caused little controversy, perhaps because the emphasis was directed from the play itself to the surrounding local colour. In part, this was Antoine's way of dealing with drama that was fundamentally uncongenial to him. Although he directed *Cinna*, *Héraclius*, *Horace*, *Le Menteur*, *Polyeucte* and *Rodogune* as well as *Le Cid*, he gave only fifty-five performances of Corneille altogether at the Odéon.

Although *Le Cid* remained in the repertoire, Antoine's attention in his subsequent staging of French tragedy shifted from the world in which the play was performed to its contemporary staging conditions in a more rigorous investigation of what authenticity might mean. Whilst an on-stage audience was used in the 1909 *Andromaque*, it engaged in much less stage business. For his production of *Britannicus* (1911), he set the stage obliquely as he had in so many of his productions of contemporary drama. He also cast women (Andrée Pascal and Marie Ventura) in the roles of Britannicus and Nero to emphasize the youthfulness which Racine had stressed in his preface to the play and which the Comédie-Française consistently muffled by casting their leading actors in the roles. Indeed, Antoine had cast the mature de Max as Nero in his Théâtre Antoine production.

Esther (1913) was approached rather differently. Whilst restoring Jean-Baptiste Moreau's music for Racine's play, he took the costumes, gestures and scenes of an eighteenth-century series of Gobelin tapestries of the story of Esther (made from designs by Jean-François de Troy) as his inspiration for the *mise en scène* of the play. A net masked the ceiling of sets designed by Paul Paquereau. Lighting created a golden glow on the stage and a halo effect around the actors, and Ibels cut the costumes from coffee sacking and then hand-painted the decoration on them as part of this venture into stylization.

The images here are reminiscent of those used for Hauptmann's quasi-symbolist *Hannele Mattern*, which Antoine had described as 'a very beautiful poem' when he first saw it in Berlin in 1893 and which he staged recurrently at Easter at the Théâtre Antoine and the Odéon, spending extravagantly in an attempt to make the spiritual substantial, experimenting with lighting and even, one year, signing up a German acrobat as a flying angel. Just as that had been a response to the activity of the new symbolist theatre, the production of *Esther* came in the wake of the Ballets Russes tour. But the religiosity and the faithfulness to a specific visual source was quite unlike the practice of the Ballets Russes.

For all his proclaimed admiration of Racine, Antoine was more convincingly inward with Molière. His Molière productions were both more confident and more creatively iconoclastic, perhaps because he felt that the spirit of the writing, which seemed rooted in the life and manners of the people, had been obscured by Comèdie-Française acting and staging. Although costumes and interiors were always accurately seventeenth-century in their detail, Antoine was much less concerned here with historical reconstruction. He wanted to restore the fun, liveliness and modernity of Molière's drama and, a frequent attender at the café-concert himself, he looked to farce and popular comedy for his means.

He claimed to have approached *Tartuffe* as if it had just been offered by a contemporary author. Placing this play in 'its true milieu' meant rejecting the long tradition that Molière should be played in a single setting, 'a Molière'.[14] He used four sets, therefore, leading the audience through successive locations as they penetrated steadily deeper into Orgon's house. Because there was so much toing and froing in the opening scene, this was set in Orgon's garden, with the family sitting talking under a tree and Orgon (Mosnier) carried on in his chaise. As habitually with Antoine, doors and windows opened, seats were for sitting on and properties accurate in their seventeenth-century detail, were indicative of daily life.

Antoine was appreciative of Molière's timing and his use of stage furniture. Tartuffe's first entrance is delayed until Act III. The staircase by which Antoine's Tartuffe (Desjardins) finally entered was so constructed that first his feet, then his body, and finally his head slowly appeared. Attentive to the fact that the play has two central male comic figures, Tartuffe and Orgon, the dupe, originally played by Molière himself, Antoine placed the famous table under which Orgon hides to overhear Tartuffe's courtship of Elmire in Act IV 'naturally' rather than, as usual in Théâtre Français productions, in an obvious mid-stage position. The naturalism, by allowing the audience a more interesting viewpoint on the action, intensified the embarrassment and absurdity of the scene and provided a tremendous opportunity for Elmire as her situation with Tartuffe becomes increasingly desperate and Orgon, apoplectic behind the table, fails to intervene. Such attention to the implications of the text has none of what Antoine dismissed as the 'realistic veneer' of Fechter's nineteenth-century production which had led to such fussy distractions as his Tartuffe making his entrance drinking a glass of wine.[15]

Although some critics attacked the production for its break with tradition, it was also widely praised. The applause from the theatre audience repeatedly interrupted the words of the actors. Faguet declared that if living now Molière would have performed it just so, and by the time Antoine directed *L'Ecole des femmes* (Nov. 1908) the critics, accustomed now to seeing Molière with modern *mise en scène*, applauded the set which used the height as well as the depth of the stage.

At first level there was an old Paris street supported by a wall, and beyond this were the flowers and climbing-plants of the ingeniously hung garden and the house of Arnolphe, so that the action could move smoothly between the street and different parts of the garden. Using modern techniques to rework an old idea, Antoine here created neither a static 'Molière' nor a series of different scenes but a plurality of acting spaces within a single set, by means of which he gained the fluency he felt comedy needed.

Beginning in 1910 with *Monsieur de Pourceaugnac* (Oct.) and *Le Médecin malgré lui* (Dec.), and following these with *Le Bourgeois gentilhomme* (Oct. 1911) and *Le Malade imaginaire* (Oct. 1912), Antoine opened three seasons with Molière farces which were presented first as matinees accompanied by an introductory lecture, and the productions were so successful that they were repeatedly revived. In his *Malade imaginaire* lecture, claiming Molière as his own with not a little impudence, he pointed out that there was no comedy as *rosse* as Molière's. Besides restoring the full spoken text, he reincorporated the fantasy and spectacle of the mime, song and dance of the interludes that would have entertained the seventeenth-century audience. Although invariably cut elsewhere, these seemed a necessary part of the texture of the drama, throwing the scurrilous wit of the spoken play into relief. In much the way that he would later insist on using the music Moreau had composed for Racine's *Esther*, he retrieved Lulli's compositions for *Le Bourgeois gentilhomme*, and restored the elaborate (Turkish) closing ceremonies. As if to emphasize the artifice, the actors playing Argan, Toinette and Béralde in *Le Malade imaginaire* watched the interludes from the auditorium.

The real iconoclasm here was Antoine's casting of music-hall performers in the principal roles. As the *Comœdia* critic put it, 'there is no more Opéra, no more Folies-Bergère, no more café-concert, André Antoine has carried them

all off to the second Théâtre Français' (Oct. 1912). After his invitation to
Vilbert of the Ambassadors had caused a sensation in August 1910, Antoine
wrote to Dranem of the Eldorado:

You know that I have invited Vilbert to come next winter to the Odéon to play Monsieur
de Pourceaugnac at one of our classical matinees.
  I have, indeed, a theory that café-concert artists would be infinitely more interesting in
works of the classic repertoire and that they are the keepers of the comic tradition.
  So now I come to you, to ask if you too wish to come to one of these lecture–matinees
to play Molière's Le Médecin malgré lui in which I know you would be marvellous.[16]

Releasing this letter to the press was a characteristic demonstration of
Antoine's ability to create a theatrical event and, indeed, the success of these
plays demonstrated to the sceptical that it was possible to make money with
the classical repertory. Dranem repeated his role of Sganarelle, both at the
Odéon and with Odéon actors at the Trocadero, and both also appeared in
contemporary plays at the Odéon. Vilbert was cast again as Jourdain in Le
Bourgeois gentilhomme and as Argan in Le Malade imaginaire with the opéra-
bouffe performer Jane Marnac to mime, sing and dance in powdered wig and
diamond-chequered costume as Polichinelle in the first interlude, whilst a
company of dancing valets appeared in the third interlude.

  Although the innovation brought a spate of vitriolic letters, all these
performers were hugely successful as were the dancers, and Vilbert's
Jourdain was punctuated throughout by shouts of laughter from the
audience, particularly in his clumsy attempts to imitate the dancing-master.
The use of professional clowns cast a revelatory light on Molière's comic
writing. It was claimed that Sganarelle had, 'never been played with such life
and truth' as by Dranem, and Léon Blum insisted that the 1911 Bourgeois
gentilhomme had been, 'mounted and played with exquisite purity of taste'.
The venture reinforced Antoine's place in popular talk and at least one stand-
up comic worked it into his patter when, seeing Antoine arrive at the
Olympia Club, he anticipated an Odéon engagement. But as Jacques
Arnavon, a Molière scholar who worked with Antoine on the text of Tartuffe
saw, the real importance of his Molière productions was that in presenting 'a
classic comedy freed from the spreading gangrene that afflicted it' they
enabled audiences and other theatre directors to see that reclamation of
revered texts as exciting theatre was possible.[17]

8   A national theatre

Imaginative programming, the juxtaposition of the well known with the less familiar, the safe with the shocking, had been a feature of the Théâtre Libre and was evident in a newly ambitious form at the Odéon. The parallel staging of an authentic and a conventional *Andromaque* was only one example of this and, indeed, Antoine complemented these with a production of Euripides' *Andromache*, with antiphonal chorus and a cast especially imported from the Comédie-Française. Before Corneille's *Le Cid*, Guilhen de Castro's *La Jeunesse du Cid* (*Las Mocedades del Cid*), an early Spanish version of the story, was staged, and before Racine's *Esther* in 1913, the André Dumas–Leconte version of the story. A series of miser plays, which oddly missed *Volpone* but included Plautus, *La Farce de la marmite*, Pushkin *Le Chevalier avare* and an ancient Chinese comedy, *L'Avare chinois* (*Kan Thsian hou*), accompanied Molière's *L'Avare*. *L'Avare* itself was hardly safe or familiar in the re-established text that Antoine played in 1911 and of which he commented to *Comœdia* that, 'like me, the House was gripped by the extreme violence, the daring vivacity of the scenes between father and son [in the usually cut IV.i]. Never in our modern plays has anyone gone further' (7 Oct. 1911).

Such exploration, revelation and comparison was, for Antoine, a crucial part of the function of a national theatre. Throughout his nine years at the Théâtre Antoine he had preserved the idea of returning to the Odéon to stage the classics. Indeed, as letters and references located by his biographer Francis Pruner have made clear, the Odéon had frequently been in Antoine's mind and in the minds of his supporters from his early Théâtre Libre days. When offered the sole directorship, he was ready with a programme policy. Besides contemporary drama by established authors which, in an age before cinema had quite taken hold, was the commercial backbone of his programme, he saw the Odéon's central role as the staging of major drama from abroad and from the past. There would be Thursday matinees in which, beginning with medieval drama, he would move via the French Renaissance through the Italian comedy, Marivaux and Beaumarchais, to Victor Hugo and Becque. On Mondays he would stage the rarely played works of major writers, beginning with Molière's *Don Juan*, and there would be five evenings a year devoted to complete newcomers. His mission was nothing less than the re-establishment of the cultural centrality of drama and the retrieval of the lost drama of the past. He claimed the right to play all genres, even vaudeville, providing it was the best of its kind.[1]

In the event, Antoine kept to these plans remarkably closely, alternating productions, playing commercially promising and more risky contemporary works and allowing no indefinite runs. Each season's programme combined major and minor works from the French drama of the past; tested revivals, including revivals of Théâtre Antoine and Théâtre Libre plays; the French premières of foreign classics; plays by contemporary writers, and a series of lectures to accompany the Thursday matinees. A play from the English repertory was introduced every year, usually Shakespeare, but Marlowe and Sheridan also figured, and there were productions of plays by Euripides, Lope de Vega, Machiavelli, Goethe, Schiller, Pushkin, as well as revivals of his Théâtre Libre productions of Tolstoi, Ibsen and Strindberg. By October 1911 he was able to report that after five seasons he had at last reached his goal for the Odéon, namely, 'a vast repertoire with alternating shows' which was, by general agreement, 'an instrument of trial and experiment as useful to authors and actors as it [was] interesting to lovers of theatre' and that a regular, informed audience had gradually been created which achieved, with the company, 'the mysterious collaboration on which was founded the success and literary influence' of his two former theatres.[2]

The programme for the 1911–12 season makes clear just how vast the repertoire was and how frequent the alternations (numbers in brackets refer to performances). Amongst the forty-five plays performed were revivals of Corneille's Le Cid (5) and Polyeucte (3); Racine's Britannicus (4) and Les Plaideurs (4); Molière's L'Avare (3), Le Misanthrope (2), Les Précieuses ridicules (3); and M. de Pourceaugnac (1). New productions were mounted of Molière's Amphitryon (3) and Le Bourgeois gentilhomme (33); of Racine's Bajazet (4); Bergerac's Le Pédant joué (2); Tristan L'Hérémit's La Mort de Sénèque (14), and of two short plays by La Fontaine (4 and 4), as well as revivals of plays by Marivaux (1 and 2), Beaumarchais (4), de Musset (1), Balzac (1) and Dumas père (31). From the foreign repertoire came Euripides' Andromache (2), Shakespeare's Troilus and Cressida (5) Lope de Vega's L'Etoile de Seville (2), and Aux jardins de Murcie, a play by Feliu y Codina (21). There were also fifteen new or late nineteenth-century plays, of which the outstanding successes were Anthelme's L'Honneur japonais (45), Maurey's adaptation of David Copperfield (51), and the Dumas–Leconte Esther (59). Les Corbeaux (1), Thérèse Raquin (1), L'Arlésienne (21), The Power of Darkness (3), and Ghosts (3) were revived from his repertoire of modern classics.

Antoine, prevented from acting by his contract, was able for the first time to put all his energy into direction. Although his name did not appear on posters or programmes, he assumed control of all elements of performance, casting, staging, set and costumes as he had at his other theatres, and every newspaper discussed his *mise en scène*. Designers Jusseaume, Paquereau, Ibels, worked to his brief. As at the Théâtre Antoine, régisseurs, including Tourneur from the Antoine, ran secondary rehearsals on the stage, in the Orangerie, in the foyer, based on his prompt books.

The intensity of the primary rehearsals in which he might spend an hour working on ten tricky lines, the attention to detail, was legendary. Rehearsals of complex new productions would run late into the night and openings were delayed, as indeed the opening of *Julius Caesar* was, if Antoine was not satisfied. René Benjamin, one of his writers, told how Antoine studied the text phrase by phrase, word by word with the actors until he found what he wanted, how, just as at his other theatres, he was 'on the stage to act, in the auditorium to watch, almost at the same time'. A commentator in 1912 could proclaim with confidence that:

There has been much discussion in Paris recently in response to the visit of the famous German director, Max Reinhardt, of the discipline and cohesion of the theatrical companies from across the Rhine: of the new troup of the innovator, Reinhardt and the old troup of the Meininger . . . discipline and cohesion are much inferior among our leading companies – except one of them, that of the Odéon, of course, which is kept in a constant state of training and order and has exactly that kind of homogeneity.[3]

Famously holding to the Meininger practice which he had developed at his other theatres, Antoine allowed no star performers. The actors were listed in alphabetical order on posters and programmes and the ensemble effect was widely acclaimed. In practice, the ideal was never quite achieved, any more than it was by the Meininger. The most demanding roles necessarily went to the most gifted actors and audiences came specifically to see them perform. As newspaper reviews make clear, Antoine himself had been the star actor at the Théâtre Libre in the minds of the press and many of the audience, and had distracted attention from the main action when he cast himself in tiny roles.

Théâtre Libre writers who met up with Antoine again in his new incarnation were moved to find their work treated with greater experience but with the same absorption and respect, clarity of judgement and eye for a visual image. Benjamin said that 'Out of nothing, he created the illusion of reality . . . there was never a poet with more fire and harmony than this man' (p. 13) and Geffroy, recalling two months' work on *L'Apprenti*, wrote that he rediscovered Antoine just as he had known him at the outset at the Passage de l'Elysée des Beaux Arts, then at the Montparnasse and the Théâtre Antoine:

He had the same passion, the same fire, with always greater knowledge, not only of material matters but of the moral significance of characters. André Antoine is a great artist, a great observer of character . . . a colorist, a musician of the first order. This man has an unparalleled, marvellously keen sense of colour and sound.

With 'colour and sound', he transformed 'the Odéon's sad and sombre stage'. He went back to sources, to Rome, to Brittany, to the Louvre not to reproduce but, through a process of selection and condensation, to create concentrated images of reality. Animation and sound as well as appearance gave the texture of life. The coming and going of numerous workers and the continual sound of hammers and a saw contributed with cranes and real site equipment to create the impression of an authentic work-site for Sudermann's *Parmi les Pierres* (1908).[4]

The burden of this study, indeed, has been that the common assumption that realism is necessarily sensuously dull is not supported by Antoine's work. Theatrical perception had intensified the dramatic moment at the Théâtre Libre: Jacques Damour framed in a doorway; lanterns punctuating the prison darkness and catching the faces of the Duc d'Enghien and his hasty judges; the *oremus* rising between the serried beds of a white hospital ward. The plasticity and visual relationships of theatre were always essential to his work even when his resources were slight. What he rejected was glamour – easy visual excitement that neither elucidated nor intensified the script.

Despite his continuing willingness to sponsor verse drama and his occasional forays into symbolist staging, he held at base to his, by now familiar, argument that:

It is only with the appearance of naturalism, introducing at last the theory of place, that one can build a truly living atmosphere around the characters of a play . . . the *mise en scène* plays the role of description in a novel, it is itself exposition and the connection between drama and milieu is unbreakable.

Even in the 1920s, when the tide had turned against realist staging and, admitting that 'the Ballets Russes has upset all our conceptions,' he offered the diagnosis that 'what we have done is exaggerate our care for realism', he nevertheless retained a fundamental belief in solidity and verisimilitude, predicting that there would before long be a 'return from the world of imagination to the real world'.[5]

It does seem to be the case, however, that in the last years at the Odéon, Antoine was increasingly drawn to contemporary texts that allowed him to create spectacle. Although his authors were quick to defend him as 'the most discreet and scrupulous' of directors who 'never let the *mise en scène* swamp the play',[6] the balance seems to have frequently tipped towards scenery as it had done only on occasion in the past. Mosnier's account makes it clear that Antoine was very conscious of the growing appeal of cinema and saw spectacle as a weapon (p. 532). The 200 costumes Ibels designed for

L'Honneur japonais (1912), meticulously based on Japanese prints and artefacts in the Musée Guimet, were lavishly trimmed and hand-painted, whilst *Antar* (1910) had mountain and desert scenes and an exotic fire-dance to a Ravel score. The *mise en scène* for Dumas's *Esther* (spring 1912) outdid all these with its massive winged statues and orgiastic crowd in the Babylon scenes, whilst for the fifth act of *Rachel* (winter 1913–14), a celebration of the nineteenth-century tragedienne, Antoine erected on the Odéon stage a mock-up of the stage, back-stage area and part of the auditorium of the Comédie-Française itself. Undeniably this is decadence, even if a surprisingly astringent kind of decadence. For all his admiration of Antoine, Copeau's insistence on simplicity was as much a reaction against Antoine's spectacular authenticity as against the glitter of mainstream theatre that Antoine himself abhorred.

During his time at the Odéon, Antoine essentially offered a performed history of drama. Some plays had only a single performance and others were not much more than staged readings, but many had several performances and were subsequently revived, and some were so successful that Antoine ran them for up to two weeks. He staged works by Boileau, Voltaire and Diderot, by Hugo and Balzac. Among the early French plays were Greban's *Le Vray Mistère de la Passion* (1906), Rotrou's *Saint Genest* (1908) and Pradon's *Phèdre et Hippolyte* (1910). His imagination was fired by comparison and retrieval. His production of a play by Cyrano de Bergerac was a characteristic response to the enthusiasm generated by Rostand's *Cyrano de Bergerac*.

The Thursday classic matinee was the core of his work, far exceeding the contractual obligation to stage four classic plays a year. Although he never managed to build a Petit Odéon, an experimental house within the confines of the main house, the idea was established in these matinees, which included the staging of many works normally encountered only on the page, and in the programme of 'Unpublished Saturdays', introduced in the 1910–11 season, to give new authors an opportunity to try out their work. Only under Barrault, Director of the Odéon between 1959 and 1968, was a small experimental house finally achieved. In 1906–14 experimental work that might have packed a Petit Odéon, a Pit, a Cottesloe as it once had a Théâtre Montparnasse and soon would a Vieux Colombier left empty seats in the huge Odéon auditorium and proved a drain on Antoine's resources.

But Antoine did revive certain works he particularly valued, even when he knew there was no possibility of a capacity audience. Calderón's *La Dévotion à la croix* was played twice in 1908 and revived twice more in 1909 and 1913. Although *Ghosts* was much better received than *The Wild Duck* both were revived two or three times most years. Besides being one of the few houses to give a space to verse plays, he ran an annual spring poetry competition and, in autumn 1908, a series of fortnightly poetry readings on themes such as 'Time' or 'The Sea'. Many of Antoine's individual productions were celebrated, but what distinguished his Odéon directorate from his predecessors' and claimed the attention of his successors was the continual investigation of what a national theatre should be, an investigation accompanied by a constant stream of letters from him to the ministry explaining the need for a more realistic subsidy. Benjamin noted that Antoine never thought of the theatre as a diversion; the word 'battle' was continuously on his lips (p. 12).

The matter of the run is, of course, at the heart of the continuing debate about subsidy and government responsibility for the arts and Antoine's attitude to it is telling. Whereas theatre managers in the commercial theatre increasingly looked for plays that would run indefinitely Antoine, convinced that long runs were inimical to good live theatre, resisted and always had new work in rehearsal. His practice was to run a very successful production for up to a fortnight and then to revive it for occasional performances in subsequent years. In the 256 performing weeks of his tenure between October 1906 and March 1914, 231 different plays were performed at the Odéon, an astonishing average of just less than one new production a week. Pressure for tickets did lead him to allow a few productions a longer run, although even this would be interspersed at least 50 per cent with other productions. There were, for instance, 30 performances of Dumas fils' *Les Danicheff* in 1909 and 70 of *Antar*, a semi-operatic Egyptian life of Muhammad, in 1910; 60 of *Rachel*, in 1913–14, whilst *Vieil Heidelberg*, a translation of a recent successful German play, produced in 1906 (5 performances), was revived in 1907 (16); 1908 (16); 1910 (34); 1912 (21), and 1913 (30).

Some classics, notably *Julius Caesar* (30), *King Lear* (17) and the Molière farces, ran and were repeatedly revived and *Faust* held its place for four months in 1913 (65), but the very successful plays did tend to be bourgeois drama of ideas or exotically located verse plays which, if more worthy and more authentically set, were not much more demanding on their audience than the theatre against which so much of Antoine's earlier work had been pitted. That he did play these works suggests he was rather more commercially alert than his critics allowed. That he resisted pressure to play them all the time, whilst no doubt commercially short-sighted, was a sign of his seriousness and creative energy.

The ministry report at the end of Antoine's first season, besides remarking the 'excellent impression' he had made with his resolution to 'create an ensemble company', to 'vary his programmes and create a strong repertoire that is both classic and modern', had noted that, 'M. Antoine began by altering the austere and chilly auditorium of the Odéon and the public has found it light, bright and spacious' (fig. 29). It noted, too, that receipts had trebled, rising to an average of 2,504 francs 52c per performance, compared with the 815 francs averaged during the previous season under Ginisty's directorship. But the renovated house, the stable company, the exciting programme, the marvels of the *mise en scène* which brought in the audiences and made the Odéon a centre of France's cultural life all had to come from the scanty subsidy and receipts which frequently did not cover costs, even with capacity houses.

The question of costs deserves fuller investigation, since it is one that remains pressing today and affects even the most gifted directors. The success of the Odéon under Antoine does seem to have been closely tied up with the vast sums of money spent there. The renovation of the theatre, mentioned in the Budget Report, although hugely expensive, had achieved a combination of light and intimacy that attracted the public as well as democratizing the auditorium, while the spectacular scenography on which so much of his popular success was based depended on the modernization of the stage.

Similarly, the solid and accurate decor Antoine demanded, with walls that did not shudder if brushed by an actor, came at a price, being time-consuming to build and heavy to move. 'Three boards and a passion' might or might not make for better theatre but they are undeniably cheaper. An element in the failure of the first Odéon administration had been a strike by stage-hands, unprepared for the demands made on their time and energy and resentful of the incomer's authoritarian manner. The financial troubles of the second administration were exacerbated by escalating labour costs at a time when unionization was leading to widespread improvements in pay and conditions and the film studios were competing for skilled craftsmen. Antoine became, in 1912–13, the first French theatre director to pay a liveable retainer during the summer recess instead of laying his staff off. Furthermore, the lack of back-stage depth at the Odéon necessitated an unusually large stage crew to effect the complete removal of all scenery at each change of show.

The rich and varied programme was taxing on actors, who might be holding a dozen major roles in readiness for revival whilst keeping up a gruelling schedule of rehearsals for current and new productions, but it gave them a range and intensity they could have got nowhere else and welded them into a remarkable and long-serving ensemble. There was, undeniably, an element of wilfulness in Antoine's programming policy. The speed with which some productions came and went defeated all but the most watchful in the potential audience and the frequent striking and erection of scenery exacerbated the practical problems. Antoine's insistence on completely new decor and costumes for each production was also expensive and whilst works were, very occasionally, played in the set built for other productions – *Mandragora* in the *Romeo and Juliet* set, for instance – this was uncommon even for single fleeting experiments. Was this self-indulgent extravagance or a crucial element in retrieving and exploring the play?

Although success was real, costs were crippling and recurrent. *Julius Caesar*, whose record-breaking receipts had averaged 3,975 francs in December 1906, had still failed to break even. Despite a lucrative tour of the provinces in June and August, Antoine had begun his second season still in debt to the Magasins du Louvre for the theatre refit. In 1908, at the end of the second season, after the commercial failure of *Ramuntcho*, with 400,000 francs worth of debts, he had been ready to resign. In his lecture before *L'École des femmes*, early the next season, he announced himself 'completely ruined' and invited the audience to inspect the models for the decor he had been unable to afford. The situation was saved by the intervention of Louis Benière, a businessman who had made his debut as a writer at the Théâtre Antoine and whose one-act *Les Goujons* had run in harness with a Brieux play for forty-nine performances in 1907.

In April 1914 the government voted an *allocation extraordinaire* of 125,000 francs to bail out the Odéon and to show sympathy in a practical way for 'an artistic effort which certainly [had] no equivalent in the whole history of contemporary theatre'. But Antoine's debts were more than treble that. The grant covered only the unpaid wages of the Odéon company, then running at 50,000 francs a month, and did little to alleviate the other outstanding debts or the continuing daily expenses and, on 6 April, finding it too little and too late, Antoine resigned, seeing the necessity of abandoning his 'dream of an artistic and prosperous theatre'.[7]

In his own account of his failure, Antoine pointed out that the subsidy which had remained the same for 50 years was simply insufficient to support an adventurous programme and that his allocation of the total was disproportionately small. The Opéra subsidy was 400,000 francs a year and the Comédie-Française 240,000 francs, compared with the Odéon's 100,000 (figures for 1912). Despite reiterated praise of Antoine's work by the ministry and despite Antoine's continual appeals for an increase, the disparity remained. Clearly, he did not cut his cloak according to his cloth. Whether he could have made the Odéon the cultural centre it became had he done so is improbable.

How justified was Antoine's continual challenge to the subsidizing agency? In its 1914 report, the Budget Commission acknowledged that one of the chief problems was the location of the Odéon itself and its costly running charges. Even in the ruinous year of 1908, his debts had not exceeded the 400,000 francs subsidy granted each year to the Opéra whose achievements in these years by no means matched those of the Odéon.

True to form, the costs of *Psyché*, Antoine's final production, far outweighed possible receipts. Although acclaimed and drawing capacity houses, it lost between 1,000 and 2,000 francs a night. That he chose this as his Molière production for 1914 is interesting in view of what does appear to have been a growing emphasis on spectacle in his recent contemporary productions. For *Psyché* is not a play but a masque-like confection conceived for Louis XIV's court by Molière, Corneille, Quinault and Lulli, which had only been performed once since 1715. Antoine's notion of modelling Pyrrhus in *Andromaque* on Louis was extended here to an attempt to recreate the ambience of the Versailles which could have generated such a work.

Almost six months' preparation preceded the production, with five tailors working eight hours a day for 124 days on the 150 costumes, which were designed by Ibels and an assistant from illustrations of seventeenth-century court entertainments. As in the previous year's production of Racine's *Esther*, Antoine again turned from his long-held belief that the original stage directions were a vital part of the text. Instead of placing the Prologue in a rustic place with a rock and the sea in the background, he placed it on the terrace of Versailles and some aspect of the palace and gardens – the fountain of Neptune, the avenues of trees, the night brightened by torches – was present in each of the nine different decors. The ballet-master from the Opéra was brought in to choreograph the dances and used thirty-two singers and forty musicians to perform the twenty-nine musical sequences. *Psyché*, like *Esther*, was staged after the first French performances of the Ballets Russes. If this was an attempt, as Oscar Brockett has suggested, to incorporate a new vision of theatre into his own, it was a final, overwhelming and self-destructive attempt, albeit hugely successful with press and public.[8]

The resignation led to an eruption of press articles; to surveys of Antoine's career and denunciations of the ministry and the fashionable audience; to discussions of the difficulties of running the Odéon; to a number of emotional demonstrations, and to a benefit gala at the Opéra (the receipts of which, ironically at some 110,000 francs the equivalent of a year's subsidy of the Odéon, had to be handed over to the creditors after the official bankruptcy). Antoine himself acknowledged the reproaches about his spending on decor but was quite unrepentant, citing both the needs of the play and the competition from the cinema, whose luxury, ingenuity and variety of *mise en scène* threatened to lure away the popular audience.[9]

Paradoxically, given Antoine's life-long belief in the primacy of the dramatist's script, his work at the Odéon was conclusive in shifting the balance of power and establishing the supremacy of the director in French theatre. Under him, the rule of the actor gave way, not to the rule of the dramatist as he had anticipated, but to the rule of the director. Although his name appeared on neither the hoardings nor the programme for the Odéon, discussion in the press and among the audience turned not on the capacities of individual actors nor even, finally, on the qualities of the play itself but on the authenticity, the conviction and the coherence of Antoine's *mise en scène* and the remarkable ensemble acting of his company. The director's interpretation of Renard, Molière or Shakespeare was what caused excitement. In this, Antoine's work endorsed and ran parallel with that of other theatre directors whose own careers had begun in the burst of theatrical activity following the foundation of the Théâtre Libre — Reinhardt in Germany, Granville Barker in England, Stanislavski in Russia.

Antoine's Odéon work was no less significant because it was often problematic. The Odéon he inherited was primarily a show-place for famous and upcoming actors to perform in the most renowned and popular plays of the French repertoire. Under his direction, it became a theatre which asked questions about appropriate performance styles and about the repertoire. New ways of staging Racine and Molière were explored which reanimated works become inert through years of traditional and increasingly ossified stage method. Lesser-known works of the masters or works of their lesser-known contemporaries and successors were reintroduced, and the openness to other European theatre that had been such a feature of the Théâtre Libre was evident in one of the temples of French national culture. Antoine engaged, too, with some of the questions about the role of a national theatre that still need answers. In what kind of new writing should a theatre interest itself? What proportion of the repertoire should be devoted to new writing and what to exploration of the drama of the past? What to abstruse and what to potentially popular work? Antoine did not solve these problems, nor did he develop a sustained taste for unusual work in the large proportion of the Odéon audience, but they were matters to which he gave continual attention and offered a challenging series of answers.

9   Antoine and cinema

In the course of Antoine's film, *L'Hirondelle et la mésange* (*The Swallow and the Bluetit*),[1] two characters hitch themselves to the towropes of their barges and, lacking animals to do it for them, heave their barges along the canal (fig. 47). The detailed accuracy of what is shown, the actors' exact knowledge of what to do and doing it without fuss, the characters' bent backs and absorption in their labour all work to establish our acceptance of this as an habitual and necessary part of these people's lives. The sequence catches the essence of Antoine's realism both because the seeming authenticity of what is shown compels audience belief and because the composition of the frames demonstrates an alertness to the possibilities of the medium: to the use, for example, of close-ups and camera angles, which emphasize the physical effort and the sensitivity of the man to the presence of the woman, and of panning shots of the affluent landscape beyond the towpath which the characters, absorbed in their labour, ignore but the camera and, therefore, the audience, perceive. Artifice intensifies belief. The shaping imagination of the director is at least as crucial in the cinema as in the theatre.

The SCAGL (Société Cinématographique des Auteurs et Gens de Lettres), a subsidiary of Pathé, employed Antoine after his return from Turkey in 1914 specifically to work on Albert Capellani's film version of Victor Hugo's *Quatre vingt treize* (*1793*) after that director had left for Hollywood, but also, since he was a famous theatre director, to supply distinction to the team making 'art films'. These, like *1793*, were adaptations for the screen of classic novels — historical melodramas starring renowned Comédie actors.

Since the enterprise was modelled on the kind of escapist and spectacular theatre against which Antoine's whole enterprise had been pitted, it put him in a somewhat false position and although, when he had the opportunity to select his own scripts, Antoine turned to Zola and Daudet for plots about working people and the land, it is hardly surprising that he was continually at odds with his producers. More surprising is just how much was achieved in the eight films on which he worked. These present a continuing exploration of the possibilities of the new medium and an argument against the limitations imposed by the SCGAL; possibilities and arguments which recur in his film criticism spurred, perhaps, by the discussion of his work by younger theorists such as Delluc.[2]

After the experience gained completing Capellani's film and then directing

47 *L'Hirondelle et la mésange*. Frame still, camera, René Guychard. Michel (Alcover) and Marthe (Maguy Delyac) heave the barges. (Cliché Cinémathèque française)

an adaptation of Dumas père's *The Corsican Brothers*, more or less to the formula, he was ready to be more exploratory. *Le Coupable* (*The Culprit*) was the result, and it is a film remarkable for its exploration of the possibilities of narrative and for the potency of its visual images in a period when contemporary cinema was theatrical and studio-bound. As Ralph Stevenson has written:

cinematographic space was circumscribed to coincide with theatrical space, for, in the eyes of producers and audience, the one was a reproduction of the other.

But this was all changed when the camera freed itself (and the spectator with it) from the 'orchestral stalls viewpoint', and became mobile, either changing place between shots by cutting, or by moving during the filming of a single shot by panning or tracking.[3]

But the camera did not, of course, free itself. It was precisely because Antoine had struggled with the paradoxes of realism in the theatre that his film work played a significant part in showing how cinema could be freed from the theatrical straitjacket and still claim to be a serious art form.

Based on a novel by Coppée, *Le Coupable* opens with a trial scene in which the presiding judge addresses the court on behalf of a criminal. A series of

48 *Le Coupable*, court room close-up: the faces of the just. Camera, Paul Castenet. (Cliché Cinémathèque française)

flashbacks tells the life-stories of the judge and the criminal, his unacknowledged natural son, up to the present. A remarkable narrative fluidity is achieved. Whereas, in Antoine's theatre, the apparatus of a realistic court scene – benches, dock, lawyers, attendants, jury, crowd – meant that a trial scene would, of necessity, become the solid centre or the climax of a play, here on film the flashbacks form the greater part of the action, but the momentary intercutting of court sequences functions as a reminder of the trial in progress to which all is leading. The camera's power to focus attention and create contrasting images contributes to the narrative flow. Full shots of judge and criminal, whose bearing and gesture express individual passion, give way to sequences in which the screen is filled with the faces of the just, the vengeful or the merely curious who throng the court. White faces starting out of a black background supply crowd scenes that make an impact, can be called in at will, but last for only a moment (fig. 48).

The story has a melodramatic predictability. It tells of courtship and desertion; of the loving mother of the illegitimate child of the liaison, Auguste; of the harsh stepfather from whom, after the mother's death, the child runs away to a vagrant life in the city, a stretch in the reformatory,

casual employment as a theatre extra and the all-but-accidental theft which
has brought the natural son before his father, and it ends with the father's
public acknowledgement that the guilt is only his. But cliché is avoided
because, although some sequences run for longer than they would today, the
speed and detail of the narrative, the internal contrasts and the selection of
significantly representative scenes express potently the simple happinesses
and miseries of the lives depicted. Cliché is avoided, too, because the film
creates acute consciousness in the audience of the social and cultural context
within which those lives are lived. The evocation of the past resulting from
the cutting and interweaving (*découpage et entrelacement*) of scenes seemed to
a contemporary viewer to proceed with a 'simplicity and breadth that was
more and more touching'.[4]

The principles of Antoine's theatrical naturalism are evident but they are
freshly informed by the new medium. There is, for example, a brief and
moving scene of the abandoned girl's lying-in, in a bare room with metal
frame beds and a tormented figure tossing in the next bed. It is as terse as it is
effective. After a quick cut back to the court we return not to the hospital, but
to the girl making artificial flowers for a living, with her baby beside her. This,
in turn, gives way to a series of shots in which children are seen coming out of
school and then to the mother and Auguste, now about six years old, sailing
down the Seine and walking in the park of St-Cloud. The leaping and
lingering technique registers succinctly both the emotional security and the
financial stringency of Auguste's infancy.

Similarly, shifts in life chances are registered through a succession of
mealtime sequences. First, in a convivial scene, the young law student is
welcomed into the girl's family, then, in a desperately harsh scene after his
mother's death, Auguste and his stepfather confront each other over a
miserable table; finally the one-time student, now an eminent lawyer, on a
merry social occasion reads with shock of the arrest of the son he abandoned
long ago. Just as the lying-in scene echoes more sharply and poignantly the
hospital scene of *Sœur Philomène*, so this sequence adopts one of Antoine's
recurrent stage settings, the gathering around a meal-table that he had used
repeatedly from *En famille* in the first days of the Théâtre Libre to *La Terre* and
La Bonne Espérance, to evoke traditional associations of security and good
fellowship and to undercut them ironically.

Such an effect can be achieved in the cinema with greater speed and
subtlety. Here, and in comparable sequences in *L'Hirondelle et la mésange*, *La
Terre* and *1793*, where it is Marat, Danton and Robespierre who are so met,
the camera creates a sense of the group, but also, moving into close-up and
looking over the shoulder of one or another character, draws attention to the
particular expression or gesture of an individual within the group. In *La Terre*,

for instance, the camera, looking over the old man's shoulder, records the hostility between the generations as Lise coldly wipes the table around Old Fouan and his guest.

Environment was a crucial element in naturalist theatre and Paris itself is used in *Le Coupable* to reinforce the feeling and social texture of the action. In what seems to have been the first such filming of the city, Paul Castanet, who had worked on *1793* and became Antoine's regular cameraman, caught the life of the Paris streets: its derelict warehouses where the homeless boys sleep; its carriages, whose doors they hold open for a pittance and its barrows whose fruit they steal; its parks where lovers dream and runaways play in the swing-boats after hours; the chiaroscuro of its staircases and doorways; the barren stone of yard and walls in its reformatory where youths in clogs march to take their exercise, snow or shine, or loiter to smoke an illicit cigarette; the bustle of back-stage activity in one of its great theatres, where Auguste, among the extras, is naively delighted with his costume. The place teems with life and the life is observed on film with telling and often humorous detail.

There are three panoramic sequences. In the first, the law student and his girl, charmed with life, stroll together through the streets and sit in the Luxembourg Gardens. Later, mother and child ride on the Seine river-boat and the Paris of ancient and beautiful, derelict and war-ravaged buildings is glimpsed wonderfully as it slips by behind them. In the third Auguste, grown up, tormented after selling the stolen jewel, retreats to the hilly *banlieue* where the city is spread out before him. Paris provides a background to young love, to the strong affection of mother and child and to the miserable struggle with conscience of the adult Auguste. The reiterated presence of the great city as background to such changed circumstances, intensifies our perception both of the changes and of the city's imperviousness to the joy or suffering of the individual.

This is, I think, one of the great silent films because of the way it alerts the audience to the social and individual experience of its characters through expressive composition of the individual frame, but also because it uses the narrative potential of moving film, the fluidity and the power of telling montage, a fluidity suggested by the fact that, despite clumsy equipment, some 400 different shots were used in the film as a whole.[5] Again, this is a development of the theatrical practice. Antoine's attention to the movement and rhythm of drama had drawn frequent comment since his work on *Lear* and the succession of scenes and speed of action of one of his last stage productions, Schiller's *Guillaume Tell* (Jan. 1914), had led at least one critic to apply the cinematic metaphor to it (*Le Siècle*, 18 Jan. 1914). In the 1919 discussion of the cinema, Antoine insisted on the need to distinguish

49 *Le Coupable*, Auguste sleeps rough: chiaroscuro effects. (Cliché
Cinémathèque française)

between photography which works in individual, still images, and cinema
which is multiple and continuous, arguing fiercely that 'beautiful views do
not make a film' and that the cameraman must be at the service of the
narrative.

Varied and often breathtaking images succeed each other in his film, but
Antoine is not dealing in decoration. The power of the visual composition to
rouse our imaginative participation intensifies our response to the
desperation of the runaway boys when the moonlight shines into the depths
of their dockland hideout and, as the camera searches the shadowy buildings
for them, illumines their white faces briefly (fig. 49). Similarly, at the turning-
point of the plot, when Auguste has turned chance into theft by deciding to
sell rather than return the jewel, he and his shady confederate, recognizable at
first only by the characteristic outline of their hats, are seen silhouetted
against the light as they meet on the quayside whilst, through the arch of the
bridge, Notre Dame shows mistily in a low-angled shot. The frame-still
reproduced here (fig. 50) catches the moment at which the camera has moved
in close enough to enable us to begin to distinguish the faces and gestures of
the two men. We delight in the composition whilst responding to the human
interaction it depicts just as, at some level of consciousness, we delight in the
linguistic composition of Shakespearean dialogue whilst responding to the
grief, anger or confusion it expresses. We are touched morally and

50 *Le Coupable*, Auguste passes on the stolen item; Notre Dame is mistily present in background. Use of silhouettes and Paris landscape. (Cliché Cinémathèque française)

aesthetically even whilst we are absorbed in making sense of the on-going action of the film.

Although the intertitles are missing from the surviving print of the film, which led Richard Abel to observe in his massive study of the early French cinema that the plot is 'now close to incomprehensible', the research of the French *cinéaste* Philippe Esnault shows that once a few verbal clues to the relationships between the characters are supplied, all becomes clear, because the visual narrative line is strong. His research also demonstrates that Antoine's films can function without the sometimes excessive length to which his intertitles usually run.[6]

Antoine found film far less resistant to his wish to re-create the real than theatre with its necessary artifice had proved to be. Ideas pursued at the Théâtre Libre re-emerge in Antoine's cinema, and often the way in which they do so marks essential differences between film and theatre. The limits of realism are reached much more quickly in the live and imitative art of theatre than they are in cinema, where images of people and places that existed at a particular moment in time are fixed by light on celluloid with the documentary persuasiveness of the photograph. The virtuoso skills of the designer, the director and, particularly, the actor are indeed more apparent and more directly relished in the theatre than in the cinema. In Antoine's illusionist theatre the audience, for all it was plunged into anonymous darkness, was still interactive with the on-stage performance, ready to chill it with a hostile response or break into appreciative if illusion-shattering applause for an effective set or an especially well-performed speech or sequence of action.

Having challenged and often exposed the artifice of the theatre by bringing real plants, solid wood and painted landscapes on to the stage, Antoine could now truly imitate the impressionists and take his canvas into the open air. It had, indeed, always been the exterior scenes that lacked conviction in his theatre work. Already enthusiastic about the documentary potential of the new medium, he was the first maker of feature films in Europe to break consistently and purposely with the contemporary practice of studio filming and take his crews and actors on location: out into the streets of Paris (*Le Coupable*), to the wild Breton coast (*Travailleurs de la mer*, 1917); to the Beauce (*La Terre*, 1919); to the Flemish canals (*L'Hirondelle et la mésange*) and to the wide skies and marshes of the Camargue (*L'Arlésienne*, 1921).

Antoine pointed out that by going to real, inhabited places he avoided the horrors of the theatre scenery at Vincennes, and the old problems of shaking walls and windows through which light couldn't enter. Citing the interior used for *La Terre*, he noted 'the difficulty of taking to Vincennes the manger and the contents of this barn whose ceiling shelters real swallows' nests'.[7] Imaginative perception of the location also caught an atmosphere not realizable in the studio. Shots of villagers in their dark smocks, wearing sabots and smoking their pipes; of harvesters in the fields interrupting their work to drink from big stone jars, bring the peasant world of the Beauce, for example, sharply before the audience of *La Terre*.

A direct result of Antoine's first regional film, *Travailleurs de la mer*, which was voted among the top five films of the decade by *Comœdia* readers in 1920[8] was that within two years there were numerous units making realist and local colour films in the various French regions – although it should be admitted that the innovation was particularly welcomed by the studios because it coincided with an economic recession in the Vincennes workshops that resulted from the competition in the French cinemas of imported American films.

René Benjamin, reporting on the making of *L'Arlésienne*, noted that when Antoine travelled to Arles to search out the exact locations of the various scenes in Daudet's novel he seemed to drink in the place, missing nothing and, doing so, declared, 'I've been a fool to make decor for thirty years. Now the cinema will make it for me.'[9] The contrivance now lay in recognizing what would be an expressive or photogenic building or landscape and in composing the frame: placing objects, people and animals in such a way that they would be so caught by the camera as to seem not to have been placed at all. Antoine found that by abandoning Daudet's play-script and returning to *Lettres de mon moulin* in which the source story occurs he could rediscover the contexts of its action and re-create the visual impressionism of Daudet's book. Moments of passion or catastrophe are caught against a background of old carts and farm equipment or under the dappled shadow of trees, the old shepherd is held in silhouette against a light sky or his face and hands are lit by flickering firelight in an otherwise dark frame. In *La Terre*, the camera lingers over scythes and forks as if anticipating Françoise's death on a sickle; when Old Fouan's land is divided the camera closes in on a clod of earth pressed between a woman's hands.

Those mobile and unpredictable details, playing fountains or pecking chickens, that Antoine delighted to use in the theatre and which habitually distracted audience attention to themselves, intensify the impression of reality when caught momentarily in a photographic frame. So at the beginning of *L'Arlésienne* after panning across a landscape of wide flat fields, intercut with rivers as the camera closes in to the widow's farm, first a flock of sheep is driven briefly across the screen and then we see a woman, back to camera, feeding her chickens before moving into the farmhouse and its inhabitants. This is another version of an even more vivid sequence in *La Terre* in which the camera follows a flock of sheep as they move from their pen in a dark barn out into the circle of light made by opening the huge barn doors.

In fact, for all the camera is turned directly to nature, what we see on the screen in these films often reflects the impact of painters on Antoine's perception of landscape, just as his theatre decor had. His own imaginative vision dictates the way the landscape is framed and how the human figures are placed within it. Where, in the stage version of *La Terre*, the landscapes of Millet and Corot were reflected in the painted back-cloth, in the film we seem to see them brought to life, whilst the Swallow and the Bluetit, which at times seem to be sailing through a seventeenth-century Dutch painting, begin their journey with a down-river view of a bridge that startlingly recalls Van Gogh's *Pont d'Arles*.

The notable difference in the tone of Antoine's filmic presentation of peasant lives has less to do with the medium than with the man himself. The anger and surging activity that characterized Théâtre Libre productions has given way to a sense of resignation and endurance in the film version of *La Terre*, as if he had become reconciled to the harshness of the rural world as it receded into the past. Indeed, it was perhaps a combination of nostalgia with his characteristic literal-mindedness that fuelled his attack on Herbier's recasting of Zola's novel in the present in his version of *L'Argent*.[10]

As with the setting, Antoine's screen acting is both lifelike and rehearsed. Often berated by theatre critics because his troupe spoke so naturally that they couldn't be properly heard, Antoine realized that cinema demanded much lower-key acting than the most realistic theatre if it was to appear natural. But, always aware that the fullest illusion depended on intensive preparation, he rehearsed his cast thoroughly, working to eliminate 'opéra-comique' and the self-conscious posing that seemed to afflict actors in front of the camera. He discussed the characters' actions and thoughts with the actors, instilling consciousness of movement, gesture and relationship and asking them to observe local people carefully.

Diderot's paradox was still important to Antoine. The intelligent understanding of the character and projection of the self into the part through intensively rehearsed use of acting skills resulted, with a few worrying exceptions, in remarkably natural acting in a period of notoriously histrionic film performance. Indeed, to see Antoine's films is to catch a startling sense of what contemporary commentators meant when they exclaimed at the truth and naturalness of the acting in his theatre. The exaggerated gestures and overworked facial muscles of Gabriel de Gravonne as Frédéri are an embarrassing distraction in L'Arlésienne, where they conflict with the low-key performances of the rest of the cast. Antoine came to believe that troupes of actors should be trained specifically for the cinema. Although Pathé demanded that he use professional actors like Gravonne in leading parts, supporting roles from Travailleurs onwards were played by locals: Breton fishermen, Camargue peasants, Belgian watermen, as appropriate, plying on screen the long-tried skills of their trade and wearing their everyday clothes. The great problem of extras and authenticity was solved at a stroke.

Antoine's practice was directed always to intensifying the illusion of reality. He attacked the fixed idea of the 'orchestra stalls' attitude of contemporary cinema in which the cameramen took up their position before the acting area, as if in a theatre, whilst the actor was placed not within the four walls of his room or the four points of his horizon, but always facing the spectator. He argued that the camera might also look over a character's shoulder or follow the actors about to 'surprise their looks from whichever angle they present themselves'. Obvious as this seems today, and inflexible as his method often continued to be, the perception was a crucial step forward. As Antoine wrote:

the whole scene is composed to be seen as if from the prompter's box . . . But one of the invaluable qualities of the cinema, by contrast [with the theatre], is that it decentralizes movements, expressions, attitudes endlessly, according to distances and changing formats by the multiplication of scenes and incessant displacement of the spectator.

It was, of course, 'necessary for cinema artists to be assiduous in ignoring the cameraman' just as, in the theatre, Antoine's actors had learned not to acknowledge the presence of the audience with a glance of direct address.[11]

51 *L'Hirondelle et la mésange*, the plot. Michel is drowned, pushed under by Pieter's boathook while attempting to steal the hidden box of contraband goods. (Cliché Cinémathèque française)

L'Hirondelle et la mésange

The film which, although not his last, indicated the end of Antoine's career, *L'Hirondelle et la mésange*, has been restored for the Cinémathèque française from the six hours of rushes and the intertitles Antoine left. The birds of the title are the names of two cargo barges which, lashed together, work the canals of Belgium and France. Entirely shot on location, the film emerges as a remarkable documentary, through which winds a creaking melodrama of treachery and adulterous lust in a screenplay written for Antoine by Gustave Grillet. The film was abandoned when Antoine refused to reduce the documentary content in favour of more melodrama.

Chiaroscuro and the arrangement of the frame are handled with panache by Antoine at the emphatic moments of the plot and notably at the moment when the villain is drowned as he attempts to steal the black metal box in which his brother-in-law has concealed the contraband goods (fig. 51). But the real power of the film lies in its seeing, its rhythm and the extraordinary impression it gives of lived life. The details of everyday activity are more than ever the centre of attention: loading the cargo, operating the locks, dressing up for an outing, preparing and eating meals. These events are

52 *L'Hirondelle et la mésange*, the Antwerp Festival, 1920: the procession in long shot. The characters are at the bottom right corner of the frame. (Cliché Cinémathèque française)

observed, often from over the shoulder of the participating actor, sometimes in long shot so that the whole sequence of an activity is seen, sometimes with movement into close-up so that we are brought to sharp realization of the feeling and experience of the individual character.

The movement down the canals is reflected in the pace of the film: wide calm banks seen in panning shots from on board the barge give way to sudden bursts of activity as the barges join the Tamise fish market or find themselves part of the great Antwerp Festival which took place once every twenty-five years. Its last occurrence was this one of 1920, and in this footage alone Antoine justifies his claim that news filming should and could capture the life of events. There are splendid, Renoir-like shots of people under umbrellas facing jets of water sprayed from a giant fish, the centre-piece and ancient emblem of the procession. Groups and floats in the procession are seen in long shot, advancing on and passing the camera, which gives the cinema audience the impression of watching with the street-side observers even whilst seeing far more than any individual observer could have done. Our party mingles with the crowd. The camera seems to lose them in its long shots of the procession but picks them out at a distance and moves into close-

53 *L'Hirondelle et la mésange*: movement into close-up of the characters watching the procession.
Michel, Marthe, Griet (Maylianes) and Pieter (Ravet). (Cliché Cinémathèque française)

up as, not yet separated by mutual suspicion, they too participate in the excitement and clamour to see (figs. 52 and 53).

Although Pathé again insisted that Antoine use professional actors for the four leading parts, the naturalness of their playing is assisted by the camera-angles which make the scenes appear less contrived, although the actors had, as usual, been intensively rehearsed before shooting began. Boats, trees, bridges, even people who are not directly engaged in the action, are often only partly in frame as if to suggest that what the film registers is only a glimpse of what is there. Similarly, when characters walk off frame, Antoine tends to cut to their destination just before they reach the bottom of the stair or go through the door, which further marks the difference from the rigidity of theatre's fixed entrances and exits, its distinct on- and off-stage areas.

There are certain contradictions and problems with Antoine's films. Although the realism of his sets had been a cause of wonder, the real power of his theatrical *mise en scène* had lain in the fact that he created a harmony, an interactive mutuality between what was seen and what was heard in the theatre. Drama for him was words as well as images; words written to be

54   Antoine in his office at the Odéon, *c.1912*, working on the text. (Photo Harlingue-Viollet)

spoken within a three-dimensional space – words shaping and shaped by the relationship between characters. From the outset, he had relished the kind of perceptions and recognitions available only in the drama: the division of audience attention between speaker and hearer; the impact of including a silent listener within a scene, whose presence is perhaps unnoticed by the speaker because of stage positioning; the extraordinary range of the speaking voice and the way in which its impact is changed by its stage context; the power of a sudden silence or a pause held to the verge of unbearability. Dumas and Montigny had worked on spectacle well before Antoine. What Antoine attended to was the interaction of word and spectacle. Now, he was operating in a silent medium and there is an irritating wordiness about his intertitles. The images and intertitles of Antoine's films are often not in satisfactory balance. There is too much reading, as if Antoine was unable to let the words go sufficiently and entirely trust the cinematic image.

On the other hand, Antoine defined cinema as 'living creation' whereas theatre is 'an imitation of nature' and, since the essential creation happens during shooting and cutting, the primacy of the script, particularly in silent cinema, is necessarily undermined. In 1918 as in 1887, Antoine perceived himself as merely the *metteur en scène* of the literary text and never allied himself with the influential contemporary critic, Delluc, in arguing that the director of the film should be its 'auteur'.[12] But it was a self-deceptive position: his is the ruling imagination of his films. Although all but one of his films are derived from novels, he worked with the adaptor and in the case of *La Terre* and *L'Arlésienne* was responsible for the screenplay himself.

The way the camera is used and the film cut: the movement from long shot to middle range to close-up; shots which track over a landscape or follow a character's movements, the use of angled as well as straight-on camera positions contribute to the illusion of naturalness. Even as these elements charm and compel our watching and make the images more lifelike, they increase directorial control of viewpoint, shaping our responses. In the name of greater realism, Antoine asserted the authority of the artist-director as, indeed, he always had done but, where in his theatre this was scrupulously at the service of the play text, in his films the written script is the point of departure for a visual composition.

The failure to agree about the editing of *L'Hirondelle*, indeed, is telling and Antoine's last film, *L'Arlésienne*, although successful in its day, perhaps partly because it starred the music-hall performer, Fabris, is disappointing when compared with the earlier *La Terre*. In that film the fearful sequence of events and hostilities which culminates in Old Fouan's death by the roadside after the camera has followed him on a long and terrible walk via the homes of the children who have rejected him and across the land that has been the cause of mutual jealousy, is informed by and interactive with the evocation of landscape and daily life. In the later film, there seems to be a disjunction between the events and Antoine's interest in landscape and daily life: the plot, for all it is taken from Daudet, seems to be something of a distraction from the Camargue peasant life. A young Antoine would probably have managed to develop a strategy to enable him to operate more effectively within the new industry and to take his intuitions about the medium further.

As it was, Antoine's principal innovations in film were directed, as they had been in the theatre, to intensifying the impression of reality and, whether knowingly or not, to increasing his own control over how the audience interpreted that reality. True to his own past, he attacked mainstream cinema for its moribund theatricality, investigated the documentary possibilities of film and insisted on location instead of studio shooting which, apart from the realism of set, allowed him to use natural light instead of the customary strong studio front-lighting that flattened the image. He also moved the camera from its fixed position into the action. It was a startlingly fresh response to the possibilities of the cinema and one completely consistent with the search for truthfulness to experience that had informed his theatre work from the outset.

Antoine's film career (1915–22) was brief. As with his work on French and foreign classics, his influence on serious French cinema has been rather overshadowed by the reputation of his early work in the theatre. His influence in cinema derives partly from the presence in the new industry of actors and régisseurs – de Max, Joubé, Tourneur, Capellani, Gémier – whose theatrical training had been with Antoine, and partly from the recurrence among the early scripts of the French cinema of works that had inspired or had figured in the repertoire of Antoine's theatres, including adaptations of Zola and Daudet, Brieux's *Blanchette* (1921, director: René Hervil) and Renard's *Poil de Carotte* (1926, director: Julien Duvivier, assistant director of *La Terre*). But, even more, it derives from the integrity and activity of Antoine's own theatre work which had itself helped create a climate in which social seriousness and formal innovation were valued and interlinked.

This seriousness, coupled with the insights and achievements of Antoine's own brief excursion into film and his insistence that art lies in discovering expressive means of exploring and representing experience and particularly the experience of working people, found an immediate response in the work of other French directors such as Delluc, Epstein and Abel Gance, albeit they took the insights further and made much more demanding films.

Antoine came to cinema too early and too late. He was too early for the studios to have developed proper respect for the innovatory director and too late to be sufficiently personally adaptable to create the kind of working relationships that had enabled him to ask so much of his collaborators in the theatre. Disputes with the producers meant that *Le Coupable* was not as full as Antoine intended and *L'Hirondelle et la mésange* was never finally edited. But he was neither too late nor to early to perceive the importance and potential of the new medium and to argue its need for writing and acting that would be appropriate to film rather than theatre. Even after he abandoned film-making, Antoine retained his interest in it and played a part in establishing its claims to serious attention by reviewing films and discussing cinematic matters in his regular columns in *Comœdia*, *L'Information* and *Le Journal* as well as in invited lectures and occasional contributions to newly founded *ciné* magazines. In a lecture at the Pepinière cinema in June 1920 entitled 'Yesterday, today and tomorrow' he discussed film-making of the past dozen years in France, Italy and America with projected extracts.

He enquired into the nature of cinema as a medium, campaigned against censorship, made claims for inventive and honest films, attacked the dull and commercial, deplored the way films were cut to a standard length and, most notably, warned that the massive financial resources of Hollywood threatened to stifle the European industry, and argued for government support. Griffith's *Birth of a Nation* and Gance's *Napoléon* were held up by him as milestones in the development of cinema and in a telling article entitled 'What has happened to *Napoléon*?' he berated the distributors for allowing the American spectacular, *Ben Hur*, to displace Gance's remarkable epic, writing prophetically that,'whilst we are waiting time passes and *Napoléon* risks being lost'. He found the suggestion that people were not interested in filmed news absurd and pointed out that it was the method that needed attention, more on-the-spot reporting being essential to interest. Amongst his other campaigns were demands that actors be specially trained for film work; that there should be intelligent cinema for children with special matinee screenings and, coming full circle, he advocated the founding of a cinema club, a 'Vieux Colombier of the cinema'. He threw his weight behind Dreiser's opposition to the power of big business in Hollywood and saw that the advent of the talkies would bring cinema closer to theatre as the word struggled for dominance over the visual image. It is, in other words, an extremely fertile and stimulating response to the possibilities of film.[13]

Antoine gave up filming, claiming that he was too old to adapt to the privations of the new form and already younger men had adopted and advanced some of his methods with greater flexibility and understanding of the technical possibilities of film narrative. But, as Richard Abel has written, in an assessment that could be applied with equal justice to the theatre work, despite his personal difficulties in adapting to the film industry, 'Antoine did articulate ideas and institute practices that were fundamental to the emergence of French realist cinema'.[14] Certainly, if the *Hirondelle* story makes clear the extent to which he had moved away from the expectations of his financial backers, the film work in general is visible evidence of the kind of perception and responsiveness, the capacity to experiment, to take risks and to learn through experience that characterized so much of Antoine's work in the theatre. It also offers telling evidence of Antoine's attentiveness to his medium.

Theatre work is necessarily ephemeral. It survives in shared and often distorted memories. It can be partially recreated from written reports, prompt books, paintings, photographs and from studies such as this one which attempt to read and synthesize some of the material. Now, although the record can never be complete and the live performance never wholly recaptured, we often have, in addition, taped and filmed recordings of performances and, occasionally, of rehearsals.

Such mechanical recording did not exist when Antoine was active in the theatre, nor is there much visual evidence of the Théâtre Libre work. But these fragile and fading films do exist. Although film is evidently different from live theatre, something of the theatrical event, of what audiences found so luminous in Antoine's realism – the intensity, the sense of place, the power of the visual image – can be glimpsed in the films that survive. My own experience, indeed, of watching Antoine's surviving films quite late in my research made me realize, as no reading could have done, the kind and extent of the wonder that contemporary commentators were registering in their attempts to describe the 'truth', 'sincerity' and 'naturalness' of the performances in Antoine's theatre. It seems likely that *Coupable, La Terre* and, probably, *1793* will be recognized as among the great silent films when new prints are eventually available to enable them to be more widely shown.

Antoine's idea of an independent theatre altered the process of theatre in the twentieth century and proved a major enabling device for subsequent dramatic writing and innovation. His years at the Odéon extended the sense of what a national theatre might explore and achieve. He articulated ideas and instituted practices which have been absorbed and developed in both theatre and cinema. The man was quarrelsome, often dictatorial and his obstinate sense of what theatre could offer to society bankrupted him twice over. He abandoned his first wife and child. He adapted his memoirs to show his own actions as he thought they should have been. But even those who, like Lugné-Poë, had been most hurt by him personally acknowledged his extraordinary capacity to commit himself to the needs of a play, and found themselves won over by his self-effacing absorption in his art and the remarkable creativity of his imagination when faced with a stage and a play that he esteemed.

Appendix 1 CHRONOLOGY

Date		Theatre etc.
1858	Antoine born	*1859* Darwin *Origin of Species*
1870		FRANCO-PRUSSIAN WAR
1871	Begins work, Firmin Didot, rue Jacob	Zola begins *Rougon Macquart*
1872	Sees Manet Exhibition	Manet Exhibition, Beaux Arts
	Diction course at evening school	
1873	1st visit to Comédie-Française	*Thérèse Raquin* fails at Renaissance
		Chronegk joins Meininger
		L'Arlésienne fails at Odéon
1874	Writes to Got *et al.* about *Paradoxe*	Impressionist Salon
		Dramatic censorship reintroduced
1875	Joins Comédie-Française claque	New Paris Opéra opens
1876		Wagner's theatre at Bayreuth
		L'Ami Fritz at Théâtre Français
		(realistic scenery)
1877	Clerk at Gas Company; joins Laisné's acting class; meets Wisteaux (Mévisto)	
1878	Directs *L'Ami Fritz* for Laisné	Marie Dumas's international matinées
	Refused by Conservatoire	at Gaité
1879	Military service in Tunisia	French trans. *War and Peace*
1880	In Tunisia	Zola, 'Naturalism in the Theatre'
1881	Returns to Paris; marries	Irving remodels Lyceum stage
1882	Works 13–14 hrs daily at Gas Company, earns *c.*120 francs a month	*Les Corbeaux* fails at Comédie-Française
1883	Separates from wife	*Ghosts* premièred, Stockholm
1884	Joins Cercle Gaulois, Passage de l'Elysée des Beaux Arts	*L'Arlésienne* succeeds at Odéon
1885	Directs and acts for Cercle Gaulois	*La Parisienne* refused by Odéon
		Revue Wagnérienne founded
1886	Relationship with 2nd wife, Pauline Verdavoine (Mlle Deneuilly) begins	*Thérèse Racquin* banned
		Ghosts staged by Meininger
1887–94	DIRECTOR OF THÉÂTRE LIBRE	
1887	Mar. 1st soirée of Théâtre Libre	*Jacques Damour* taken by Odéon
	May 2nd soirée of Théâtre Libre	Opéra Comique burns, 150 die
	Jul. Leaves Gas Company	Zola's *Renée* fails at Odéon
	Oct. 1st Season: *Sœur Philomène*	Russia bans *Power of Darkness*
	Nov. Moves to Théâtre Montparnasse	
	New Programme each month (2 perfs. each)	

Date		Theatre etc.
1888	Jan. 1st tour: Brussels, then Berlin	Strindberg, *Miss Julie*
	Feb. *Power of Darkness*	Oct. over 200 subscrips too many at
	July Meininger in Brussels.	Th. Libre
	Open letter to Sarcey published	Oct. Lugné-Poë debut at Th. Libre
	Move to Théâtre Menus Plaisirs	
1889	Tour to London; sees Irving's *Macbeth*	Brahm founds Freie Bühne, Berlin
	Rejects Strindberg's *Father*	*La Parisienne* at Th. Français
	Mévisto joins Odéon troupe	Théâtres Moderne, Independent, Libre
		Ancien and d'Applic. founded in
		Paris
1890	*Ghosts*	Last Meininger tour
	3 performances each programme	Ministry subscrip. to Th. Libre
	introduced	debated in Senate
	May 1890 Manifesto, *Le Théâtre Libre*	Paul Fort founds Théâtre d'Art
1891	*Wild Duck*	Independent Theatre founded in
	Public season, Théâtre Porte Saint-	London
	Martin	Vaudeville new plays, matinees
1892	Aug.–Oct. tours French provinces, 20	Oct. Janvier to Odéon
	plays, massive public interest	Dec. Colas to Vaudeville
	Dec. tours Italy: *Blanchette, Ghosts,*	*Lady from the Sea* dir. Lugné-Poë
	Fille Elisa	
1893	*Miss Julie*	Théâtre d'Œuvre founded
	Weavers	5 Ibsen prods. in Paris
	Season at Eden and Porte	Zola's *Rougon Macquart* completed
	Saint-Martin	Curel, *L'Invitée* at Vaudeville
	Publishes open letter to Le Bargy	Death of Taine
	Nov. In Berlin for première	
	Assumption Hannele Mattern, meets	
	Hauptmann	
1894	Théâtre Libre in financial difficulties	Brahm at Deutsches Theater;
	June Resigns control to Larochelle	Reinhardt joins Brahm
	Summer and autumn tour of Europe	Strindberg's *Father* at Œuvre
	Sept. Antoine declared bankrupt	Gémier to Ambigu
1895	2-year contract with Porel at	Appia, *La Mise en scène Wagnérienne*
	Gymnase at 1,000 francs a month,	Dumas fils dies
	soon leaves	First films made
	Makes living as freelance actor	
	La Parisienne at Marseilles	
1896	June accepts Odéon co-directorship	Larochelle closes Th. Libre
	with Ginisty	
	Aug. strike of Odéon technical staff	Death of Edmond de Goncourt
	Oct. 12 Odéon season opens	*Ubu Roi* at Théâtre d'Œuvre
	Oct. 27 Agrees to take month's leave	
	Oct. 30 Ginisty sacks Gémier and	
	Barny	
	Nov. 22 Formally resigns from Odéon	
	Dec. Zola presides at banquet for	
	Antoine	

Date		Theatre etc.
1897	Jan.–May tours with Coquelin in *L'Age Difficile* and *La Parisienne* July Signs lease on Menus Plaisirs	Rostand's *Cyrano de Bergerac* Moscow Art Theatre founded Duse tours to Paris

1897–1906   DIRECTOR THÉÂTRE ANTOINE

1897	Sept. opens with *Blanchette* and *Boubouroche*	
1898	Feb. *Weavers* banned *Ghosts* revived, kept in rep. May *Weavers* licensed: demonstrations Dec. *Britannicus* fails	Zola publishes *J'accuse* Zola in exile
1899	*Miss Julie* revived *La Parisienne* great success	Irish Literary Theatre founded Death of Becque Dreyfus retrial in Rennes
1900	Awarded Legion of Honour *Poil de Carotte* staged	
1901	Renovates Théâtre Antoine *Fille Élisa* licenced Brieux, *Maternité* banned	Gémier and others leave Th. Antoine
1902	Stops advertising subscrips: always oversubscribed	Death of Zola
1903	June–Oct. Tours South America	Censorship ended in France
1904	Opens campaign for Becque memorial Dec. *King Lear*	Abbey Theatre opened, Dublin English Stage Society founded
1905	Appointed to Conservatoire jury	Grand to Comédie-Française
1906	Stages *Ghosts* as tribute to Ibsen May 31 Accepts Odéon directorship	Death of Ibsen Reinhardt's Kammerspielhaus

1906–14   DIRECTOR OF ODÉON

1906	Dec. *Julius Caesar* Refits Odéon	Gémier dir. Théâtre Antoine
1907	Extensive summer tour of provinces to recoup costs	Mévisto opens Théâtre Mévisto Intimate Theatre, Stockholm
1908	Inaugurates Odéon lectures 400,000 francs in debt Receipts 725,000 francs	Becque Memorial (by Rodin)
1909	*Andromaque*	Ballets Russes in Paris *La Parisienne* in Th. Français rep.
1910	*M. de Pourceaugnac* – Café-concert stars at Odéon Receipts 854,000 francs *Coriolanus* *Romeo and Juliet*	Death of Jules Renard
1911	Receipts 904,000 francs	1st manifesto of futurists
1913	Death of Mme Antoine (Deneuilly)	Copeau founds Vieux Colombier
1914	Apr. 3 Govt. votes 125,000 francs to Odéon Apr. 6 Resigns from Odéon: 750,000 deficit	Janvier administrator of Russian Imperial Theatres Gavrault dir. of Odéon; Mosnier régisseur-général

Date		Theatre etc.
	Apr. 20 Benefit Gala at Opéra	
	Apr. 25 Declared Bankrupt	
	Director of Conservatoire, Turkey	
	Sept. Returns at outbreak of war	FIRST WORLD WAR BEGINS
	Retained by Pathé as film director	Aug. Odéon closed to Mar. 1915
	Son Henry killed at front; son André	Vincennes Studios closed
	wounded	
1915	Various small acting roles (ovation at	Provincetown Players founded New
	Café Maynol)	York
1915–22	FILM DIRECTOR Pathé.	1917–19 Copeau's New York tour
	Completes Capellani's 1793	includes Poil de Carotte, Blanchette and
	and makes 8 films of own	Boubouroche
1918	Refuses Conservatoire Chair of	ARMISTICE
	Cinema	
1918 on	THEATRE/CINEMA CRITIC	
	Writes some 200 articles a year	
	freelance for Journal, Comœdia; Le	
	Monde illustré etc.	
1919	Joins L'Information as Critic	Gémier, 'le nouveau Théâtre Libre' at
		Th. Antoine
1921	Publ. Mes souvenirs sur le Th. Libre	Dullin founds L'Atelier
1927		Cartel: Dullin, Baty, Jouvet, Pitoëff
		established
1928	Publ. Mes souvenirs sur le Th. Antoine	
1932	Publ. Théâtre 1870 à nos jours	
1939		SECOND WORLD WAR
1941	Benefit Gala at Théâtre Français	
1943	Death of Antoine	

Appendix 2 ANTOINE'S PRODUCTIONS

THÉÂTRE LIBRE 1887–94

From January 1888 Antoine regularly toured with his company and staged invited public performances: only the most significant are noted here. Numbers in brackets refer to number of performances.
*plays subsequently taken by the Odéon or Comédie-Française.

Théâtre Passage de l'Élysée des Beaux Arts

30 Mar. 1887	Four one-act plays: Duranty and Alexis, 'Mlle Pomme'; A. Byl, 'Un préfet'; J. Vidal, 'La Cocarde'; Léon Hennique, *Jacques Damour** (after Zola)
30 May 1887	Bergerat, *La Nuit Bergamasque*; Méténier, *En famille*

1887–8

Oct.   Byl and Vidal, *Sœur Philomène* (les Goncourts); Villiers de l'Isle Adam, *L'Evasion*

Théâtre Montparnasse

Nov.	Corneau, *Belle Petite*; Mendès, *La Femme de Tabarin**; Hennique, *Esther Brandès*
Dec.	Jullien, *La Sérénade*; Banville, *Le Baiser**; Céard, *Tout pour l'honneur* (after Zola)
Feb.	Tolstoi, *The Power of Darkness*
Mar.	Bonnetain and Descaves, *La Pelote*; Margueritte, *Pierrot assassin de sa femme*; Guiches and Lavedan, *Les Quarts d'heure*
Apr.	Moreau, *Matapan*; Arène, *Le Pain du péché*
June	Salandri, *La Prose*; Ancey, *Monsieur Lamblin*; Alexis, *La Fin de Lucie Pellegrin*

1888–89

Théâtre des Menus Plaisirs, Boulevard Strasbourg

Oct.	Icres, *Les Bouchers*; Verga, *Chevalerie rustique*; Darzens, *L'Amante du Christ*
Nov.	Gramont, *Rolande*
Dec.	Porto-Riche, *La Chance de Françoise**; Hennique, *La Mort du Duc d'Enghien*; Mikhael, *Le Cor fleuri*
15 Jan.	Mendès, *La Reine Fiammette*
31 Jan.	Céard, *Les Résignés*; Jullien, *L'Echéance*
Mar.	The Goncourts, *La Patrie en danger*
May	Cladel, *L'Ancien*; Zola, *Madeleine*; Ancey, *Les Inséparables*
June	Rzewuski, *Le Comte Witold*; Méténier, *La Casserole*; Laumann, *The Tell-Tale Heart* (after Poe)

1889–90

Oct.	Aicard, *Dans le Guignol*; Aicard, *Le Père Lebonnard*
Nov.	Bois, *Au Temps de la ballade*; Ancey, *L'Ecole des veufs*
Jan.	Turgenev, *Le Pain d'autrui*; Fèvre, *En détresse*
Feb.	Alexis and Méténier, *Les Frères Zemganno*; Ginisty and Guérin, *Deux tourtereaux*
Mar.	Brieux, *Ménage d'artistes*; Jullien, *Le Maître*

2 May   Boniface and Bodin, *La Tante Léontine*; Mullem, *Une nouvelle école*; Wolff, *Jacques Bouchard*
30 May   Lorrain, *Viviane*; Céard, *La Pêche*; Ibsen, *Ghosts*
June   Bergerat, *Myrane*; Descaves and Darien, *Les Chapons*

1890–1

Oct.   Fèvre, *L'Honneur*
Nov.   Biollay, *Monsieur Bute*; Scholl, *L'Amant de sa femme*; Sermet, *La Belle Opération*
Dec.   Ajalbert, *La Fille Elisa* (after Goncourt); Linert, *Conte de noël*
Mar.   Lecomte, *La Meule*; Ginisty, *Jeune premier*
Apr.   Ibsen, *The Wild Duck*
May   Rosny, *Nell Horn*
June   Wolff, *Leurs filles*; Corbeiller, *Les Fourches Caudines*; Courteline, *Lidoire*
July   One act plays: Sutter-Laumann, *Cœurs simples*; Bourgeois, *Le Pendu*; Mullem, *Dans le rêve*

Jan.   Public season at Théâtre Porte Saint-Martin, *La Mort du duc d'Enghien*, *La Tante Léontine* and *L'Ecole des veufs*
Feb./Mar.   Tour, to Brussels (*Fille Elisa*) and to St Petersburg (*La Tante Léontine*)

1891–2

Oct.   Tabarant, *Le Père Goriot* (after Balzac)
7 Dec.   Salandri, *Un Rançon*; Vaucaire, *Un Beau Soir*; Prévost, *L'Abbé Pierre*
21 Dec.   Ancey, *La Dupe*; Marsolleau, *Son petit cœur*
Feb.   Brieux, *Blanchette*; Curel, *L'Envers d'une sainte*
Mar.   Fèvre, *L'Etoile rouge*; Guinon, *Seul*
May   Gramont, *Simone*; Wolff, *Les Maris de leurs filles*
8 June   Bourde, *La Fin du vieux temps*
30 June   Carré and Loiseau, *Péché d'amour*; Perrin and Couturier, *Les Fenêtres*; Docquois, *Mélie*

20 Aug.–1 Oct.   Tour of French provinces with twenty plays including *Ghosts*; *The Power of Darkness*; *Lidoire*

1892–3

3 Nov.   Salandri, *Le Grappin*; Biollay, *L'Affranchie*
29 Nov.   Curel, *Les Fossiles*
Jan.   Coolus, *Le Ménage Brésil*; Strindberg, *Miss Julie*; Goncourt, *À bas le progrès*
Feb.   Bruyerre, *Le Devoir*
Mar.   Lecomte, *Mirages*
Apr.   Courteline, *Boubouroche**; *Valet de cœur*
May   Hauptmann, *The Weavers*
June   Bourgeois, *Mariage d'argent*; *La Belle au bois rêvant*; *Ahasvère*

Dec.   Italian tour includes *Blanchette*; *Ghosts*; *La Fille Elisa*

1893–4

Nov.   Björnson, *A Bankruptcy*
Dec.   Perrin and Couturier, *Inquiétude*
1 Feb.   Hauptmann, *The Assumption of Hannele Mattern*; Villiers de l'Isle Adam, *La Révolte*
23 Feb.   Barres, *Une journée parliamentaire*

Apr.   Luguet, *Le Missionnaire*

June   Antoine hands control of Théâtre Libre to Larochelle, including two partly
         prepared plays, Fabré, *L'Argent*; Caraguel, *La Fumée puis la Flamme*

FREELANCE ACTOR 1895–7

Jan. 1895–June 1896   In Lemaître, *L'Age difficile* at Gymnase; in *Blanchette* for Baret; in *La Parisienne* in Marseilles and French provinces; in Curel's *La Figurante*, Théâtre de la Renaissance, for Bernhardt

Jan.–May 1897   Tour with Coquelin cadet and Dumeny in *L'Age difficile* and *La Parisienne*

FIRST ODÉON DIRECTION July–Oct. 1896

Performed (10–27 Oct):
Britannicus; *Le Médecin malgré lui*; Bergerat, *Le Capitaine Fracasse*; Schiller, *Don Carlos*; *Tartuffe*
Prepared but not performed:
Aeschylus, *The Persians*, *Eumenides*; Arnaut, *Le Danger*; Villers de l'Isle Adam, *La Révolte*
In rehearsal:
Haraucourt, *Don Juan*; Vigny, *La Maréchale d'Ancre*; Carré fils, *Les Yeux clos*

THÉÂTRE ANTOINE, 1897–1906 (Théâtre des Menus Plaisirs)

During this period Antoine played between 25 and 40 plays a year in repertory and staged 144 different plays. Théâtre Libre revivals figured largely, but there were new plays too and a few attempts at classics. I detail 1898–9 to show the pattern, and, thereafter, record only the most notable premières and revivals. Lists of all the plays produced and revived in these years are given in Mosnier.

1897–8
Repertory including:
New plays:
Curel, *Le Repas du lion*; Fabré, *Le Bien d'autrui*; Veber, *Dix ans après*; Dreyfus, *Les Amis*; Porto-Riche, *L'Infidèle*; Edmond Sée, *La Brebis*; Villeroy, *Heakléa*; Becque *La Parisienne*; Travieux, *Joseph d'Arimathée*; Marsolleau and Byl, *Hors les lois*; Lemaire and Bournet, *Le Petit Lord*; Bernard, *Le Fardeau de la liberté*; Mirbeau, *L'Epidémie*; Marsolleau, *Son petit cœur*; Labruyere, *Le Retour de l'aigle*; Becque, *Le Départ*
Théâtre Libre revivals:
Blanchette and *Boubouroche*; *Sœur Philomène*; *Ghosts*; *Jacques Damour*; *The Weavers*

1898–9
Repertory:
New plays:
Loti, *Judith Renaudin*; Courteline; *Le Gendarme est sans pitié*; *Gaités de l'Escadron*; Ancey, *L'Avenir*; Jullien, *Le Doute*; Kahn and Tailhade, *La Farce du Polchinelle*; Coolus, *Cœur blette*; Vaucaire, *Les Girouettes*; Alexis, *Vallabra*; Brieux, *Résultat des courses*; Curel, *La Nouvelle Idole* (great success); Donnay and Descaves, *Une pièce nouvelle*; Hermant, *L'Empreinte*; Trarieux, *La Mort d'Hypathie*; Depré and Charton, *Père naturel*; Bruyère, *En paix*
New productions:
Racine, *Britannicus*; Molière, *L'Ecole des femmes*
Théâtre Libre revivals:

The Weavers; *Ghosts*; *Wild Duck*; *The Power of Darkness*; Hauptmann, *The Assumption of Hannele Mattern*; Björnson, *A Bankruptcy*; Strindberg, *Miss Julie*; Turgenev, *Le Pain d'autrui* Curel, *Le Repas du lion*; Ancey, *La Dupe*; Fabré, *L'Argent*, *L'Ecole des veufs*; Louis de Gramont, *Rolande*; Rzewuski, *Le Comte Witold*; Byl and Vidal, *Sœur Philomène*; Brieux, *Blanchette*; Courteline, *Lidoire*; Courteline, *Boubouroche*; Perrin and Couturier, *Les Fenêtres*; Fèvre, *En détresse*; Darzens, *L'Amante du Christ*; de l'Isle Adam, *La Révolte*
Théâtre Antoine revivals:
Dreyfus, *Les Amis*; Porto-Riche, *L'Infidèle*; Edmond Sée, *La Brebis*; Villeroy, *Herakléa*; Becque, *La Parisienne*; Travieux, *Joseph d'Arimathée*; Marsolleau and Byl, *Hors les lois*; Lemaire and Bournet, *Le Petit Lord*; Bernard, *Le Fardeau de la liberté*; Mirbeau, *L'Epidémie*; Marsolleau, *Son petit cœur*; Labruyère, *Le Retour de l'aigle*; Becque, *Le Départ*

1899–1900
Repertory including:
Premières:
Jules Renard, *Poil de Carotte* (125 perfs.); Richepin, *La Gitane*; Donnay and Descaves, *La Clairière*; Bernstein, *Le Marché*; Bruyère, *En paix*
Revivals:
La Fille Elisa; *L'Argent*

1900–1
Repertory including:
Premières:
Courteline, *L'Article 330*; Travieux, *Sur la foi des étoiles*; Brieux, *Les Remplaçantes*; Hennique, *La Petite Paroisse* (after Daudet)
New production:
Hauptmann, *Drayman Henschel*
Revivals:
La Mort du Duc d'Enghien; *La Fille Elisa*; *La Révolte*

1901–2
Repertory, with fifteen premières, including:
Premières:
Sudermann's *L'Honneur*; Courteline, *Les Balances*; Curel, *La Fille sauvage*, *La Nouvelle Idole*; Hugot and St-Arroman, *La Terre* (after Zola); Schnitzler, *La Compagne*; Méténier, *Boule de Suif* (after Maupassant)
Public reading:
Brieux, *Les Avariés*
New production:
La Parisienne
Revivals:
La Nuit Bergamasque; *La Fille Elisa*; *Jacques Damour*; *Blanchette*; *Boubouroche*; *Poil de Carotte*; Pierre Wolff, *Leurs filles*

1902–3
Repertory of some twenty plays, including:
Premières:
Heijermans, *La Bonne Espérance*; Sée, *L'Indiscret*; Renard, *M Vernet*
Revivals:
Poil de Carotte; *Boubouroche*; *L'Honneur*; *Leurs filles*; *La Parisienne*

1903–4
Repertory, with ten premières, including:
New plays:
Courteline, *La Paix chez soi*; Donnay and Descaves, *Oiseaux de passage* (plays for 4 months);
Trarieux, *La Guerre au village*; Brieux, *Maternité*
New productions:
Schnitzler, *Le Perroquet vert*; *Power of Darkness*
Revivals:
Renard, *M. Vernet*; Darzens, *L'Amante du Christ*; *Ghosts*; *Duc d'Enghien*; *La Fille Elisa*; *La
Parisienne*; *Drayman Henschel*; *L'Honneur*

1904–5
Repertory, with 10 premières, including:
Premières:
Maindron, *Le Meilleur Parti*; *Les Avariés*
New production:
King Lear (60)
Revivals:
Tante Léontine; *Power of Darkness*

1905–6
Repertory, with five new plays in alternation including:
New plays:
Gandillot, *Vers l'amour*; Curel, *Le Coup d'aile*; Leblanc, *La Pitié*
New production:
Meyer-Förster *Vieil Heidelberg* (50)
Revivals:
Ghosts; *Wild Duck* (month's run)

THÉÂTRE NATIONAL DE L'ODÉON 1906–14

Antoine directed 232 plays in this period. I give the full programme for one season,
1910–11, as an example, and otherwise list notable productions. Where a play was much
revived/performed I note this. A complete list of all Antoine's productions in these years
is given by James B. Sanders.

1906–7
Forty-one plays in repertory, including:
New productions:
Shakespeare, *Julius Caesar* (53); 1908; 1909; Becque, *Les Honnêtes Femmes*, *La Parisienne*;
Molière, *Les Précieuses ridicules*, *Don Juan*; Corneille, *Polyeucte* 1907; 1909; 1912; Racine,
Britannicus 1907; 1908; 1911; *Andromaque*, *Les Plaideurs* (4); 1908 (3); 1909 (4); 1910 (5);
1911 (1); 1912 (3); Sudermann, *L'Honneur*; Marivaux, *Le Jeu de l'amour et du hasard*;
Beaumarchais, *Le Barbier de Seville* (5); Hugo, *La Grand'mère* (13); Daudet, *L'Arlésienne* (21);
1908 (18); 1909 (30); 1910 (24); 1911 (30); 1912 (22); 1913 (20); Musset, *Le Chandelier*;
Gréban, *Le Vrai Mystère de la Passion* 1908; 1909; 1910, 1913
Eight new plays, including:
Lucien Descaves, *La Préférée* (16); Busnach, *La Faute de l'abbé Mouret* (after Zola) (29);
Brieux, *La Française* (49)
Théâtre Libre/Antoine revivals:

Donnay and Descaves, *Oiseaux de passage* (11); Brieux, *Les Avariés*; Tolstoi, *The Power of Darkness* 1908; 1913; 1914; Meyer-Förster, *Vieil Heidelberg* (5); 1907 (16); 1908 (16); 1910 (34); 1912 (21); 1913 (30)

1907–8
Forty-two plays in repertory, including:
New productions:
Molière, *Tartuffe*, *L'Avare*, *L'Impromptu de Versailles*; Corneille, *Le Cid* 1908; 1909; 1910; 1912; Racine, *Phèdre*; Pushkin, *Le Chevalier avare*; *L'Avare chinois*; Plautus, *La Farce de la marmite*; Euripides *Electra*; Aeschylus, *Eumenides*
New plays:
Geffroy, *L'Apprentie* (48); Sacha Guitry, *Petite hollande*; Loti, *Ramuntcho* (21)
Théâtre Libre/Antoine revivals:
King Lear (17); 1913 (10); *Wild Duck*; *Ghosts*; *The Assumption of Hannele Mattern*

1908–9
Thirty-five plays in repertory, including:
New productions:
Racine, *Andromaque*; Molière, *L'École des femmes* (3); 1909 (1); 1910 (3); 1911 (2); 1913 (2), *La Critique de l'école des femmes*, *Les Femmes savantes*; Calderon, *La Dévotion à la croix* (2); 1909 (1); 1913 (1); Sudermann, *Parmi les Pierres* 1910 (70); Pierre Newsky/Dumas fils, *Les Danicheff* (30); *Les Corbeaux* 1910 (20); 1911 (2); 1912 (1); 1913 (17)
Nine new plays:
Guiraud, *Le Poussin* (34); Fauchois, *Beethoven* (66)
Revivals:
Poil de Carotte

1909–10
Fifty plays in repertory, including:
New productions:
Aeschylus, *The Seven Against Thebes* (2); Corneille, *Horace*; Racine, *Athalie*; Molière, *Le Malade imaginaire*; 1912 (31); 1913 (2); Shakespeare, *Coriolanus* (16); Dumas père, *Charles VII* (2); Pradon, *Phèdre et Hippolyte*
Five new plays:
Renard, *La Bigote*; Chekri-Ganem, *Antar* (70); Hennique, *Jarnac*

1910–11
Full repertoire:
New productions:
Molière, *Monsieur de Pourceaugnac* (21), *Le Misanthrope* (5); Shakespeare, *Romeo and Juliet* (46); Racine, *Iphigénie en Aulide* (4); Corneille, *Le Menteur* (4), *Rodogune* (5); Voltaire, *Zaïre* (5); Marivaux, *L'Épreuve* (10); Boileau, *Chapelain décoiffé* and *Les Héros de Romans* (2); Verlaine, *Les Uns et les autres* (3); Favart, *Les Trois Sultanes* (10); Dancourt, *La Femme d'intrigue* (2); Gandillot, *Vers l'amour* (39); Regnard, *Le Joueur* (2)
New plays:
Trarieux, *Un Soir* (22); Jean Richard, *L'Inquiète* (2); Marie Lenéru, *Les Affranchis* (16); Jean Marlet, *La Boulangère* (3); René Benjamin, *Le Pacha* (8); Mme Dick May, *Mère* (10); Lecomte du Nouy, *Maud* (11); P. de Puyfontaine, *La Cour d'amour de Romanin* (9); Jules Romaine, *L'Armée dans la ville* (5); Réné Fauchois, *Rivoli* (21); Traversi, *Les Plus Beaux Jours* (24); J. Galzy, *La Revanche de Boileau* (2); Duhamel, *La Lumière* (2); Oscar Franck, *Cœur*

maternel (1); P.-H. Loyson, *L'Apôtre* (1); Schneider, *Les Mages sans étoiles* (1); Ernest
Raymond, *L'Assomption de Verlaine* (3); Maurice Faramond, *Diane de Poitiers* (1)
In repertory:
Molière, *L'Ecole des femmes* (14); *La Critique de l'école des femmes* (2), *Le Médécin malgré lui*
(3); *Les Fourberies de Scapin* (1); *Les Femmes savantes* (1); *Le Misanthrope* (5); Racine,
Andromaque (5); *Phèdre* (1); Corneille, *Horace* (1); Verga, *Chevalerie Rustique* (21); Meyer-
Förster, *Vieil Heidelburg* (34); Daudet, *L'Arlésienne* (40); Becque, *Les Corbeaux* (2); Chakri-
Ganem, *Antar* (5); Arnoux, *La Mort de Pan* (6)

1911–12
Forty-eight plays in repertory, including:
New productions:
Molière, *Amphitryon* (3); *Le Bourgeois Gentilhomme* (24); *Les Précieuses ridicules*; Corneille,
Rodogune; Racine, *Bajazet*; Lope de Vega, *L'Étoile de Seville* (2); La Fontaine, *La Coupe
Enchantée*; Shakespeare, *Troilus and Cressida* (5); Cyrano de Bergerac, *Le Pédant joué*;
Euripides, *Andromache*
Eleven new plays:
Max Maurey, *David Copperfield* (60); André Dumas–S.-C. Leconte, *Esther, Princesse d'Israel*
(59); Anthelme, *L'Honneur japonais* (45); Brieux, *La Foi* (9)

1912–13
Forty-nine plays in repertory, including:
New productions:
Molière, *Le Dépit amoureux*; Corneille, *Héraclius* (1); Racine, *Esther*; Aeschylus, *The Persians*;
Bergerat, *La Nuit florentine* (after Machiavelli) (4, not revived); Goldoni, *La Locandiera*;
Goethe, *Faust* (65); Sheridan, *School for Scandal* (1)
Ten new plays

1913–14
Forty-one plays in repertory, including:
New productions:
Diderot, *Il est bon? Il est méchant?* (3); Schiller, *William Tell*; Molière, *Le Mariage forcé,
L'Étourdi, Don Juan; Psyché* (21); Musset, *Il ne faut jurer de rien*
Series of nineteenth-century reconstructions:
Picard, *La Petite ville* (1801); Scribe, *Le Diplomat*; Labiche, *Poudre aux yeux* (1861); Labiche,
L'Homme n'est pas parfait (1864)
New plays:
Gustave Grillet, *Rachel* (100); Brieux, *Le Bourgeois aux champs* (42)

CINEMA DIRECTOR, 1915–22:

Films in order of shooting. Date of release where different in brackets.
1915 *Les Frères corses* (1916)
1916 *Le Coupable* (1917)
1917 *Les Travailleurs de la mer*
1918 *Israël* (made in Turin for Itala Tiber)
1919 *La Terre* (1921)
1920 *Madame de Seiglière* (1921)
1920–2 *L'Hirondelle et la mésange* (1984)
1921 *L'Arlésienne*
[Capellani's *1793*, completed by Antoine, was released in 1921]

Notes

All translations are my own except where otherwise stated. Where plays are known in English, I have used the usual English title. All books published in Paris except as noted.

Preface

1 Henderson, *The First Avant-Garde* (London, 1971), p. 10.
2 *The Road to the Temple* (London, 1926), p. 195.
3 The major French sources are the early study by Thalasso; the seven-volume manuscript account of Antoine's life and work by Charles Mosnier, actor and régisseur at the Théâtre Antoine and the Odéon; the detailed and extensive research of Francis Pruner which resulted in a number of books and editions relating to Antoine and James Sanders' revelatory work on Antoine's letters and his period at the Odéon. Quotations from Antoine's letters are taken from Sanders' edition of the letters to 1894, unless otherwise stated. At a late stage of my research James Sanders drew my attention to A. Ambach, 'Antoine et le mise en scène', a master's thesis which includes a collection of some 106 photographs reproduced mainly from Mosnier and the journal, *Le Théâtre*.

1 Who would give the signal?

1 Reprinted in A.I. Miller, *The Independent Theatre in Europe* (New York, 1931), p. 33.
2 Shaw, *Our Theatres in the Nineties* (26 June 1897), vol. III, p. 174.
3 Henry James, *The Scenic Art*, ed. Allan Wade (New York, 1957), p. 8. Amongst the most renowned of the plays were Dumas fils, *La Dame aux camélias* (1852) and Augier, *Les Fourchambault* (1878).
4 To Wisteaux (14 Jan. 1884; of *Ventre de Paris* at the Théâtre des Nations, to Pauline (Feb. 1887), 'they murdered this fine book'.
5 Strindberg, 'First Letter to the Intimate Theatre' (1908), trans. and ed. A. Paulson, *The Strindberg Reader* (New York, 1968), p. 66; Antoine: *Bulletin de la Société des Amis de Zola* (1923), no. 2; Ibsen, *Letters and Speeches*, ed. Evart Sprinchorn (New York, 1965).
6 *Mes souvenirs sur le Théâtre Libre* (1921), p. 9, from which subsequent quotations of Antoine up to 1896 are taken unless otherwise stated. Quotations from Antoine dated from 1896 are from *Mes souvenirs sur le Théâtre Antoine* (1928).
7 Diderot, 'Premier entretien', *Œuvres complètes*, vol. IV, p. 286; Zola's citation of, in 'Le Naturalisme au théâtre', p. 186; Got, *Journal* (1910); Antoine, 'Mounet-Sully et le paradoxe sur le comédien', *L'Information* (July 1919). Cf. also letter to Mounet-Sully (15 Jan. 1876).
8 *The New Review* (Dec. 1889), reprinted in James, *The Scenic Art*, p. 35.
9 Sarcey, *Le Temps* (17 Sept. 1887). Quotations from Sarcey are from *Le Temps*. Many of Sarcey's reviews of the Théâtre Libre are collected in Sarcey, *Quarante ans de théâtre* (1902), vols. VII and VIII. I do not give dates for press quotations which occur in the week following a performance under discussion.
10 Bergerat, *Souvenirs d'un enfant de Paris*, vol. IV (1913), pp. 111, 114.
11 Céard (7 Nov. 1887); *Lettres inédites à Émile Zola*, ed. C.A. Burns (1958), p. 340.

2 The fourth wall: Antoine and the new acting

1   *Journal* (11 Oct. 1887). 'Goncourt' refers throughout to Edmond de Goncourt. Cf. also *Le Soleil*: 'one cannot treat it as the pastime of amateurs'; *Chat Noir*, 'Who knows? This little kiosk in the passage de l'Elysée des Beaux Arts is perhaps the Conservatoire of the future.'

2   Quotations from: Sarcey (17 Oct. 1887); *Gaulois* (12 Oct. 1887); Ganderax, *Revue des deux mondes* (15 Nov. 1887), p. 456; Goncourt, *Journal* (11 Nov. 1887).

3   Dumas fils, quoted by Marvin Carlson, *The French Stage in the Nineteenth Century* (New Jersey, 1972); *Nouveaux entr'actes* (1890), trans. M. Carlson, p. 124; *Théophile Gautier* (1858), trans. M. Carlson, p. 70; Antoine, *Conferencia* (1 Mar. 1923).

4   *Le Théâtre vivant* (1892), p. 11.

5   'Some furniture remained along the curtain line, which was always treated as an invisible but inviolable fourth wall', O.G. Brockett and R.R. Findlay, *Century of Innovation* (New Jersey, 1973), p. 90.

6   'Le Théâtre vivant', *Art et critique* (9 Aug. 1890), p. 500.

7   Méré, in interview with Mosnier (1906), Mosnier, p. 31; audition notes unearthed by Pruner, *Les Luttes d'Antoine* (1964), pp. 25, 143, in a remarkable piece of detective work; Sarcey (17 Dec. 1888).

8   Moore, 'The Patron of the Great Unacted', *Pall Mall Gazette* (5 Feb. 1889) p. 4.; Antoine, 'Le Mise en scène', *Les Annales* (21 June 1914); Jullien, 'Le Théâtre vivant' (1890), p. 501.

9   E. Fogarty, Principal, Central School of Speech and Drama, introducing her translation of C. Coquelin, *The Art of the Actor* (London, 1932), pp. 11, 13. Antoine's attack on the Conservatoire is most readily accessible in the May 1890 manifesto.

10 Sarcey (21 Jan. 1889; 17 Dec. 1888); Goncourt, *Journal* (26 Dec. 1890); Fay, 'Some Thoughts on Acting', quoted in B.K. Clark, *The Emergence of the Irish Peasant Play at the Abbey Theatre* (London, 1982), p. 42; Antoine to Pauline (2 Apr. 1887).

11 Saxe-Meiningen letter: *Le Temps* (23 July 1888).

12 James, *The Scenic Art*, p. 16; Hennique, *Comœdia* (22 Sept. 1927); La Pommeraye, *Paris* (26 Sept. 1887); *La République française* (29 Sept. 1887).

13 Sarcey (12 Apr. 1888); Doumic, quoted in Pruner, *Les Luttes*, p. 387; Pessard, quoted *Souvenirs* (14 Nov. 1890); Antoine (14 Nov. 1890); and cf. Jullien, 'It is only *chez* Antoine that these effects are rendered with satisfactory intensity', *Art et critique* (20 Dec. 1890).

14 *La Vie moderne* (28 Oct. 1888).

15 Moore, *Impressions and Opinions* (London, 1913), p. 164; *Souvenirs* (30 May 1890).

16 Lemaître, in interview, trans. Belloc, *New Review* (Feb. 1894), p. 214; letter to Le Bargy (24 Oct. 1893), reprinted, *Le Théâtre Libre* (1893–4) and Curel, *Théâtre complet*, 6 vols. (1919), vol. I, pp. 50–2.

17 Manifesto, May 1890; Curel, *Théâtre complet*, vol. II, p. 9.

18 Lugné-Poë, *Sot de tremplin* (1931), p. 192.

3 Extending the repertoire

1   Reviews, 12 Feb. 1888; Vogüé, *La Revue des deux mondes* (15 Mar. 1888), p. 434. See also, 'a success, do I say? A triumph', *La République française*; 'a truly theatrical work of great simplicity and sinister reality', *L'Intransigeant*; 'Tolstoi's drama created a huge success of curiosity, of sympathy and of emotion . . . made a great impression on a paying audience in which Russian high society was strongly represented', Lemaître, *Le Journal des débats* (13 Feb. 1888).

2   *L'Information* (7 Mar. 1921).

3   Faguet, *Notes* (1888), p. 11.

4   Antoine, *L'Information* (19 Mar. 1928); Tolstoi letter, quoted in Méténier, 'Le Théâtre Libre', *La Vie moderne* (11 Feb. 1888), p. 88; Ibsen correspondence, reprinted *Souvenirs* (20 Apr. 1890; 25 July 1890).

5   20 Jan. 1888.

6   Edouard Noël and Edmond Stoullig, *Les Annales du théâtre et de la musique* for Feb. 1888 (hereafter *Annales*). Also, Courteline's capitulation to Antoine's choice of cast for *Boubouroche*, *Souvenirs* (15 Apr. 1893)

7   *Sot de tremplin*, p. 51. See also *Gil Blas* (12 Feb. 1888), 'an artist without equal. His gesture, his diction, his mime have inexpressible strength.'

8   Pruner, *Le Répertoire étranger* (1958), which includes detailed discussion of the play and its context.

9   J.L. Styan, *Max Reinhardt* (Cambridge University Press, 1982), p. 17.

10 *Répertoire bibliographique des traductions et adaptations françaises du XVᵉ siècle à nos jours*, vol. VII, p. 6; Céard to Zola, 2 Sept. 1888; Lugne-Poë's first Ibsen production was *Lady from the Sea* in 1892.

11 Production information from Paul Ginisty, *La République française* (14 Aug. 1889); Pruner, *Le Répertoire étranger*, pp. 234–5. Antoine's letters *re Ghosts*: to Zola (6 June 1888), *Correspondance*, ed. J. Sanders, p. 140; to Sarcey (July 1888), *ibid*: p. 146; to Hessem (26 July 1888 and 30 Apr. 1889), *ibid.*, pp. 156, 187–8.

12 Armand Ephraim to Antoine, quoted Sarcey (4 May 1891). And see Pruner, *Le Répertoire étranger*, pp. 77–9.

13 Moore, *Impressions and Opinions*, pp. 162–7.

14 Darzens, *Théâtre Libre illustré* (27 Apr. 1891) ser. 2, no. 5.

15 Preface to *Miss Julie*, trans. Michael Meyer (London, 1982), pp. 101–2.

4 Experiments with the *mise en scène*

1   *Le Temps* (23 July 1887), trans. Judith Braid; *Souvenirs* (23 July 1888; 10 Feb. 1887); to Zola (6 July 1888). Antoine's May 1890 manifesto includes a detailed discussion of the *mise en scène*.

2   *Annales* (1888), p. xvii.

3   'After the Play' (1889), reprinted in James, *The Scenic Art*, p. 45.

4   Archer, 'The Dying Drama', *The New Review* (Sept, 1889); James, *The World* (12 Feb. 1889).

5   *La Mort du Duc d'Enghien*, 1st and 2nd editions (1886; 1889).

6   *Encyclopaedia Britannica*, 1911 edition, vol. XII, p. 231.

7   To Goncourt (6 July 1888), *Correspondance*, p. 139.

8   Goncourt, *Journal* (14 Mar. 1889); other quotations about *La Patrie* are from the Antoine or the Goncourt memoirs for February and March 1889 and from press reports of the week beginning 20 Mar. 1889.

9   Faguet, *Notes* (23 Mar. 1889).

10 *Conferencia* (1923).

11 *Goya and the Impossible Revolution* (London, 1976), p. 177.

12 Antoine, 'Les Coulisses des coulisses' *Je sais tout* (15 Feb. 1907), pp. 15–22.

13 *Le Temps* (5 June 1893), pp. 388–94.

14 (2 May 1898), *Mes Souvenirs sur le Théâtre Antoine*.

15 Trans. M. Boulby, *Die Weber* (London, 1962), p. 41. Sarcey discusses the song, as does Pruner in *Le Répertoire étranger*, pp. 147ff.

16 1885, trans. L.W. Tancock (London, 1954), p. 20.

17 *Je sais tout* (15 Feb. 1907).

5 Playwrights' theatre

1   Introduction, *Théâtre complet* vol. 1 (1919). Other quotations from Curel from these volumes. See too, Paul Alexis dedicating *La Fin de Lucie Pellegrin*, 'without you I would never have written this play'.

2   Sarcey, *Quarante ans*, vol. VII, p. 181.

3   Salandri, *Le Courrier français* (1 Aug. 1892); Goncourt, quoted in M. Belloc, *New Review* (Feb. 1894), pp. 205–14, p. 210.

4   Archer, *The World* (13 Feb. 1889); quotation about scripts, *Le Temps* (25 June 1887; 4 July 1887).

5   Curel, *Le Temps* (3 May 1919); Mendès, Preface to *La Femme de Tabarin*, quoted in the 1887–90 manifesto; Faguet, *Notes* (3 Dec. 1886), p. 376; Antoine reported in *Le Courrier français* (5 July 1891).

6   André Paul Antoine, *Antoine, père et fils* (1962); 'The Painter of Modern Life' (pub. 1863) trans. in P.E. Charvet, *Baudelaire: Selected Writings on Art and Artists* (Cambridge University Press, 1981), p. 435; T.J. Clark, *The Painting of Modern Life* (London, 1985), p. 49.

7   Zola, 'Naturalisme au théâtre', p. 260; Jullien, *Le Théâtre vivant* (1892), p. 17; Zola, 'Le Naturalisme au salon', *Le Voltaire* (19 June 1880).

8   Oscar Méténier, *Les Voyous au théâtre* (Brussels, 1891), pp. 61ff. Méténier notes that La Roquette had 45,000 inhabitants as compared with the 35–40,000 of other poor quarters. Information from text with *mise en scène* (ART, Historique); Flammarion illustrated edition: photographs too dim for adequate reproduction; and Méténier, 'À propos de *La Casserole*', *Art et critique*, no. 3 (1889), pp. 45–7.

9   Jan. 1890: *La Fille Elisa* ban reported throughout the press.

10 Press reports, week beginning 24 Dec. 1887; Verlaine in *Chat Noir* (Nov. 1889), quoted Pruner, *Les Luttes*, p. 142; Jullien, 'Le Théâtre moderne', *Revue encyclopædique* (1896), p. 245.

11 Rolland–Lugné-Poë, *Correspondance 1894–1901* (1957), p. 17; Antoine to Linert, *Le Théâtre Libre illustré*, no. 3 (Dec. 1890), p. 86.

12 Pessard, *Annales* (1888), p. x; Noël and Stoullig, *Annales* (1888), pp. 333, 327; on *Pierrot: Le Temps* (26 Mar. 1888) and Ganderax, 'Le Répertoire du Théâtre Libre', *Revue des deux mondes* (1 Sept. 1888), p. 220; Faguet, *Notes* (6 May 1890), p. 162.

13 Saverne, 'Dix ans à l'école d'Antoine', *Comœdia* (25 Sept.–12 Nov. 1913).

14 Shaw, Preface, *Three Plays by Brieux* (London, 1911), p. ix; Mosnier, vol. I, p. 32.

15 'L'Ouverture du Théâtre Antoine', *La Quinzaine dramatique* (1897), p. 147–9. Also Sarcey (4 Oct. 1897); *Le Théâtre* (Oct. 1903), p. 4.

16 Scepticism, in Michael Hays, *Public and Performance* (Michigan, 1981), p. 142; Albert Carré, *Souvenirs* (of Vaudeville), p. 143.

17 *Politiken* (17 Sept. 1888), trans. B.G. Madsø, p. 111.

18 Moore, *Impressions*, p. 167; J.T. Grein, quoted Michael Orme, *J.T. Grein* (London, 1936), p. 70; Shaw, introduction to J.T. Grein, *The World of Theatre* (London, 1921); Fay quoted by B.K. Clarke, *Irish Peasant Play*, p. 63; W.G. Fay and C. Carswell, *The Fays of the Abbey Theatre* (London, 1935), pp. 108–9.

19 Moore, 'The Patron of the Great Unacted', *Pall Mall Gazette* (5 Feb. 1889); on *Rolande*, to Hennique (16 Oct, 1888); Antoine quoted, *Souvenirs* (12 Dec. 1888; 31 Jan. 1891).

20 Quoted, Belloc, *New Review* (Feb. 1894), p. 212.

21 Copeau, *Nouvelle Revue française* (Sept. 1913), trans. John Rudlin. For details of the Vieux Colombier programme see Rudlin's *Jacques Copeau* (Cambridge, 1986).

6 Director's theatre

1   A. Aderer, *Théâtre à coté* (1894), p. 119.
2   Goncourt (31 Jan. 1891); Antoine, *Le Théâtre de 1870 à nos jours* (1932), pp. 419, 486.
3   *Le Théâtre*, vol. 138, p. 17; extract trans. Mrs G.B. Shaw, *Three Plays*.
4   'Le Miroir de succès, André Antoine', *Le Miroir* (13 Oct. 1912). The cigarette recurs in virtually all the cartoons.
5   Saverne, 'Dix ans': unattributed quotations from Antoine in this chapter are from Saverne's series of articles.
6   A number of these régisseur's copies of plays (including those for *La Nuit Bergamasque*, *Poil de Carotte*, *Julius Caesar* and *King Lear*, discussed in this book) are deposited in the Bibliothèque Historique de la Ville de Paris by the Association des régisseurs du théâtre. Rostand, quoted R. Coursaget, *Cent ans de Théâtre* (1947), p. 108.
7   *L'Art du théâtre* (1903–4).
8   *Souvenirs* (20 Jan. 1902); Noël and Stoullig, *Annales*, p. 28.
9   Jules Renard, 'A propos Poil de Carotte', *Théâtre complet* (1959). p. 312.
10   Letter to Maire Garvey (30 June 1904), quoted in B.K. Clark, *Four Plays of the Free Theatre* (Cincinnati, 1915).
11   Antoine, *Le Théâtre*, pp. 409–10.

7 Staging the classics

1   'Le Roi Lear', *L'Illustration théâtral* (17 Dec. 1904); *L'Information* (16 Nov. 1920). Notable among the small amount written on Antoine's Shakespeare productions are Oscar Brockett, 'Antoine's Experiments in Staging Shakespearean and Seventeenth-Century French Drama' in Brockett (ed.), *Studies in Theatre and Drama* (The Hague, 1972), André Paul Antoine, 'Les Mises en scène Shakespeariennes d'Antoine', *Theatre Survey* (May 1958), and James Sanders, *Antoine à l'Odéon*.
2   *Comœdia* (6 Aug. 1925); *L'Information* (5 May 1919).
3   Quotations from a discussion in *L'Art du théâtre* (1904), p. 4.
4   *L'Information* (16 Nov. 1920).
5   Léon Blum, *Au théâtre* (1906), p. 257.
6   'Conference prononcé à l'Université des Annales' (1922).
7   'Les Coulisses des coulisses', *Je sais tout* (15 Feb. 1907). The words 'admirable', 'superb', 'marvellous' recur in press comment, also 'spurred on by his subject he has passed the rubicon', *Figaro* (5 Dec. 1906); 'the effect on the public was considerable' (*L'Illustration théâtral* (8 Dec. 1906).
8   *Jules César*, Odéon 1906. Collection ART Bibliothèque Historique: includes Antoine's typescript with music cues, the prompt copy, and a copy of the translation printed in *L'Illustration théâtral* with *mise en scène* sketches and instructions interleaved with the text. Technical details and rehearsal illustrations are from Antoine's discussion of his production in *Je sais tout* (15 Feb. 1907).
9   '*Jules César* au théâtre de l'Odéon, *L'Illustration théâtral* (Dec. 1906).
10   Brockett, 'Antoine's Experiments', p. 201.
11   'Extreme simplicity', *Comœdia* (22 Apr. 1910). See too, Noël and Stoullig, 'gripping modernity' *Annales* (21 Apr. 1910); Brisson, 'Stupefying modernity', *Le Temps* (25 Apr. 1910). Copeau's comments on the production here and elsewhere in the chapter are from *Le Théâtre* (June 1910).
12   Quotations, in order: *Souvenirs* (24 Nov. 1890); *Conferencia* (1 July 1923); *Je sais tout* (5 June 1914); *Britannicus*, discussed *Souvenirs* (4 Dec. 1898). Besides Sanders' detailed account, *Antoine à l'Odéon*, to which I am indebted, the main source of information for the

Odéon work are Mosnier, and Ibels, 'La Carrière d'Antoine', *Je sais tout* (25 May 1914), as well as press accounts.

13   'Causerie sur la mise en scène', (1903).
14   'True milieu' – Ibels, *Je sais tout* (May 1914), p. 651.
15   Interview in *Comœdia* (1907). See too: 'Molière has had, in Antoine, the most respectful of admirers' (*Comœdia*); 'go to applaud and go to acclaim this thrilling creation by Antoine' (*L'Humanité*)..
16   19 Aug. 1910, reprinted *Comœdia* (29 Aug. 1910)
17   Quotations from *Comœdia* (14 Nov. 1910; 8 Apr. 1911 and 28 Oct. 1911); *Journal des débats* (2 Dec. 1907); Arnavon, *Notes sur l'interpretation de Molière* (1923), p. 47.

8 A national theatre

1   Information here from *Souvenirs*; Pruner *Le Répertoire étranger* and *Les Luttes*; a long interview with Paul Mortier in *Je sais tout* (1906); and Adolphe Brisson's article on the Odéon, *Le Temps* (22 Oct. 1917).
2   *Journal des débats* (24 Oct. 1911).
3   R. Benjamin, *Antoine enchaîné* (1929), p. 14; Gaston Sorbet, *L'Illustration* (15 June 1912).
4   Geffroy, *Comœdia* (5 Jan. 1908); accounts of *mise en scène*: Filax, *Les Hommes du jours*, no. 47, *André Antoine* (12 Dec. 1908); and Antoine, *Le Journal* (11 July 1925).
5   'La Mise en scène', *Paris le soir* (10 Mar. 1921); Lecture, 1922, quoted Brockett, 'Antoine's Experiments', p. 208.
6   G. Duhamel, letter to *Comœdia* (13 Apr. 1914).
7   Antoine's resignation letter and the report of the secretary of the Budget Commission of the Ministry of Fine Arts quoted Mosnier, vol. VII; see, too, Sanders, *Antoine à l'Odéon*, pp. 267ff.; discussion throughout the French press in April 1914, and Antoine's own account, *Le Journal* (April 1914), and 'Dossier Antoine'. The Budget Report for 1906–7 is in Mosnier, vol. v.
8   *Le Temps*; *Comœdia*; *Figaro* etc. week beginning 2 Apr. 1914; Brockett, 'Antoine's Experiments', Noël and Stoullig, *Annales* (24 Apr. 1914).
9   Mosnier, p. 770; Donnay, 'Mon journal de guerre: tableaux de la vie de Paris', *Le Journal de l'université* (15 Apr. 1916).

9 Antoine and the cinema

1   Shot 1921, restored and edited 1983–4 for the Cinémathèque française by Henri Colpi, adviser Philippe Esnault (shown London National Film Theatre, 28 Sept. 1985). I was able to see *Le Coupable* and *1793* at the Cinémathèque française. The newly restored print of *1793* was shown in the NFT's 'Revolution Revisited' season, April 1989. The Cinémathèque française does not have a print of *La Terre*, but the London NFT gave a single showing of one in 1987, *L'Arlésienne* was shown at the NFT in 1987. The newly located print of *Travailleurs de la mer* was shown at the Musée d'Orsay in May, 1990.
2   Delluc, 'Antoine travaille', *Le Film*, no. 75 (20 Aug. 1917), reprinted in R. Abel, *French Film Theory and Criticism: 1907–29* (Princeton, 1988).
3   Ralph Stevenson and J.R. Debrix, *Cinema as Art* (London, 1965), p. 55.
4   *Le Temps*, quoted Mosnier, p. 810.
5   Philippe Esnault, 'Propos d'Antoine', *La Revue du cinéma*, 271 (April 1973), and personal communication. Esnault is engaged on a full-length study of Antoine's films.
6   Richard Abel, *French Cinema: The First Wave 1915–29* (Princeton, 1984), p. 121. I was fortunate that Philippe Esnault, who attended my showing of the film at the Cinémathèque française, provided a whispered but lucid commentary on the film.

7   'L'Avenir du cinéma', *Lectures pour tous* (Dec. 1919), copy in Mosnier, p. 909.

8   Mosnier, p. 909; Abel, *French Cinema*, p. 98.

9   R. Benjamin, 'Antoine déchaîné', *Les Œuvres libres*, no. 3 (Sept. 1921), p. 343.

10   R. Abel, *French Cinema*, p. 513.

11   'Le Film' (Dec. 1919), reprinted in J. Mitry, *Histoire du cinéma II, 1915–25* (1969), pp. 250–2.

12   Delluc, 'Cinéma et cie: d'où viennent ou où vont nos metteurs en scène?', *Paris-Midi* (17 Aug. 1918), p. 3.

13   'Cinéma d'hier, d'aujourd'hui, de demain' was published in *Le Journal du ciné-club*, no. 24 (25 June 1920) pp. 3–4. Amongst the more notable of the articles, 'Tripatouillages', *Cinémagazine*, no. 1 (25 Mar. 1921) pp. 5–6. A number of undated articles by Antoine, including 'Que devient *Napoléon*?' are collected in the Dossier Antoine in the Bibliothèque de la Ville de Paris.

14   R. Abel, *French Cinema*, p. 95.

Select bibliography

All books are published in Paris except where otherwise stated. The Auguste Rondel Collection in the Bibliothèque de l'Arsenal in Paris, an important source of articles, press cuttings and play texts, includes marked scripts of *Ghosts* and Charles Mosnier's seven-volume manuscript study of Antoine's life and work.

The collection of the Association des Régisseurs du Théâtre (ART) in the Bibliothèque Historique de la Ville de Paris has cuttings files (Dossier Antoine); play texts, including Flammarion illustrated texts, and marked scripts and prompt books of, amongst others, *La Nuit Bergamasque*, *Blanchette*, *Poil de Carotte* and *Julius Caesar*.

Notable among Antoine's many articles and open letters, a selection of which is currently being prepared by James B. Sanders, are:

On the Saxe-Meiningen Company: *Le Temps*, 23 July 1888
'À Monsieur Le Bargy', printed *Le Théâtre Libre*, 1893–4
'Causerie sur la mise en scène', *La Revue de Paris*, 1 Apr. 1903
'Les Coulisses des coulisses' [on Julius Caesar], *Je sais tout*, 15 Feb. 1907
'Le Journal de ma vie', *Je sais tout*, 5 June 1914
'L'Avenir du cinéma', *Lectures pour tous*, Dec. 1919
'Mounet-Sully et le paradoxe sur le comédien', *L'Information*, July 1919
'La Mise en scène', *Conferencia*, 1 Mar. 1923
'Emile Zola et le théâtre', *L'Information*, 4 Aug. 1924; 11 Aug. 1924; 18 Aug. 1924
Le Théâtre Libre (manifestos), 1887; 1887–90; May 1890; Oct. 1891; 1893–4

Abel, R., *French Cinema: The First Wave, 1915–29*, Princeton, 1984
Aderer, A., *Le Théâtre à Côté*, 1894
Ambach, A., 'Recherche sur la conception de la mise en scène d'Antoine', master's thesis, 1968–9, Bibliothèque Gaston Baty
Antoine, André, *Mes Souvenirs sur le Théâtre Libre*, 1921
   Mes Souvenirs sur le Théâtre Antoine et sur l'Odéon (1er Direction), 1928
   Le Théâtre de 1870 à nos jours, 1932
   Lettres à Pauline, ed. F. Pruner, 1962
   La Correspondance d'André Antoine: le Théâtre Libre, ed. James B. Sanders, Quebec, 1987
Antoine, André Paul, 'Le Naturalisme d'Antoine: une legende', in *Réalisme et poésie au théâtre*, ed. J. Jacquot, 1960, pp. 233–40
   Antoine perè et fils, 1962
Belloc, M., 'The Théâtre Libre of Paris', *The New Review*, Feb. 1894, pp. 205–14
Benjamin, R., 'Antoine déchaîné', *Les Œuvres libres*, 3, Sept, 1921
   Antoine enchaîné, 1929
Brieux, Eugene, 'Maternity', trans. Mrs G.B. Shaw in *Three Plays*, London, 1911
Brockett, Oscar, 'Antoine's Experiments in Staging Shakespearean and Seventeenth-Century French Drama', in Brockett (ed.) *Studies in Theatre and Drama*, The Hague, 1972, pp. 195–209
Carlson, Marvin, *The French Stage in the Nineteenth Century*, New Jersey, 1972
Copeau, Jacques, *Nouvelle Revue française*, Sept. 1913
Coquelin, C., *The Art of the Actor* (1894), trans. E. Fogerty, London, 1932

Curel, François de, *Théâtre complet*, 6 vols., 1919–24

Darzens, R. (ed.) *Le Théâtre Libre illustré*, 1889–91

Esnault, P., 'Propos d'Antoine', *La Revue du cinéma*, 271, Apr. 1973, pp. 45–8

Faguet, E. *Notes sur le théâtre contemporain*, 1886; 1888; etc.

Goncourt, Jules and Edmond de, *Journal*, vols. VII and VIII, 1894; 1895

Got, E., *Journal*, 1910

Henderson, John A., *The First Avant-Garde*, London, 1971

Hobson, Harold, *French Theatre Since 1830*, London, 1978

Horn-Monval, M., *Répertoire bibliographiques des traductions et adaptations françaises du théâtre
    étranger*, 8 vols., 1958– 66

James, Henry, *The Scenic Art*, ed. Allan Wade, New York, 1957

Jullien, Jean, *Le Théâtre vivant*, 1892

    'Le Théâtre moderne et l'influence étranger', *La Revue encyclopædique*, April 1896, pp. 245–7

Lugné-Poë, A., *Le Sot du tremplin*, 1930

Méténier, Oscar, *Les Voyons au théâtre*, Brussels, 1891

Miller, A.I., *The Independent Theatre in Europe*, New York, 1931

Moore, George, *Impressions and Opinions*, London, 1913

Noël, E. and E. Stoullig, *Les Annales du théâtre et de la musique*, 1876–1901

Paulson, A. (ed.), *The Strindberg Reader*, New York, 1968

Prince, F., *André Antoine et le renouveau du théâtre hollandais, 1880–1900*, Amsterdam, 1941

Pruner, Francis, *Le Théâtre Libre d'Antoine: le répertoire étranger*, 1958

    Les Luttes d'Antoine. Au Théâtre Libre, 1964

Renard, Jules, *Théâtre complet*, 1959

Roussou, M., *André Antoine*, 1954

Rudlin, John, *Jacques Copeau*, Cambridge University Press, 1986

Sanders, James B., *André Antoine, directeur à l'Odéon*, 1978

Sarcey, F., *Quarante ans de théâtre*, 8 vols., 1900–2

Saverne, G., 'Dix ans à l'école d'Antoine', *Comœdia*, 25 Sept.–12 Nov. 1913

Shaw, G.B., *Our Theatre in the Nineties*, 3 vols., London, 1931

Stokes, John, *Resistible Theatres*, London, 1972

Strindberg, A., *Open Letters to the Intimate Theatre*, trans. Walter Johnson, Seattle, 1966

Thalasso, A., *Le Théâtre Libre*, 1909

Veinstein, A., *Du Théâtre Libre au Théâtre Louis Jouvet*, 1955

Waxman, S.M., *Antoine and the Théâtre Libre*, Harvard University Press, 1926

Zola, Emile, 'Le Naturalisme au Théâtre' in *Le Roman Expérimental*, 1882

    Lettres inédites à Henry Céard, 1958

Index